Emotions and Virtues in Feature Writing

Jennifer Martin

Emotions and Virtues in Feature Writing

The Alchemy of Creating Prize-Winning Stories

Jennifer Martin
Faculty of Arts and Education
Deakin University
Melbourne, VIC, Australia

ISBN 978-3-030-62977-9   ISBN 978-3-030-62978-6   (eBook)
https://doi.org/10.1007/978-3-030-62978-6

© The Editor(s) (if applicable) and The Author(s), under exclusive licence to Springer Nature Switzerland AG 2021
This work is subject to copyright. All rights are solely and exclusively licensed by the Publisher, whether the whole or part of the material is concerned, specifically the rights of translation, reprinting, reuse of illustrations, recitation, broadcasting, reproduction on microfilms or in any other physical way, and transmission or information storage and retrieval, electronic adaptation, computer software, or by similar or dissimilar methodology now known or hereafter developed.
The use of general descriptive names, registered names, trademarks, service marks, etc. in this publication does not imply, even in the absence of a specific statement, that such names are exempt from the relevant protective laws and regulations and therefore free for general use.
The publisher, the authors and the editors are safe to assume that the advice and information in this book are believed to be true and accurate at the date of publication. Neither the publisher nor the authors or the editors give a warranty, expressed or implied, with respect to the material contained herein or for any errors or omissions that may have been made. The publisher remains neutral with regard to jurisdictional claims in published maps and institutional affiliations.

Cover illustration: bgblue, Getty Images
Cover design: eStudioCalamar

This Palgrave Macmillan imprint is published by the registered company Springer Nature Switzerland AG.
The registered company address is: Gewerbestrasse 11, 6330 Cham, Switzerland

For Marty. A man whose virtue matches my emotion and who, best of all, shares my vices.

Foreword

Mention the word journalism and most people think of the news. But journalism comes in all shapes and sizes, from tweets marked "Breaking" to 24-hour cable news channels and from podcasts like *This American Life* to books written by the world's most famous print journalist, Bob Woodward. That's far from the extent of journalism's range—journalists commonly ghost-write the memoirs of the famous and infamous alike and equally commonly create content for organisations, whether banks or sporting clubs—but still it is the news of the day that characterises journalism in the public mind. Is this a problem? Well, just as using the words journalism and news interchangeably short-changes the richness and diversity of journalism as a form, so the form of news short-changes the richness and diversity of life. How can it not, when everything from the rescue of a lost pet to the outbreak of war is rendered into a news item that is short, terse and impersonal. It is true that for well over a century news written to what is known as the inverted pyramid has been the most efficient way to communicate noteworthy happenings. And it is still is; Twitter is tailor-made for breaking news. It has deficiencies, though. News side-steps analysis, strips away context and cauterises emotion. The impersonal tone is aimed at convincing readers of the news outlet's commitment to neutrality and fairness which is a plausible strategy, but for decades comedians have poked fun at the gap between the solemnity of newsreaders and the reality of life. "And now for something completely different," intoned Monty Python's Eric Idle, "a man with three buttocks" before throwing to John Cleese interviewing a man with a "50 per cent bonus" in the derrière department.

Apart from being the, ah, butt of jokes, the form of news reinscribes a worldview that places most value in information, and certain kinds of information at that—bushfires, assaults, election results, scientific breakthroughs, official reports, leaked reports and so on. The push in newsrooms is always to find the news before your competition and get it to the public as soon as possible. Accuracy is of prime importance too, but it's not hard to see how the newsroom imperative, combined with the formulaic nature of newswriting, inculcates an approach to events, issues and people that tends to reduce them to "12 snappy pars" as my first news editor at *The Age*, Mike Smith, used to call them. It was while working at *The Age* that I first bumped into the limits of seeing the world through the prism of hard news. A month after completing a cadetship at the newspaper, I was among a number of staff sent to cover what became known as the Ash Wednesday bushfires, the worst natural disaster in Victoria, Australia, in nearly five decades. After interviewing survivors in Lorne and Anglesea, on the coast south-west of Melbourne, what struck me most and what I still remember today is the gap between the enormity of the event and the means at my disposal to communicate it—a short news article. The people I interviewed, which included a family with two teenage children and a builder who had all lost their homes, were in what I now see was a state of shock. They could not find the words to express how they felt, but emotion was fairly radiating from them in waves. Confusion, emptiness, a sense they had been picked up like a flake of ash and thrown helter-skelter; that's what I intuited, but that could not be put in a news piece so I pushed more questions on them and eventually got some "quotes", and duly filed. As "quotes" they were fine, but they fell far short of conveying what I thought needed to be reported that day, which was at least some sense of the intense emotions survivors experienced.

In the years since, whether in other newsrooms, or teaching journalism, or writing about it, the stories I've found most rewarding to work on are those that seek to portray events in their complexity and people in their full humanity. To give just one example from the many I've read, I've never forgotten being deeply moved reading "Hiroshima", John Hersey's account for *The New Yorker* of how six people survived the dropping of the first atomic bomb, on 6 August 1945, on the Japanese city. It was more than half a century later and I was half a world away, sitting in the Australian bush on a summer holiday, but Hersey's lyrically spare prose first made me feel the human cost of the bomb; then it helped me understand its alarming importance as a categorically different kind of bomb—one with the potential to destroy the entire planet.

I've set "Hiroshima" in classes since and, overwhelmingly, students are bowled over by it. Lesley Blume's excellent book about its creation, *Fallout*, published in 2020, sent me back to the original and I was struck again not only by Hersey's importance as a pioneer of long-form journalism but by his ability to honestly and accurately convey what it was like to experience the bomb's destructiveness. Here's a paragraph from "Hiroshima" that, once read, is hard to forget. It concerns the efforts of one of the survivors, Reverend Kiyoshi Tanimoto, to save others:

Mr Tanimoto found about twenty men and women on the sandspit. He drove the boat onto the bank and urged them to get aboard. They did not move and he realized that they were too weak to lift themselves. He reached down and took a woman by the hands, but her skin slipped off in huge, glove-like pieces. He was so sickened by this that he had to sit down for a moment. Then he got out into the water and, though a small man, lifted several of the men and women, who were naked, into his boat. Their backs and breasts were clammy, and he remembered uneasily what the great burns he had seen during the day had been like: yellow at first, then red and swollen, with the skin sloughed off, and finally, in the evening, suppurated and smelly.

By now the tide has risen, making it harder for him to get across the water. Hersey continues:

On the other side, at a higher spit, he lifted the slimy living bodies out and carried them up the slope away from the tide. He had to keep consciously repeating to himself, "These are human beings." It took him three trips to get them all across the river.

By bringing readers down from the bomber's aerial view of the city to people on the ground, Hersey opened space for them to imagine themselves in the shoes of a people whose military just a few years before had bombed Pearl Harbor, killing 2400 people and bringing the United States into the Second World War.

Jennifer Martin's book, *Emotions and Virtues in Feature Writing*, is about how the richness and diversity of journalism as a form enables it to explore and illuminate the richness and diversity of life. Her chosen focus is award-winning feature stories—or long-form journalism—and she is particularly interested in how journalists can and should report on and convey the emotional life of those they write about. She is interested too in journalists finding and reporting the right facts but taking a creative approach to structuring and telling a true story does not mean a licence to make things up. She has created what she terms a "virtue map", drawn from Aristotle's philosophical writings, augmented by later scholars' work, that includes the virtues of courage, empathy, honesty, responsibility, resilience and "phronesis", or practical wisdom. These qualities are included in most codes of ethics for journalists but tend to be implicit rather than stated out loud. And most journalists seem more comfortable with that than with trumpeting their own virtues, especially when they know the many constraints imposed on them, whether in dealing with sources, the pressures of time and space, overbearing editors or interventionist proprietors. Nor are they fond of talking up their literary aims or aspirations. As Paul McGeough, a Walkley award-winning journalist, once told the Australian scholar, Sue Joseph, if he walked into a bar and announced he was a "literary journalist", he'd get punched.

Jennifer Martin is not worried about that prospect; she is happy, keen even, to explore the literary elements of journalism. She badges up the various virtues and identifies exactly where and how they are practised by journalists as well as by those they write about. Further, she applies the virtue map to close readings of a range of articles, examining how various journalists achieve the literary effects they have. She devotes chapters each to Helen Garner's "Did Daniel Have to Die?" for *Time Australia* magazine, published in 1993, Chloe Hooper's "The Tall Man" for *The Monthly*, published in 2006, and Hannah Dreier's "A Betrayal" for *ProPublica*, published in 2018. Each of the articles is about achingly emotional topics: the death of a 2-year-old boy, Daniel Valerio, at the hands (and feet) of his stepfather, Paul Aiton; the death of an Indigenous Australian, Mulranji Doomadgee, at the hands (and knees) of "the tall man", police Senior Sergeant Chris Hurley, and the callous indifference of customs officers in the United States that nearly led to the death of a 17-year-old Salvadorean immigrant, Henry Triste, who informed on members of a murderous teenage gang to which he once belonged, MS-13.

I would not want to suggest, and nor would she either I imagine, that when journalists include their subjects' emotional lives in their stories they only write about painful, wrenching emotions, but as a journalist who worked primarily in community media, as a journalism teacher, a feminist scholar and as someone whose life was touched by trauma as a child, Jennifer Martin gravitates towards topics that many prefer to avoid. I found this myself when we collaborated on two feature articles for *Inside Story* about the findings of the multi-volume final report of the Royal Commission into Institutional Responses to Child Sexual Abuse in 2017. Not exactly Monty Python silly newsreader material, to be sure, but as Jennifer Martin reminds us here, it was the dogged investigative work of journalists like Joanne McCarthy of *The Newcastle Herald* that spurred the then Labor prime minister, Julia Gillard, to set up the royal commission in the first place. There is little doubt the royal commission's five years of work fundamentally shifted public awareness and knowledge about the scourge of child sexual abuse. Similarly, I have little doubt that Jennifer Martin's book makes a valuable contribution to exploring and explaining how and in what ways feature stories help fulfil journalism's vital role in society.

Deakin University   Matthew Ricketson
Melbourne, Australia
January 2021

PREFACE

I live and earn my living on the lands of the Wurundjeri people of the Kulin Nation, otherwise known as Melbourne, Australia. I'd like to acknowledge that the lands were stolen, and sovereignty was never ceded, and I pay my respects to the elders, past, present and emerging.

Courage. Empathy. Honesty. Responsibility. Resilience. And of course, *phronesis*, which is what the Greek philosopher Aristotle called 'practical wisdom'. While writing this book I've sidled up to, glanced at warily, walked around and looked at those six words from every angle, and even hurled a few soundly unvirtuous phrases at them in frustration more times than I'd like to admit. For these character traits are the co-ordinates of my 'Virtue Map', which I developed in order to help me better understand how prize-winning feature writers make us feel something when we read their work. It wasn't until I came to write this book that I seriously questioned why it was I was so fascinated with the feature article. I am always surprised at how an honest story, well told by a beautiful writer, can make me look at the world, or myself, with different eyes, no matter how many times I have read the story. Which is why, in addition to my three in-depth case studies in Part II, I have included a list of additional recommended readings of feature articles for each chapter. Each story on that list has informed this book and expanded my view of what it means to live together in a community. I am deeply indebted to each of those writers.

This book is about the journey of the story and what we can learn from it. For me, the brief moments of true *eudaimonia*, of joy, of insight, of connection, happen down in the muck of our everyday lives as we try to show *courage* against the odds, we take time to extend *empathy* to those in

xiv   PREFACE

need, we're *honest* when it isn't convenient, we take *responsibility* for our mistakes and we are *resilient* when faced with the inevitable and shocking indifferences and disappointments of life. It is in the endless striving towards eudemonia or the claim of being a 'phronimos' that defines our collective humanity. Which is why I argue that long-form feature articles, well-researched and honestly told stories by journalists who know how to wield words as weapons or cast them as spells that expose our own prejudices, are narrative maps that can help us find our individual and collective way.

Nor do I want the pursuit of virtues to be seen as some lofty aspiration that exists only in some imaginary philosophical high-ground. When I began this preface, Melbourne, like so many cities around the globe, entered a strict lockdown in a bid to turn back the rising tide of the Covid-19 pandemic. We weren't allowed to travel more than five kilometres from home. We could only leave to get food, or medicine or to exercise for one hour a day. Masks were mandatory. We couldn't have visitors to our homes. In what was one of the world's longest and strictest lockdowns, wearing a face mask and keeping our distance from each other became daily acts of virtue—small but crucial displays of kindness and consideration that kept complete strangers safe and well. Yes, it was a mandated virtue and we faced fines if we didn't comply. But the fines themselves were also the unequivocal message from our elected leaders that 'this is who we are, and this is what we must do'.

So, when I ventured outside and joined my masked neighbours, I began to see a community collectively committing phronetic acts of practical wisdom, striving to protect each other, acting in good faith. That didn't mean we weren't exhausted as the weeks turned into months. It didn't mean we weren't angry at the inevitable failures of an under-funded and under-resourced health system, or the government's scrambling to improve contact-tracing. But we continued to strive. And now, as we ride the roundabout of the lifting and imposing of travel restrictions, I quietly think of mask-wearing as 'virtue signalling' in the true sense of the word. Wearing a face mask is 'unfunded empathy' on a grand scale, rather than the term being used as a cheap political pot-shot, fired across the aisle in a neo-liberal, 'post-truth' world. *Courage. Empathy. Honesty. Responsibility. Resilience. Phronesis.* As I completed this preface, the United States elected a new president who evoked the virtues of decency and fairness in his victory speech. The vice-president is Kamala Harris, an African American woman of South Asian descent and the daughter of immigrants. Rioters stormed the Capitol, sending shockwaves around the world. But then 22-year-old Youth Poet Laureate Amanda Gorman at the Presidential Inauguration proclaimed her countrymen 'will rebuild, reconcile, and recover'. A new horizon is coming into view. And we need journalists to help us see what lies ahead. But more than this, we need journalists who can use their storytelling skills to ignite our emotions, to help us experience empathy and encourage us to turn emotions into virtues by taking action. This is why emotion in journalism matters. In skilled hands, it is the fuel that can fire the engine of social change. So, to all of those wonderful feature writers who have helped us imagine a new horizon and encouraged us to look beyond it, to who we are and who we want to be, thank you. And to those writers who have yet to tell their own honest stories that will change how we see the world: I eagerly await your words.

Melbourne, VIC, Australia   Jennifer Martin

Acknowledgements

I am indebted to all of the journalists whose rigorous reporting and sublime writing have informed this book and particularly to Helen Garner, Chloe Hooper and Hannah Dreier, whose articles are the subject of my case studies. It has been such a privilege to read, study and live with your stories. Your work has transported and transformed me. Thank you.

This book simply could not have been written without the generous guidance and support of Carolyne Lee, my former PhD supervisor, colleague and friend. Carolyne, I remember exactly where I was standing, coffee in hand, in the shadow of Melbourne University's John Medley building, when you planted the seed for what would become my PhD. And when that project was complete, you had faith in me that I would write a book and you have since read through every draft of every chapter until it was so. Thank you. To Denis Muller, for the sharing of your extensive knowledge about ethics and the media and your kind and wise insights into this messy business we call life—I treasure our conversations. To Lisa Waller, thank you for all of your encouragement and wisdom in knowing what it takes to do the hard work and letting me know that I could do it. And to Matthew Ricketson, thank you for being so generous with your time and knowledge and for always answering my knocks on your office door and letting me plunder your bookshelves. To Kristy Hess, who provided such valuable feedback on my work and has given me both encouragement and inspiration. To Margaret Simons, thank you for your ability to know how to fix it, and when to put it down and eat a scone, and for your support for this project from its beginnings as a PhD.

I also want to thank Deakin University's 'Warrnambool Writers' Collective' (TWC) for running their annual writing retreats where I found the rare treasures of friendship, fellowship and time to write. Also, from Deakin, my 'SUAW' (Shut Up and Write) buddies who kept me turning up to the page both in and out of lockdown and reminded me what it was all for, exactly when it counted. Likewise to my 'Writer's Circle': Meg and the gang, for being there when I finally understood that creating something from nothing is hard—and worth it. Thank you also to my dear friends and fellow writers, Nadia and Kym, for never doubting.

I am indebted to the expertise and professionalism of Juliet Richters for her proof-reading and copy editing of my book, as well as Alisa Dodge for her preparation of the index. Such safe hands! And to Palgrave's excellent editorial team, Lucy Batrouney, Mala Sanghera-Warren, Bryony Burns and Emily Wood. Thank you for being so supportive of my work. I am also indebted to the Walkley Foundation, especially Barbara Blackman and Helen Johnstone who answered all of my requests with patience and grace. Thank you. And to my intellectual 'home away from home', the International Association of Literary Journalists, who welcomed me as a PhD candidate, I value your intellectual rigor and generosity.

Finally, thanks to my now-adult children, Zeke, Atticus and Keziah for always asking 'how's the book going?' and then having the patience to listen to the answer for much longer than they needed to. Atticus, thank you for your brilliant cover design of me as a rock star. It was perfect and you were robbed. And to Martin Armstrong, thank you for quietly making a liar of me by bringing the eudemonia, every day.

CONTENTS

Part I	Theory	1
1	Why We Need a Map	3
2	Navigating Narrative Journalism: Blurred Boundaries and Uncertain Beginnings	17
3	The Virtue Paradigm: The Feature and Democracy	45
4	The Virtue Paradigm: A New Framework	65
5	The Virtue Map: The Walkley Project	81
6	The Virtue Map: Emotions and Virtues	109
Part II	Case Studies	145
7	Children: A Case Study	147
8	Disadvantaged or Socially Marginalized: A Case Study	181

9	Citizen, Nation, World: A Case Study	209
10	Conclusion	237

Appendix: List of Recommended Reading by Chapter 247

Index 253

LIST OF TABLES

Table 5.1	The Virtue Map: a study of Walkley Award-winning features 1988–2014	100
Table 7.1	Individual Virtue Map, Helen Garner 'Did Daniel Have to Die?'	149
Table 8.1	Individual Virtue Map, Chloe Hooper 'The Tall Man'	182
Table 9.1	Individual Virtue Map, Hannah Dreier 'A Betrayal'	216

PART I

Theory

CHAPTER 1

Why We Need a Map

Throughout this book I address a deceptively simple question which I first asked as a reader, then as a reporter and finally as a researcher. That is 'How do journalists make us feel emotions when we read their work?' How do journalists bring their writing and reporting skills together to construct compelling narratives that communicate emotions to readers, and permit readers to empathize with those people who are the subject of the stories? The Scottish philosopher and neo-Aristotelian theorist Alasdair MacIntyre declared in his seminal work, *After Virtue*, first published in 1981, that 'man is in his actions and practice, as well as in his fictions, essentially a story-telling animal' (2007, 215–216). Yet the way in which a journalist attempts to provoke readers' emotions is an important but often unacknowledged and untheorized factor in the construction of award-winning, magazine-style feature articles (Aare 2016; Coward 2013; Shapiro 2005, 2006; Wahl-Jorgensen 2013a, b, 2018, 2019). While this kind of close textual analysis of writing devices, which highlights how the fiction writer engages readers by making them care, has been an essential component of literary studies, this focus has not been applied as consistently and rigorously in journalism scholarship (Fursich 2009; Keen 2006; Lee 2011). In this book, I examine how journalists tell their stories and, through that process, I consider what those stories may say about who we are. I argue that among the best examples of prize-winning magazine-style narrative journalism, readers are given the much-needed opportunity to

© The Author(s), under exclusive license to Springer Nature Switzerland AG 2021
J. Martin, *Emotions and Virtues in Feature Writing*,
https://doi.org/10.1007/978-3-030-62978-6_1

contemplate what it means to be a good person living well with others in a community.

The purpose of this book is to propose a timely new method of understanding some of the 'best' examples of long-form magazine-style literary journalism, or, 'long-form', a form that is celebrated with awards and honours around the globe, including, to name a handful, the US Pulitzer Prize, the British Press Awards, the European Press Prize and Australia's Walkley Awards. These exemplars of the form transcend the news cycle and are considered beacons of journalism's higher purpose, which includes helping people to grapple with the deeper questions of what it means to be human, a purpose that aligns with Kovach and Rosenstiel's argument that a journalist's first duty is to her citizens (Kovach and Rosenstiel 2014, 9). Whereas much of the existing literature on long-form has focused on journalism's normative fourth estate role of holding power to account, my focus is on investigating how its creators wield reporting and narrative tools to harness emotion, in the process addressing issues of social inclusion and cohesion.

Connections between human beings are forged by the sharing of stories. At the most fundamental level it is telling each other what we have been through and articulating how those experiences have shaped us that define who we are, as individuals, communities and nations. In an increasingly networked world, these stories are delivered to us across a vast array of platforms and devices, while many traditional print or legacy media outlets continue to struggle or fail to keep pace with the unrelenting fallout from the fourth revolution, the internet (Dowling 2014; McChesney 2013; Hendrickx 2020; Ricketson et al. 2020). As Anderson, Bell and Shirky proclaimed in their 2015 'part survey and part manifesto' about how journalists in the United States could adapt to the present, 'the future is already here' and 'there is no such thing as the news industry anymore' (Anderson et al. 2015, 32). But within this time of unprecedented change, award-winning long-form narrative journalism continues to survive and thrive, both in print and online, providing a rich and dynamic field of scholarship (Bak and Reynolds 2011; Roberts and Giles 2014; Hartsock 2016; Keeble and Tulloch 2012, 2014; Ricketson 2014; Ricketson and Graham 2017). A close study of those stories judged to be among the best examples of the form is both fitting and overdue. It is also important in helping us understand why this style of journalism resonates with readers and how such resonance is achieved.

While this book had its foundations in a larger study of 23 feature articles that had won Walkley awards, Australia's equivalent of the US Pulitzer Prize, my findings on how journalists communicate emotions to readers on topics of social significance can be used to inform a deeper understanding of narrative journalism around the globe. During my research into these magazine-style articles, it became clear there was no single theoretical framework that could adequately hold the complexity of a journalist's process of building narratives that communicate emotions and virtues to readers, much less, one that could explore how these stories may contribute in a positive way to society. In an effort to address this lacuna I turned to theorists from sociology as well as literary and media studies, which led me to develop my own framework, the Virtue Paradigm, and a new analytical tool, the Virtue Map. The latter divides award-winning features first into broad subjects: children, the disadvantaged or socially marginalized, the citizen and the nation. Then the stories are read for evidence of six main virtues: *courage*, full *empathy* (which comprises sympathy, compassion and kindness), *honesty*, *resilience*, *responsibility* and, finally, my reconceptualization of Aristotle's master intellectual virtue of *phronesis* or practical wisdom (Aristotle 2019, 104–106 [VI.5, 1140a–1140b29]).

Throughout this book I will show how the journalist's mastery of a range of narrative and reporting techniques allows us, the readers, to be transported into the story, permitting us to experience people, places and situations often far beyond our own lives. It is in this writing that journalism's greatest gift to society is revealed—which is providing us with the opportunity to consider and perhaps even change our view of the world and our place in it. One of the central arguments in this book is that within these richly textured stories readers are effectively given permission to consider the primarily Aristotelian question of what it means to live well together as a society. I argue that award-winning long-form journalism, those stories that transcend the daily news cycle, provides textual guides for us to contemplate virtues and to consider how we may harness those virtues to steer us towards a modern equivalent of what Aristotle referred to as *eudemonia*, a term that is often translated as 'happiness' but is best understood for the purposes of our discussion as 'flourishing' (Kristjánsson 2018, 1; Aristotle 2019, 414). This book considers to what extent prize-winning features contribute towards the nourishing of community by performing the important cultural work of helping people live well together, to flourish, both with and through the media (Couldry 2012; Couldry et al. 2013, 1). It is my hope that the Virtue Map will provide a compass with which scholars, students and readers of long-form features can better map how journalists write award-winning stories and perhaps, through that process, more deeply understand why some stories resonate with them or challenge their own personal, political and community landscape. The Virtue Map also provides a means by which to appreciate the emotional labour of the journalist and provides a more multifaceted perspective of emotional work within contemporary journalism.

Although there has been considerable scholarly debate surrounding definitions of what comprises *literary* and *narrative* journalism or *reportage*, this book moves beyond concerns about how these articles are labelled to consider how they are constructed (Bak and Reynolds 2011; Hartsock 2016, 83; Ricketson 2014; Ricketson and Graham 2017; Zdovc 2008). In constructing a feature story, a writer communicates emotions through the employment of a range of specific narrative and reporting devices that have the potential to transport readers into an imagined world that is, like all instances of journalism, bound by time and space (Hartsock 2016, 150). My focus on award-winning long-form, magazine-style journalism, through a discussion in Part I of my larger study of the 23 magazine-style feature articles from Australia's Walkley awards between 1988 and 2014, and my 3 specific case studies in Part II, ensures that the stories may reasonably be considered to be compelling narratives—having been judged as exemplars of the form (Martin 2017).

Throughout this book, I argue that it is only through experiencing emotions as part of the complex act of reading that people are encouraged by the journalist to consider virtues such as empathy, courage or responsibility. Among the best examples of narrative journalism are feature articles that I consider to be *phronetic journalism*, a term I based upon the attribute that Aristotle considered the most important of the intellectual virtues, phronesis, which is commonly translated as prudence or 'practical wisdom' (Aristotle 2019, 104–106 [VI.5, 1140a–1140b29]). By this term, I mean narrative journalism that can encourage a person to engage with issues that concern their community. In Aristotle's terms, such a person was referred to as a 'phronimos', someone who was considered 'a fully virtuous person, guided by phronesis' (Kristjánsson 2018, 27). Phronetic journalism refers to a 'deliberation that is based on values, concerned with practical judgement and informed by reflection' (Kinsella and Pitman 2012, 2), and arises from a synergy of well-written prose with the practical skills of reporting, which include fact finding and interviewing, or Aristotle's *techne* (Aristotle 2019, 104–117 [VI.5–3]). This virtue of phronesis is found in stories in which the writer strives to connect people with conversations about important issues, such as the treatment of Aboriginal Australians, refugees and vulnerable children, issues generating conversations that help to construct the constantly evolving identity of a modern democracy.

I advocate that there are some prize-winning features that can be considered examples of phronetic journalism—that is, journalism that has contributed to effecting a positive change in society. An Australian example is the reporting of *Newcastle Herald* journalist Joanne McCarthy, who won the Walkley Foundation's top honour, a Gold Walkley, in 2013, for her coverage of institutional child sexual abuse (Walkley Foundation 2013). McCarthy's extensive reporting (2020) was instrumental in the establishment of Australia's Royal Commission into Institutional Responses to Child Sexual Abuse (2017). It is this concern for others, combined with a desire to effect change, which is a key component of phronetic journalism. Its function is to construct a narrative that successfully communicates important civic concerns to readers. The Virtue Map may provide insight into what kind of readers journalists have in mind when they construct their narratives. Reading Benedict Anderson's seminal theory on imagined communities has informed my notions of nationalism, and, combined with my own two decades of experience as a journalist, has led me to consider that journalists may well be writing for an 'imagined *virtuous* community of readers'. By 'imagined virtuous community' I refer to readers who the writer perceives identify with a shared concept of what kind of moral behaviour is expected of citizens within a modern democracy such as Australia (Anderson 1983). I argue throughout this book that in order to write feature articles that are celebrated with awards for excellence in journalism, the author must have a clear idea of who it is they are writing for.

This book is organized into two sections. Part I orientates readers within the discipline of narrative journalism and introduces the Virtue Map, while Part II presents three detailed case studies that demonstrate how the Virtue Map can be operationalized. Chapter 2 of the first section of the book traces the origins of the feature article and the possibility that the provenance for literary journalism can be found beyond American shores, before Wolfe's famous essay, 'New Journalism', published in the edited anthology of the same name (Wolfe 1973), and even before Dickens or Defoe, back to fifth-century Athens and the communication of Ancient

8 J. MARTIN

Greek myths (Connery 2011; Hartsock 2000; Marsh 2010; Cawthon 2012). The discussion then shifts to addressing the particular demands upon the feature writer, specifically the contract with the reader to tell a compelling story using narrative devices while still remaining aligned with the principles of accurate and fair reporting. Readers are then introduced to the need to critically evaluate terms such as 'impact' and 'quality' as measures of the success of a journalistic narrative as well as the particular characteristics of 'prize culture' (English 2008; Street 2005; Willig 2019). I also discuss how Bourdieu's field theory can help us appreciate the cultural and symbolic capital of journalism awards (Bourdieu 1996, 4; Bourdieu and Johnson 1993; Couldry 2003, 653–677; Willig 2019). The awarding of prizes is a public declaration of what an organization considers valuable and worthy of celebration. In this way, journalism prizes, such as the Pulitzers, the British Press Awards and Australia's Walkley Awards, 'create winners, not just in the obvious sense, but also by establishing the rules and conditions that define the *type* of winner' (Street 2005, 833). At this chapter's end, readers will have a deeper understanding of the current discussions surrounding the proliferation and prestige of awards and their cultural significance (Street 2005; English 2008; Willig 2019).

Chapter 3 considers the feature article and its relationship with democracy and society, with a focus on some of the key debates about what it means to be a 'good person' living alongside others. The theoretical scaffolding of the Virtue Paradigm, upon which the Virtue Map rests, is introduced. The chapter begins with Habermas's notion of the public sphere and his complex theory of what he refers to as 'the ideal speech' situation (Habermas 2001). I introduce the neo-Aristotelian theorists MacIntyre, Preston and Couldry, and discuss how their notion of a person's desire to live a 'good life' intersects with my reconceptualization of Aristotle's virtue of phronesis as a means of encapsulating journalism's function to encourage good citizenship, a concept that is discussed in-depth in Chap. 6 (MacIntyre 2007; Preston 2007; Couldry et al. 2013). Anderson's conceptualization of 'imagined communities' is discussed alongside Australian anthropologist and social theorist Ghassan Hage's views on what he describes as 'the rise of paranoid white-nationalism' which he argues has left Australia's Aboriginal population as outsiders in their own land (Anderson 1983; Hage 2003).

Chapter 4 outlines the research methods applied throughout this book, beginning with a discussion on how close textual analysis, discourse analysis, critical discourse analysis and transportation theory also inform this work. Then the widely accepted role of objectivity as a cornerstone of journalistic practice is contextualized within the more recent turn in journalism scholarship towards the study of emotions (Pantti 2010a, b; Papacharissi 2014, 2015; Beckett and Deuze 2016; Wahl-Jorgensen 2019). The chapter concludes with an introduction to how the Greek philosopher Aristotle's virtue of phronesis has been reconceptualized by scholars in the last 50 years and provides a valuable framework for ensuring ethics inform our professional endeavours.

In Chap. 5 I explain how the Virtue Map emerged as a result of my earlier study into the role of emotion in a selection of Walkley award-winning long-form features. The chapter begins with a description of the unique genesis of long-form journalism in Australia and a brief history of the Walkley Awards, including their humble beginnings in 1956 when they were set up by oil baron William Walkley with a cash prize and a trophy for just five categories (Hurst 1988, 9–10). Now more than 1300 entries are received each year across 30 categories for the awards, which are often compared to the prestigious American Pulitzer Prize for journalism (Walkley Foundation 2020). After a description of how the landscape of feature writing in Australia has changed in recent times, I outline my pilot study and explain how I selected the 23 Walkley winning stories from 1988 to 2014 that comprised my final project. I discuss how I decided upon my chapter themes for the Virtue Map, including my rationale to change these themes to better demonstrate the potential for a wider application of the model in Part II of this book, in particular to Hannah Dreier's 2019 Pulitzer Prize-winning feature article, 'A Betrayal' (Dreier 2018).

Finally, this chapter closes with the inclusion of a table showing how the Virtue Map was operationalized in my original Walkley study. The Virtue Map lists, along the vertical axis, the four thematic categories of children, disadvantaged or socially marginalized, citizens and the nation. Alongside the themes are listed the virtues of courage, empathy, honesty, resilience, responsibility and the master virtue of phronesis. In Chap. 6, the final chapter in Part I, the Virtue Map is contextualized within the recent emotional turn in journalism studies, providing insight into the nature of emotions and their function and role in relation to the construction of virtues. I expand upon our foundational conceptualization of phronesis, or 'practical wisdom', as discussed in Chap. 4, before shifting the discussion to the specific function of emotion in narrative journalism. The narrative tools and writing devices journalists use in constructing their feature articles are discussed and then the chapter concludes by defining the six virtues of the Virtue Map.

Part II of the book is devoted to three case studies and includes recommendations for further reading of award-winning journalism. In this section of the book, I demonstrate how the Virtue Map can be operationalized as a tool to help understand the role of emotion and virtue in award-winning, long-form journalism. In addition to identifying the six virtues from my Walkley study I also found that each of the 23 stories could be categorized under the story themes of 'children', 'Aboriginal Australians', 'citizens' and 'the nation', with 9 articles including at least 3 of the themes. The 'nation' theme applied to 20 stories, the 'citizen' theme to 16 and the 'children' theme to 12, and 6 stories specifically concerned Australia's Aboriginal population. I had originally considered a 'social justice' theme but I decided the term, although relevant, was too broad within the context of my smaller, national study to recognize the unique historical and ongoing hardships experienced by Indigenous Australians. But, as outlined in Chap. 5, I made the decision to broaden the category themes to better demonstrate the global relevance of the Virtue Map model. I had initially planned to replace the 'Aboriginal Australians' category with 'First Nations People' but I wanted to include those stories about displaced people such as immigrants. For this reason, I decided upon a separate category for stories about those who were disadvantaged or socially marginalized. The advantage of the Virtue Map is that the model is flexible, which affords the researcher the authority to argue for and choose specific categories that best illuminate the chosen article. In the same way, the researcher is responsible for the inclusion or exclusion of individual virtues. I am not advocating the Virtue Map as an all-encompassing, 'one-size-fits-all' model to be applied uncritically to any example of award-winning long-form journalism. Rather I am suggesting that the Virtue Map provides readers and researchers with a fresh lens to view the role of emotion in writing that is celebrated for its ability to engage readers in compelling narratives about important topics.

Chapter 7, 'Children', is the first of three chapters dedicated to demonstrating how the Virtue Map can be used as a tool to deepen our understanding of how journalists use reporting and narrative tools to communicate emotions to readers. The case study chosen for this chapter is Helen Garner's 1993 article for *Time Australia Magazine* 'Did Daniel Have to Die?', which tells the story of the brutal death of a two-year-old boy at the hand of his mother's de facto husband (Garner 1993; Garner 2017, 181–188). This chapter explores in detail how Garner, through her combining of narrative and reporting devices, provides readers with pathways to vicariously experiencing the pain of people they have never met who have found themselves in situations they would never want to imagine. Or, as I discovered, Garner's story navigated me back to my own childhood trauma of a violent father, providing me with insight into the dynamics of my family. In this chapter I contextualize Garner's story as a part of the successful push by the mainstream media, in particular the Murdoch owned, tabloid *Herald-Sun* newspaper, for the subsequent government introduction of the mandatory reporting of child abuse in Victoria. As is the case with each of the three chapters that comprise Part II, my analysis is informed by my larger study of award-winning feature articles and my ongoing research and application of the Virtue Map to narrative journalism. Although only 23 articles were included in my final research project, I had read (and continue to read) many more Walkley winning magazine and newspaper features, as well as magazine-style entries that had won in other categories, such as investigative, business, Indigenous affairs and sports journalism (Walkleys 2020). My insights into each of the three articles I have chosen as case studies for my Virtue Map model are further enriched by my past 25-years' experience as a journalist and my great love of narrative journalism from around the globe. In the past decade, I have also had the privilege of teaching feature writing and journalism to university students.

Chapter 8 is dedicated to an analysis of Chloe Hooper's 2006 long-form feature, 'The Tall Man', about the death in custody of an Aboriginal man on Australia's remote Palm Island. The case study of Hooper's story exemplifies the Virtue Map's disadvantaged or socially marginalized theme. This category recognizes the strong social justice themes that drive many award-winning long-form narratives. It also highlights the role of journalism in holding the powerful to account and giving a voice to the silenced. For example, the most recent publicly available data for Australia shows that 31 per cent of Indigenous people are living in poverty (Markham and Biddle 2018) compared with a poverty rate for the whole population of 13 per cent (ACOSS & UNSW 2020). Waller and McCallum have found, based upon their research into more than 30 years of Australian media coverage on Indigenous issues, that reporting routinely frames Indigenous people as victims of discrimination and that this portrayal is a source of shame for the nation (Waller and McCallum *forthcoming* 2021: 9). Waller and McCallum refer to this framing as 'the Social Justice narrative that draws on the values of collective responsibility to support those more disadvantaged', arguing that this narrative embodies the belief that it is 'a matter of social justice for governments to help those most unfortunate in the society and it was the whole community's responsibility to solve the problems Indigenous people experienced' (9). In this book, I have drawn upon the Social Justice narrative in order to internationalize the Virtue Map for a broader audience by replacing the 'Aboriginal Australian' category with the theme of 'disadvantaged or socially marginalized' in a way that maintains a sense of collective responsibility for the wellbeing of all members of society. In common with Waller and McCallum, I draw on the work of North American scholar Mark Rifkin and his theory of 'settler common sense' as a helpful framework for a critical discourse analysis of Hooper's writing (Rifkin 2014). In her story Hooper positions herself as keenly aware of her privileged white status, which has the effect of providing readers with the opportunity to examine their own privilege and how their own 'settler common sense' may have informed their judgement of Aboriginal Australians.

In Chap. 9, 'Citizen, Nation, World: A Case Study', I conclude my analyses by exploring how the Virtue Paradigm and the Virtue Map can be useful in understanding how journalists of long-form use their writing and reporting skills to convey emotion, creating compelling narratives about what it means to belong to a local, national or even global community. This chapter provides insight into some of the international prizes for long-form feature writing, highlighting the need for scholarship to extend the study of narrative journalism beyond what has been a largely Anglo-centric focus to one which includes writing from a diverse range of cultural, social and geographical backgrounds. In this chapter, I demonstrate the relevance of the Virtue Map by analysing the 2019 US Pulitzer Prize winning feature article by Hannah Dreier, 'A Betrayal' (Dreier 2018). My final analysis chapter combines a discussion of the 'citizen' and 'nation' categories introduced in Chap. 5 and examines how these two themes entwine in Dreier's article about the plight of an immigrant teenage boy in the United States caught up in the notorious gang, MS–13. While I do not suggest that the Virtue Map should and even could be used as a universal model to neatly expose how journalists make readers feel emotion, I do argue that it is a valuable tool for understanding how writers construct compelling narratives that transcend the daily news cycle.

Chapter 10 concludes the book by summarizing my argument on the usefulness of the Virtue Map in helping readers identify how, in the process of communicating these emotions, journalists may also be framing a particular set of values for their imagined readership. I also acknowledge the great need for further scholarship into the way in which journalists around the globe use narrative and reporting devices to help readers feel emotion—and, importantly, how it is in the experiencing of that emotion that readers are given the opportunity to change their world view. The

Virtue Map, through identifying when and how journalists insert themselves into the narrative, is a powerful vehicle that has potential to provide insight into this significant emotional investment and may even help, in some instances, to identify the risks of this labour to the writer's own safety and wellbeing. Nor is the model limited to award-winning long-form journalism. Indeed, it could just as effectively identify emotions and virtues—or a lack of them—across a range of media forms that employ narrative storytelling such as entertainment writing, television, podcasts or documentary. The Virtue Map's contribution to the field of journalism studies is as a tool that helps us better understand the synergy that is created when forensic reporting skills are fused with well-written prose that has the potential, through the communication of emotion, to spark the imaginations of readers and encourage them to consider what it means to be a citizen in this globalized, mediatized society.

References

Aare, C. 2016. A Narratological Approach to Literary Journalism: How an Interplay between Voice and Point of View May Create Empathy with the Other. *Literary Journalism Studies* 8 (1): 106–139.

Anderson, B. 1983. *Imagined Communities: Reflections on the Origin and Spread of Nationalism*. London: Verso.

Anderson, C.W., E. Bell, and C. Shirky. 2015. Post-Industrial Journalism: Adapting to the Present. *Geopolitics, History, and International Relations* 7 (2): 32–123.

Aristotle. 2019. *Nicomachean Ethics*. 3rd ed. Translated by T. Irwin. Indianapolis: Hackett Publishing.

Australian Council of Social Services [ACOSS] and the University of New South Wales [UNSW]. 2020. Poverty in Australia 2020. Sydney: ACOSS and UNSW. Accessed 21 May 2020. http://povertyandinequality.acoss.org.au/wp-content/uploads/2020/02/Poverty-in-Australia-2020_Part-1_Overview.pdf.

Bak, J.S., and B. Reynolds. 2011. *Literary Journalism across the Globe: Journalistic Traditions and Transnational Influences*. Amherst, MA: University of Massachusetts Press.

Beckett, C., and M. Deuze. 2016. On the Role of Emotion in the Future of Journalism. *Social Media and Society* 15 (July–Sept.): 1–6.

Bourdieu, P. 1996. *On Television and Journalism*. London: Pluto Press.

Bourdieu, P., and R. Johnson. 1993. *The Field of Cultural Production: Essays on Art and Literature*. Cambridge: Polity Press.

Cawthon, D. 2012. Some Things Never Change: Myth and Structure in Pulitzer Prize Winning Stories, 1997–2012. MA thesis, University of Missouri-Columbia.

Accessed June 19, 2020. https://mospace.umsystem.edu/xmlui/bitstream/handle/10355/33132/research.pdf?sequence=2andisAllowed=y.

Connery, T.B. 2011. *Journalism and Realism: Rendering American Life*. Evanston: Northwestern University Press.

Couldry, N. 2003. Media Meta-Capital: Extending the Range of Bourdieu's Field Theory. *Theory and Society* 32 (5–6): 653–677.

———. 2012. *Media, Society, World: Social Theory and Digital Media Practice*. Cambridge: Polity Press.

Couldry, N., M. Madianou, and A. Pinchevski. 2013. *Ethics of Media*. New York: Palgrave Macmillan.

Coward, R. 2013. *Speaking Personally: The Rise of Subjective and Confessional Journalism*. Basingstoke, UK: Palgrave Macmillan.

Dowling, D. 2014. Escaping the Shallows: Deep Reading's Revival in the Digital Age. *DHQ: Digital Humanities Quarterly* 8 (2) https://www.digitalhumanities.org/dhq/vol/8/2/000180/000180.html.

Dreier, H. 2018. A Betrayal. *ProPublica*, April 2. Accessed February 6, 2020. https://features.propublica.org/ms-13/a-betrayal-ms13-gang-police-fbi-ice-deportation/.

English, J.F. 2008. *The Economy of Prestige: Prizes, Awards, and the Circulation of Cultural Value*. 2nd ed. Cambridge, MA: Harvard University Press.

Fursich, E. 2009. In Defense of Textual Analysis. *Journalism Studies* 10 (2): 238–252.

Garner, H. 1993. Did Daniel Have to Die? *Time Australia Magazine*, March 8, 22–27.

———. 2017. Killing Daniel. In *True Stories: The Collected Short Non-fiction*. Melbourne: Text Publishing, 181–188.

Habermas, J. 2001. Truth and Society: The Discursive Redemption of Factual Claims to Validity. In *On the Pragmatics of Social Interaction: Preliminary Studies in the Theory of Communicative Action*, ed. B. Fultner, 85–103. Cambridge, MA: MIT Press.

Hage, G. 2003. *Against Paranoid Nationalism: Searching for Hope in a Shrinking Society*. Sydney: Pluto Press.

Hartsock, J.C. 2000. *A History of American Literary Journalism: The Emergence of a Modern Narrative Form*. Amherst: University of Massachusetts Press.

———. 2016. *Literary Journalism and the Aesthetics of Experience*. Amherst and Boston: University of Massachusetts Press.

Hendrickx, J. 2020. Trying to Survive While Eroding News Diversity: Legacy News Media's Catch-22. *Journalism Studies* 21 (5): 598–614.

Hooper, C. 2006. The Tall Man. *Monthly*, March, 34–53.

Hurst, J. 1988. *The Walkley Awards: Australia's Best Journalists in Action*. Melbourne: John Kerr.

Keeble, R., and J. Tulloch, eds. 2012. *Global Literary Journalism: Exploring the Journalistic Imagination*. Vol. 1. New York: Peter Lang Publishers.

————, eds. 2014. *Global Literary Journalism: Exploring the Journalistic Imagination*. Vol. 2. New York: Peter Lang Publishers.

Keen, S. 2006. A Theory of Narrative Empathy. *Narrative* 14 (3): 207–236.

Kinsella, E.A., and A. Pitman, eds. 2012. *Phronesis as Professional Knowledge: Practical Wisdom in the Professions*. Rotterdam: Sense Publishers.

Kovach, B., and T. Rosenstiel. 2014. *The Elements of Journalism: What Newspeople Should Know and the Public Should Expect*. 3rd ed. New York: Three Rivers Press.

Kristjánsson, K. 2018. *Virtuous Emotions*. Oxford: Oxford University Press.

Lee, C. 2011. *Our Very Own Adventure: Towards a Poetics of the Short Story*. Melbourne: Melbourne University Press.

MacIntyre, A. 2007. *After Virtue: A Study in Moral Theory*. 3rd ed. Notre Dame, IN: Notre Dame Press.

Markham, F., and N. Biddle. 2018. Income, Poverty and Inequality. CAEPR 2016 Census Paper No. 2. Canberra: Centre for Aboriginal Economic Policy Research. Accessed 23 June 2020. https://caepr.cass.anu.edu.au/research/publications/income-poverty-and-inequality.

Marsh, C. 2010. Deeper than the Fictional Model: Structural Origins of Literary Journalism in Greek Mythology and Drama. *Journalism Studies* 11 (3): 295–310.

Martin, J. 2017. Inscribing Virtues in Australian Literary Journalism: An Investigation into How Journalists Communicate Emotions to Readers of the Magazine-style Walkley Award Winning Features, 1988–2014. PhD dissertation, University of Melbourne.

McCarthy, J. 2020. Joanne McCarthy: The Irony of the Past 40 Years Is That I'm a Journalist because of the Catholic Church. *Newcastle Herald*, February 23. https://www.newcastleherald.com.au/story/6639444/joanne-mccarthy-40-years-ago-i-wrote-the-worlds-worst-job-application-and-a-few-weeks-later/.

McChesney, R.W. 2013. *Digital Disconnect: How Capitalism Is Turning the Internet Against Democracy*. New York and London: New Press.

Pantti, M. 2010a. Disaster News and Public Emotions. In *The Routledge Handbook of Emotions and Mass Media*, ed. K. Doveling, C. von Scheve, and E.A. Konjin, 221–236. London: Routledge.

————. 2010b. The Value of Emotion: An Examination of Television Journalists' Notions on Emotionality. *European Journal of Communication* 25 (2): 168–181.

Papacharissi, Z. 2014. *Affective Publics: Sentiment, Technology, and Politics*. Oxford Studies in Digital Politics. New York: Oxford University Press.

————. 2015. Toward New Journalism(s). *Journalism Studies* 16 (1): 27–40.

Preston, N. 2007. *Understanding Ethics*. Sydney: Federation Press.

Ricketson, M. 2014. *Telling True Stories: Navigating the Challenges of Writing Narrative Non-fiction*. Sydney: Allen & Unwin.

Ricketson, M., and C. Graham. 2017. *Writing Feature Stories*. 2nd ed. Sydney: Allen & Unwin.

Ricketson, M., A. Dodd, L. Zion, and M. Winarnita. 2020. 'Like Being Shot in the Face' or 'I'm Glad I'm Out': Journalists' Experiences of Job Loss in the Australian Media Industry 2012–2014. *Journalism Studies* 21 (1): 54–71.

Rifkin, M. 2014. *Settler Common Sense: Queerness and Everyday Colonialism in the American Renaissance.* Minneapolis: University of Minnesota Press.

Roberts, W., and F. Giles. 2014. Mapping Nonfiction Narrative: A New Theoretical Approach to Analyzing Literary Journalism. *Literary Journalism Studies* 6 (2): 101–117.

Royal Commission into Institutional Responses to Child Sexual Abuse. 2017. *Final Report: Preface and Executive Summary.* Attorney-General's Department, Commonwealth of Australia, Canberra. https://www.childabuseroyalcommission.gov.au/final-report.

Shapiro, S. 2005. *Reinventing the Feature Story: Mythic Cycles in American Literary Journalism.* Baltimore, MD: Apprentice House.

———. 2006. Return of the Sob Sisters. *American Journalism Review* 28 (3): 50–57.

Street, J. 2005. 'Show Business of a Serious Kind': A Cultural Politics of the Arts Prize. *Media, Culture and Society* 27 (6): 819–840.

Wahl-Jorgensen, K. 2013a. The Strategic Ritual of Emotionality: A Case Study of Pulitzer Prize-Winning Articles. *Journalism* 14 (1): 129–145.

———. 2013b. Subjectivity and Story-Telling in Journalism: Examining Expressions of Affect, Judgement and Appreciation in Pulitzer Prize-Winning Stories. *Journalism Studies* 14 (3): 305–320.

———. 2018. Media Coverage of Shifting Emotional Regimes: Donald Trump's Angry Populism. *Media Culture and Society* 40 (5): 766–778.

———. 2019. *Emotions, Media and Politics.* Cambridge, UK, and Medford, MA: Polity Press.

Walkley Foundation. 2013. Joanne McCarthy: 'Living a Nightmare', Public Service Journalism Winner. Accessed May 11, 2020. https://www.walkleys.com/award-winners/joanne-mccarthy-living-a-nightmare/.

———. 2020. Categories Explained. https://www.walkleys.com/awards/walkleys/categories/.

Waller, L., and K. McCallum. Forthcoming 2021. Settler Colonial Representations of Indigenous Disadvantage. In *The Routledge Companion to Media and Poverty,* ed. S. Borden. London: Routledge.

Willig, I. 2019. Ideals of Journalism the Historical Consecration of Media Capital in Prize Awards and the Case of the Danish Cavling Award 1945–2016. *Media History.* Online May 6, 2019. https://doi.org/10.1080/13688804.2019.1608169.

Wolfe, T. 1973. The New Journalism. In *The New Journalism,* ed. T. Wolfe and E.W. Johnson, 3–36. New York: Harper and Row.

Zdovc, S.M. 2008. *Literary Journalism in the United States of America and Slovenia.* Lanham, MD: University Press of America.

CHAPTER 2

Navigating Narrative Journalism: Blurred Boundaries and Uncertain Beginnings

Much of the scholarship on the topic of the origins and definitions of literary or narrative journalism has been focused on links with the American tradition of 'New Journalism', which is widely accepted to have begun with the writing of journalists such as Tom Wolfe, Gay Talese, Truman Capote and Joan Didion (1979). However, as will be discussed in this chapter, the narrative story-telling tradition has a far older, more expansive and richer lineage than can be seen through a primarily western, United States, Anglocentric lens that dates the form as beginning in the 1960s (Calvi 2010, 2019; Connery 2011; Hartsock 2000; Keeble and Tulloch 2012, 2014; Laughlin 2002; Zdovc 2008). In the 2009 inaugural edition of the International Association for Literary Journalism Studies (IALJS) journal, *Literary Journalism Studies*, Norman Sims (who was IALJS president from 2014 to 2016) called for 'an international scholarship that recognises there are different national manifestations' (Sims 2009, 9). He declared that, 'In the United States we finally understand that literary journalism has a long history' and that he believed that 'we should base the history of literary journalism on a broad time frame—not assuming, for example, that all literary journalism descended from the New Journalism of the sixties' (Sims 2009, 10). Writing in 2016, fellow IALJS member John Hartsock proclaimed: 'I write as an American scholar. I say that in all humility, and certainly not triumph. This is because one thing I have learned in recent years as a scholar and editor is just how much literary values can shift and change between cultures' (Hartsock 2016, 7).

© The Author(s), under exclusive license to Springer Nature
Switzerland AG 2021
J. Martin, *Emotions and Virtues in Feature Writing*,
https://doi.org/10.1007/978-3-030-62978-6_2

Before I embark upon a discussion about what long-form is, I must establish at the outset what it is not. In order to illuminate my discussion of magazine-style features, otherwise referred to as long-form narrative journalism (or 'long-form'), I will include, as examples of how some writers cross the line from fact to fiction, a necessarily brief discussion of three examples of well-known, book-length journalism. The first is Truman Capote's *In Cold Blood* (1966), the second is Michael Herr's *Dispatches* (1977) and the third is Helen Garner's *The First Stone* (1995). I have included these three particular books in my discussion, as they are well-known and engaging examples of beautiful writing about real events. All three books provide a means of illuminating the challenges for both readers and researchers in navigating the boundaries between what is journalism and what is fiction.

In 1972 Tom Wolfe wrote a 13-page essay, 'The Birth of the New Journalism: Eyewitness Report by Tom Wolfe', which he then used to open his 1973 anthology of 23 long-form writers, titled *The New Journalism* (Wolfe 1972; Wolfe and Johnson 1973). But it is important to note that Wolfe never claimed that 'New Journalism' was new, instead, what he did declare was 'the first new direction in American literature in half a century' (1973, 3) and that was that it was possible to write 'journalism that would read like a "novel" or "short story"' (1973, 9). As Australian journalism scholar Sue Joseph explained, what Wolfe was advocating was 'really a fresh attempt at a certain form of journalism which took on a life of its own in the 1960s and 1970s, more because of the controversy surrounding certain assumptions about its celebrity, and the celebrity of its proponents, than anything else' (Joseph 2010, 83.) Joseph also asked the question: was it Wolfe's 'seminal work that planted the seed to focus on the American canon, and investigate the history and develop the discourse around the genre?' (Joseph 2010, 84).

As fellow Australian journalist and journalism scholar Matthew Ricketson has argued, another consequence of Wolfe's description of journalism that reads like a novel (or at least the subsequent interpretations of Wolfe's original essay) is the misconception that it is somehow acceptable for the writer to fictionalize the events and people who are the subject of the article (Ricketson 2001, 156–161, 2010).

Speaking as part of the President's panel at the 14th IALJS conference, held in 2019, Norman Sims said that while he did *not* excuse writers of long-form 'making stuff up', he had become, in some instances, 'more forgiving' of the transgression in particular cases (Sims 2019). In his 1984 book, *The Literary Journalists*, Sims was unequivocal in his censure of

2 NAVIGATING NARRATIVE JOURNALISM: BLURRED BOUNDARIES… 19

invention in long-form. He wrote: 'Should I discover that a piece of literary journalism was made up like a short story, my disappointment would ruin whatever effect it had created as literature' (Sims 1984, 5). More than three decades later Sims explained that he now divided writers into two types, 'frauds' and 'freaks'. The frauds encompassed journalists like Claas Relotius and Jayson Blair, reporters who simply invented facts when real life failed to cooperate, deceiving their editor and their readers (Barry, Barstow, Glater, Liptak and Steinberg 2003; Klusmann and Kurbjuweit 2018). But Sims suggested that the freaks made things up for different reasons and, 'in some cases that makes them interesting'. The freaks, he argued, operated 'in a different place psychologically'. To prove his point Sims cited two examples of book-length journalism. While book-length journalism is beyond the scope of my book, which is concerned with magazine-style features, the examples *are* helpful in demonstrating the particular challenges faced when a writer endeavours to follow a journalistic method to tell a compelling narrative that spans 100,000 words or more (Ricketson 2004a, 2014, 2019; Boynton 2005). Sims's first example of a 'freak' was Truman Capote, who has famously justified inventing scenes in his book *In Cold Blood* because he was 'loyal to fiction' and believed he was creating a new way of writing and that it was also 'the route to fame and glory' (Sims 2019, 5). Like Sims, I agree that Capote's inventions were 'both unnecessary and silly', and although *In Cold Blood* is an engrossing read, it is not journalism. But despite factual inaccuracies and pure invention, Capote's version of the murder of a Kansas family of four in 1959 *is* the most widely told story, raising important questions about the *responsibility* of the writer to hold themselves to an honest accounting of events.

Another example Sims provided was *Esquire* magazine's former Vietnam War correspondent, the late Michael Herr, who admitted to inventing parts of his 1977 book, *Dispatches*. It took Herr, who also wrote dialogue for the war films *Apocalypse Now* and *Full Metal Jacket*, eight years to write his book after a war that had left him suffering terribly with what would now be diagnosed as post-traumatic stress disorder. In an interview in 1992, Herr explained:

> I don't think it's any secret that there is talk in the book that's invented. But it's invented out of that voice that I heard so often and that made such penetration into my head … I don't really want to go into that no-man's-land about what really happened and what didn't happen and where you draw the line. Everything in *Dispatches* happened for me, even if it didn't necessarily happen to me. (Schroeder 1992, 46)

Herr's explanation of his decision to invent 'talk' in his book *is* fascinating precisely because of the context in which it was written, amid the horrors of war. Herr's striving to capture in words the extremity of his experience and those around him is compelling, his voice hypnotic, making him a worthy bearer of Sim's title of 'freak'. But is it journalism? In the following excerpt, he writes about 'that voice' that he heard so often in his head:

> After a year I felt so plugged in to all the stories and the images and the fear that even the dead started telling me stories, you'd hear them out of a remote but accessible space where there were no ideas, no emotions, no facts, no proper language, only clean information. However, many times it happened, whether I'd known them or not, no matter what I'd felt about them or the way they'd died, their story was always there and it was always the same: it went, 'Put yourself in my place'. (Herr 1977, 30–31)

While I am beguiled by the power of Herr's writing and Capote's prose. I am unwilling, in the final analysis, to define either *Dispatches* or *In Cold Blood* as journalism. While both authors attempted to create works of journalism, and there are examples in their narrative of the employment of journalistic method, both books ultimately fail to meet what the *New York Times* referred to as 'the cardinal tenet of journalism, which is simply truth' (Barry et al. 2003). I will return to Sims's decision to be 'more forgiving' of Herr's and Capote's inventions, but first let's push the boundaries of the discussion by introducing what I argue is the engrossing but flawed 1995 book, by much-celebrated Australian writer Helen Garner, *The First* Stone (Garner 1995). It is worth noting, as is discussed in Part II of this book, that Garner has also, deservedly, been celebrated for her journalism, winning two Walkley awards for feature writing, the first in 1993 for an article about Daniel Valerio, a toddler who died from injuries received after repeatedly being bashed by his mother's de facto. The second Walkley was for her 2017 feature about Akon Guode, a South-Sudanese refugee who drove her car into a lake, killing 3 of her 7 children, 4-year-old twins, Hangar and Madit, and her 17-month-old son Bol. Her five-year-old daughter Alual survived after being pulled from the water (Garner 1993, 2017).

Having established that Garner is deservedly celebrated for her writing about actual events, let us now briefly examine *The First Stone*, about the sexual harassment claims made in 1992 by two female students against a professor who was the master of the University of Melbourne's Ormond College residence (Garner 1995). In Garner's *The First Stone*, we have a salient example of the damage that can result when fabrication is swathed in exquisite prose and is presented and accepted as journalism. The controversy surrounding Garner's book erupted when Dr Jenna Mead, a senior scholar at Ormond College who one of the young women confided in, wrote a letter that was published in Melbourne's *Age* newspaper on 16 August, 1995, which exposed Garner as having 'split' Mead into six or seven people (Mead 1998; Ricketson 1997, 89). Garner subsequently acknowledged she had done as Mead accused but did not apologize. Then, as Ricketson describes in Mead's edited book, *Bodyjamming*, Garner, in the reprint of her 1996 book, *True Stories*, added a 'remarkable' paragraph to the speech she gave in response to Mead's revelations (Ricketson in Mead 1997, 91). In the amended version, Garner blames the publisher's defamation lawyers for her decision, saying they had 'obliged' her to 'blur' Mead's identity. She also dismissed claims that the book was a work of fiction: 'It is not a novel. Except for this one tactic to avoid defamation action, it is reportage' (Garner 1996; Ricketson 1997, 91).

If we even *can* push broader moral considerations aside, in pure journalistic terms Garner was unequivocally wrong to present her narrative to readers as an account of real events. That 'one tactic' is enough to declare her book a failed attempt to produce a work of journalism. Ultimately Garner made the decision to put herself, not the event she was writing about, at the centre of her story, a decision that Ricketson summarized as her doing precisely what renowned literary journalist John McPhee advised against. Garner 'hitchhiked on the credibility of writers who earn the reader's trust', (Ricketson 1997, 100). Sims argued that the writing of 'freaks' such as Capote and Herr leads to valuable questions about the complex 'mental states and cultural or status surroundings at the time and circumstances' of their writing (Sims 2019, 10). According to Sims's classification, I argue that the compelling power of Garner's writing and the controversy that *The First Stone* ignited in Australia's culture, entitles Garner to be in the 'freak' category. Unlike Sims, I may be delighted by Capote's insights, transfixed by the prose of Herr, and captivated by Garner's ability to construct a sublime sentence, but I have not 'become more forgiving in certain cases' (Sims 2019, 10). Instead I agree with Sims's earlier view that any fabrication ruins the impact of a piece of literary journalism (Sims 1984, 5). The more accomplished the writing, the more risk there is that the writer's falsehoods may be believed by readers. As cultural theorist Jen Webb wrote of Garner's *The First Stone*: 'If such a work is more truly fiction, or essay, and if it is also superbly written, it can persuade readers that the author's personal sociopolitical views are a kind of "truth", which can leave them feeling either convinced or betrayed' (Webb 2017). My position, in the case of Garner in particular, must be framed within my own lived experience as a University of Melbourne alumna, a journalist and a feminist scholar. I do, however, in common with both Sims and Ricketson, embrace the challenge:

> That the representing of actual people and events in words is subject to complex questions about the difficulty or even the possibility of separating people and events from our perception and construction of them behoves us to make every effort to be clear about these complexities rather than to shrug our shoulders and say, well we all know the line between fiction and nonfiction is blurred beyond recognition. (Ricketson 2010, 4)

Returning now to the question of definitions, what our previous discussion has established at the very least is that narrative journalism, by virtue of being concerned with events that have happened, is necessarily contained by its reference to time and place, whereas conventional fictions are not limited by this consideration (Hartsock 2016, 150). Put simply, a novelist can create worlds and re-imagine history, inhabiting their narrative with characters who serve their plot but have never existed. Journalism, on the other hand, is, at its essence, a 'discipline of verification' whose very worth is built upon the foundation that what is written about has happened (Kovach and Rosenstiel 2014, 71). To return one final time to Sims's analogy, whether the writer is a 'fraud' or a 'freak', the contract with the reader *is* broken when events or people are invented, no matter how beautiful or affecting the prose. Whether the writing spans 100,000 words or less than 10,000 words, if it is not based upon verifiable facts it is not journalism.

Terms such as 'feature article', 'literary journalism', reportage and creative non-fiction, while often vaguely defined, are not always synonymous and are often contested (Ricketson 2001). Joseph has noted too that, in Australia at least, the journalists themselves often resist being labelled (Joseph 2010, 2016). She quoted as an example, Walkley-winning journalist Paul McGeough, who, as a panellist at the 2009 Sydney Writer's Festival, said: 'I think the sense amongst Australian journalists, if you dare to sit down on any bar stool in this country and say "Well, actually I'm a literary journalist", you'd get hit' (Joseph 2010, 93). In the introduction to her 2016 book, *Behind the Text, Candid Conversations with Australian*

Creative NonFiction Writers, Joseph explained that two of the authors of the case studies included in Part II of this book, Helen Garner and Chloe Hooper, declined to be involved in her book and questioned the label of 'creative nonfiction'. Garner told Joseph: 'I don't know why there would be such a group [of creative nonfiction writers in Australia]. There isn't one in fiction that I'm aware of, or, if there is, I'm not part of it' (Joseph 2016, 15). Garner told Joseph that when she is asked what sort of writer she is, 'she always answers in the same way: "I just say I 'write books and journalism'. If anyone presses for further details, I say I write fiction and nonfiction"' (Joseph interview with Garner in 2010, cited by Joseph 2016, 15). Chloe Hooper also dismissed the term creative non-fiction outright to Joseph, telling her that the label 'seems slightly laughable, almost twee. The term is silly and I'd never say that's what I'm doing; I write fiction and nonfiction (Joseph, interview with Hooper 2010, cited by Joseph 2016, 15). Like Garner, Hooper views herself as a writer, not a journalist, telling Joseph, 'I'm not a journalist by training, and I've never worked for a big media outlet, so I don't feel I can refer to myself as such' (Joseph 2016, 16). But whether or not Garner or Hooper define themselves as journalists, the fact remains that they are committing acts of journalism by writing about actual events and the people involved. From any theoretical perspective, they are writers of creative non-fiction and, as my discussion of their specific Walkley winning articles in Part II will demonstrate, their work is celebrated as exemplars of long-form.

While labels such as literary journalism, reportage, literary non-fiction, creative non-fiction and narrative journalism are commonly used by those of us who conduct research into these genres, for the purposes of this book the writing we are concerned with can be defined as non-fiction narrative writing that has been produced for a journalistic purpose, that has the hallmarks of accurate reporting and that encompasses various literary devices such as scene setting, dialogue, status markers and narrative perspective. The stories in this book are further differentiated as being magazine-style features. My aim in the following chapters and through the three in-depth case studies in Part II (the analysis of which is informed by my larger study of 23 prize-winning magazine-style features) is to move the discussion beyond any debate surrounding definitions or even the legitimacy of the form. I advocate a position that unequivocally accepts narrative journalism as a much-loved writing style the world over, one that deserves serious thought about how some of the most celebrated of these stories are constructed. In short, I am heeding the advice given a decade ago by John Bak, one of the founding members of the IALJS, who urged scholars within the then emerging field of literary journalism to:

> stop writing definitional manifestos that show by default that literary journalism lacks cohesion, take charge of the discipline ourselves, conduct the research that needs to be conducted, and wait for the rest to catch up with us. They will, eventually. (Bak, in Bak and Reynolds 2011, 19)

An approach such as Steensen's, in which features are viewed as a 'family of genres', allows a more fluid analysis of this complex category than has been previously canvassed by theorists such as Taylor, whose delineation of features into four types—info-based, opinion-making, entertainment and literary journalism—can create false separations (Steensen 2011; Taylor 2005, 118–128). Taylor's system of effective elements to be found in features—that they, 'campaign, entertain, shock, explain, reveal, respond, caution, inspire, inform, enlighten'—is, however, not only useful as a broad template but also provides helpful signposting of how a broad range of emotions are employed across the wide category of features (Steensen 2011; Taylor 2005). Within the form itself, moreover, there is rich evidence to support the 'elasticity' of what Hartsock (2016, 82) describes as 'narra-descriptive journalism'. Hartsock contends 'that there can never be a single designating terminology for the form' (85) and I argue that a singular definition is neither possible nor desirable. Throughout this book, I deliberately avoid the phrase 'fictional techniques' to describe the devices employed by journalists in constructing their articles, preferring instead to use the term *narrative tools*. This is to avoid any conflation of journalism, a process concerned with events that have happened, with fiction, which is concerned with 'invented people, events and issues' (Ricketson 2010). For the same reason I prefer to use the term 'subject' or 'interviewee' rather than 'character', because 'character' suggests the journalist's efforts to describe a living person to readers is a fiction.

When writing long-form journalism, the author may employ a range of narrative tools and devices that are commonly found in works of fiction, such as scene setting, the use of dialogue in the form of direct or reported speech, and description based upon evidence of a person's status markers. The purpose of these narrative devices is to engage readers and impel them to contemplate their own emotional lives and to consider how they in turn experience life in their community (Sarbin 1995). Finally, I argue that a close textual analysis of award-winning journalism may provide an important counterpoint to theorists such as Couldry, who, despite his masterful argument for the potential of journalism to achieve great social good, and his acknowledgement of journalism as a 'part of human excellence' nonetheless focuses firmly on the failures of the media (Couldry, in Couldry, Madianou and Pinchevsky 2013, 3, 49). An examination of some of the best examples of the form by scholars such as Taylor (2005, 119) has resulted in the acknowledgement of the genre/form as having certain unique properties: 'however compromised by the commodification of the marketplace, the best and ground breaking features certainly possess the power to challenge received ideas and even act as catalysts of change'. Or, as put succinctly by Ricketson and Joseph (2015, 27), 'When it is done well, literary journalism offers us both journalism's revelatory bite and literature's artful exploring of human complexity. Maybe, in the end, there is no right or wrong way of naming it'.

ORIGINS

Media scholar Shapiro noted it was journalist John Helleman, in a 1981 article, who gave New Journalism a 'bona fide birth certificate', saying the movement began in 1965 with Wolfe's publication of the *Kandy-Kolored Tangerine-Flake Streamline Baby* and Truman Capote's *In Cold Blood* (Shapiro 2005, 91). But if we consider the possibility that narrative journalism, which in the broadest of terms can be considered the art of telling true stories through the written word, then we should acknowledge a much older provenance than the impressive writing of New Journalists such as Hunter S. Thompson, Normal Mailer, Joan Didion and Gay Talese. In his 2000 book, *A History of Literary Journalism*, John Hartsock argued that narrative journalism, 'or at least its roots', extended 'as far back as there has been the perception that an accounting of phenomena in the temporal and spatial world had value to the individual and the community' and that it was 'inaccurate to suggest that narrative literary journalism is an aberrant form that, like some tumor, grew out of the side of mainstream American journalistic practice' (Hartsock 2000, 81–82). Hartsock points out Plato 'added literary embellishment' to his account of the death of Socrates in 399 BCE and the Romans used *acta*, or gazettes, to convey not just information but human interest stories to the people (82–83).

A case has also been made that the non-fiction, storied plots of narrative journalism can be traced all the way back to the myths presented in the Greek tragic plays of the fifth century BCE (Marsh 2010). This is the argument of Charles Marsh, who suggests that the comparison of narrative journalism to a literary tradition has led to 'allegations of inferiority' (2010, 297). This inferiority is supported by Wolfe's own claim (1973, 25) that 'the literary upper class were the novelists. The lower class were the journalists, and they were so low down in the structure that they were barely noticed at all'. The contribution to journalism by writers such as Elizabeth Cochrane Seaman, an American reporter born in 1864 who wrote under the pen-name of Nellie Bly and pretended to be mentally ill in order to write about what it was like in an insane asylum (Bly 2018), have been rightly acknowledged by scholars such as Shapiro and Schudson (Shapiro 2005; Schudson and Anderson 2008). At the time of writing, a monument to celebrate Bly's journalism had been commissioned at the site of her famous investigation, on what is now known as Roosevelt Island (Hester 2020).

In his seminal 2011 work, *Journalism and Realism,* Thomas B. Connery describes the period between 1850 and 1900 as a time when a 'paradigm of actuality' emerged within journalism in the United States. He says there was 'a focus on the actual and real, on people, events and details that are verifiable and based on experience', which included 'common things and common people' (Connery 2011, 14). Early examples of such 'cultural reporters' writing pre-1890s include Walt Whitman, Mark Twain, George G. Foster, William Cullen Bryant, Henry Mills Alden, Lafacadio Hearn, Jacob Riis, Josiah Flynt, Stephen Crane and Abraham Cahan (Connery 2011, 10). John Hartsock notes David Thoreau's *Cape Cod* sketches published in 1835 and Augustus Baldwin Longstreet's *Georgia Scenes* of the 1830s as even earlier examples of literary journalism (Hartsock 2000, 23). He also includes writers such as Ernest Hemingway, Sherwood Anderson, Erskine Caldwell and James Agee as exponents of the form (Hartsock 2000, 169). In 1925 the *New Yorker* was founded by Harold Ross who announced the publication would be 'interpretive rather than stenographic' (Hartsock 2000, 170). In 1933 William Shawn became editor of the *New Yorker* and the magazine's stable of writers came to include George Orwell, Morris Markey, E.B. White, Joseph Mitchell, Lillian Ross, A.J. Liebling, John McNulty and St. Clair McKelway (Hartsock 2000, 170). And in 1946 the magazine famously devoted an entire issue to John Hersey's 'Hiroshima' (Hersey 1946; Blume 2020). As demonstrated clearly in the research by Connery (2011) and Hartsock (2000), literary journalism, as noted by Norman Sims, 'already had a respectable history: it didn't arrive full grown with the new journalists of the 1960s' (Sims 1984, 5). Examples of the literary journalism form can also be traced beyond

American shores to England, such as the nineteenth-century journalism of Charles Dickens or the seventeenth-century writing of Daniel DeFoe (Michael 2001, 149–170; Cawthon 2012; Tulloch 2014). The growing body of research by literary journalism scholars, both from within the US and beyond, advocates a more nuanced approach, acknowledging the limitations of comparing narrative journalism to the novel and short story as 'most of the tropes associated with chronotopic documentary existed well before the modern fictional novel and short story' (Hartsock 2016, 83).

The understanding that the provenance for narrative journalism can be found beyond American shores, before Wolfe's *New Journalism*, and even before Dickens or Defoe, provides the opportunity for a deeper appreciation of this journalistic form. The argument that narrative journalism's lineage can be traced back to Ancient Greek myths encourages an examination of the ways in which journalists utilize mythic themes to construct their articles. My study of 23 Walkley winning magazine features, which informs my 3, in-depth case studies in Part II of this book, provided some strong examples of writers drawing upon mythic themes. One such example was Gary Tippet's 1997 winning article about an Aboriginal man, Tony Lock, who killed his childhood abuser with an axe. His opening paragraphs, in which he refers to Lock's abuser as 'The Monster', provide a powerful illustration of just how compelling an evocation of mythic imagery can be:

> These were the creatures of Tony Lock's stolen childhood: The Rainbow Bird of his daydreams and The Monster of his nightmares.
>
> The Rainbow Bird was big and bright and beautiful. He'd climb on its back and be lifted high above the paddocks and cold, wet forest, far from the lonely timber huts and the hard, rough-handed men, away to somewhere he wanted to be: to the Safe Place.
>
> But it could never keep him there.
>
> And at night The Monster would come. (Tippet 1997, 1)

In Chap. 8 I will discuss how Chloe Hooper's article, 'The Tall Man', about the death of an Aboriginal man in custody, weaves in elements of the Palm Island community's myths into her narrative (Hooper 2006).

By drawing upon mythic themes, modern non-fiction journalist narratives are able to provide readers with 'revelations of important cultural standards and beliefs' (Marsh 2010, 295). As a framing mechanism or vehicle for communicating the journalist's narrative to readers, myth has the advantage of being sufficiently ambiguous to entice readers without prescribing that they react to the story in a particular way. This is because myths 'do not tell a culture's simple truths so much as they explore its central dilemmas' (Schudson 1992, 33). These 'central dilemmas' are expressed to readers by the journalist through the communication of emotion and notions of virtue. A mythic theme is deeply informed by emotion; indeed, it is not sustainable without it, as the central theme of any myth is the struggle of the individual to either master, accept or deal with the consequences of their emotions.

As I argue in Chap. 4, considering virtue ethics alongside mythic themes may provide further insight into why these award-winning articles came to be judged as 'compelling narratives' that resonate with readers (Walkley Foundation 2020a; Ettema 2005, 134). These stories matter because they help us to understand who we are while also pointing to ways in which we can, as a community, strive to be better. As Couldry et al. argue:

> However much we disagree on specific moral issues and priorities, we may agree on one fact: that we inhabit a world connected by a common media fabric. Just as we need to show care in using the shared institution of language, so we need to be disposed to show care in our use of media, because through media we can harm each other, and in the long run harm the fabric of public life. (Couldry et al. 2013, 52)

Celebrated long-form journalism constitutes a section of this 'common media fabric' that does indeed demonstrate the careful use of this 'shared institution of language'. Rather than 'harm each other', it can be argued that these meticulously researched and eloquently expressed articles may help us, as individuals and as members of a larger society, to live well, with and through the media (Couldry et al. 2013, 1). For the purposes of our discussion, the sense of being 'well' is used as equating to Aristotle's concept of 'eudemonia', which we will recall from Chap. 1 is often translated as 'happiness' and is understood as meaning a state of 'flourishing' (Kristjánsson 2018; Aristotle 2019, 414).

Finally, Cawthon (2012, 63) argues that 'Myth, like frames, are a part of "dominant" meanings that serve as scaffolding for a story because such meanings are difficult to resist, which alludes to their pervasiveness as well as their tendency to be embedded within texts'. Myth is, however, in their study not connected back to Ancient Greece and Aristotle. Instead the researchers argue that narrative journalism is primarily an American tradition that reprises the invention of the novel; as discussed, this position ignores the contribution of writers of narrative journalism from around the world, from countries such as Brazil, Slovenia, China, Australia, Portugal, France or Germany, to name a few. The argument also does not consider the fascinating possibility of a longer lineage stretching back to the beginnings of the classical Western tradition in Ancient Greece and Rome, as argued by Marsh and Hartsock (Marsh 2010; Hartsock 2000). While there is a growing and dynamic body of research that challenges ethnocentric attitudes towards literary journalism, Cawthon's study does lay the basis for more in-depth research on the winners of the Pulitzer Prizes, as well as providing a helpful model for research into other prize-winning work (Bak and Reynolds 2011; Hartsock 2016; Dow 2016). In common with Cawthon I use Lule's definition of myth as a 'powerful, timeless drama that made sense and gave meaning to events that seemed beyond meaning and sense' and Lule's subsequent conclusion that it is this ability to convey and explain that is the 'driving force behind myth's continued use in journalism' (Cawthon 2012, 102; Lule 1988). The decision of the writer to draw upon mythic themes to create an engrossing narrative story is an important element in understanding how narrative journalism may potentially help us to live well, to achieve a state of eudemonia, of flourishing, with and through the media. This will be discussed in Chap. 6.

Features: Discourses of Impact and Notions of Quality

Journalism prizes around the world, including Australia's Walkley awards, list 'impact' as a key judging criterion (Walkley Foundation 2020a) but, similar to the phrase 'quality journalism', this is a term that is often held to be self-evident or used in a way that, as Tofel (2013, 2) suggests, is 'loose, and often confusing, sometimes so much so that one is left to wonder if the effect is not intentional'. There is a growing body of research on how to measure the impact of the media, particularly in the context of the collapse of traditional print business models and the ongoing quest for media outlets to thrive, or even survive, online, and researchers have highlighted a lack of empirical data on the subject (Napoli 2014; Simons et al. 2017; McChesney and Pickard 2011; Schudson, M. 2003a, b; Tofel 2013; Carson et al. 2016). A result of these studies has been a more thoughtful analysis of the term 'impact', defined in the *Macquarie Dictionary* as 'the influence or effect exerted by a new idea, concept, ideology, etc.' (Butler 2017). In line with such scholars as Napoli and Simons I define impact as a measure that extends beyond a simple analysis of readership size, or reach, to take into account the extent of the 'engagement' of the readers with the story. Put simply, a small audience of powerful readers such as politicians, community, industry and corporate leaders can lead to a story having more impact than if it were simply widely circulated to the general population. Further evidence of the importance of the quality of impact to the Walkley Features is the judging criterion that the articles must demonstrate 'public benefit and audience engagement' (Walkley Foundation 2020a).

Just as the word 'impact' is a contested term, the term 'quality writing' when applied to journalism is also worthy of critical analysis, both for the profession and for research purposes (O'Donnell 2009; Carson 2019; Schudson and Anderson 2008; Ricketson 2004b; Franklin 1986). Writers, editors, media owners, readers and researchers will all discuss the *value* of quality journalism but there is no agreement—and perhaps there never will be—on what the term 'quality' really means. For a media owner, quality may tie directly to financial success. For journalists, it is the calibre of the research and it is how well they feel they have arranged words on a page to captivate readers; or it could be the winning of a prestigious award, like a Pulitzer. As authors of one American study stated, 'in one sense, people feel about quality the way Justice Potter Stewart felt about pornography: they know it when they see it' (Lacy and Fico 1990).

When looking towards prize-winning journalism for evidence of the ways in which the media are engaging in a positive way with society, it is important that we rigorously analyse the basis on which these judgements rest. A salutary example is the Pulitzer Prize for journalism, often described as the profession's 'highest honour' and used as a benchmark against which other awards around the world measure themselves; however, historically, this prize has had a very narrow remit. Pulitzer prizes in journalism were traditionally given to 'the most disinterested and meritorious public service rendered by any American newspaper during the preceding year', the 'best editorial' and 'the best example of a reporter's work ... the test being strict accuracy, terseness, the accomplishment of some public good commanding public attention and respect'. A consequence of the exclusivity of the awards was the establishment of other prizes to celebrate journalism ignored by the Pulitzer Board. In 1966, the American Society of Editors established the National Magazine Awards, known as the Ellie

Awards, in order to have their own prize to honour feature writing (National Magazine Awards 2020). The Pulitzer did not introduce its feature-writing prize until 1979. The National Association of Broadcasters established their own equivalent of the Pulitzers, awarding the first Peabody prize for excellence in broadcast in 1941 (Peabody Awards 2020). In 2006, the Pulitzer Board allowed online content to be submitted in all 14 journalism categories (Pulitzer Prize 2020). It was not until 2020 that the Pulitzer Board awarded a prize for broadcasting, with the honour going to the long-running National Public Radio (NPR) podcast, *This American Life*, for an episode about life at the Mexican border under the Trump administration (This American Life 2020).

A 2006 study investigated the question 'What Makes Journalism "Excellent"?', by examining the judging criteria of Canada's National Newspaper Awards and National Magazine Awards (Shapiro et al. 2006). This study found that the literature on this topic was insubstantial, and the authors concluded the link between 'quality' and 'excellence' was 'murky', pointing out that scholars tended to settle on a definition of excellence as being 'quality in abundance' (Shapiro et al. 2006, 1). A salient finding was that 'writing style' was prominent, along with 'reporting rigour' (12). Where 'more than one story demonstrated excellence in reporting and in other aspects, judges will probably favour the one that they consider "better written". In this sense, form seems to trump content' (12). The authors, although not defining what 'better written' meant, concluded that the judges' notions of excellence were 'as sketchy as the literature on quality standards' (3). In the main, media researchers have tended to gloss over what exactly constitutes excellence, a fact noted by Penny O'Donnell, who focused on the winners of the Walkleys' top prize, the Gold Walkley, and argued more than a decade ago that the Awards:

> offer a new and under-researched starting point for thinking about journalism practice, including the profession's processes of self-evaluation, the public's ideas about journalism, and the relationship between journalism prizes and public understanding of news quality. (O'Donnell 2009, 48)

When prize-winning journalism is studied, with the notable exception of scholars such as Street, English and Willig, it tends to be on the basis that the winning of an award speaks for itself (Street 2005; English 2008; Willig 2019). This also applies across the journalism profession as a whole. O'Donnell (2009, 48) notes 'in the literature there is little evidence of consensus on how to define professional journalism standards, the concepts of quality and excellence, or the parameters for empirical investigations of these categories'. I agree with O'Donnell that 'quality journalism emerges as a complex practice that resists quantification and monetisation' (47), but I contend that there is a need to keep striving towards a definition, despite this clearly being a problematic area, judging by the gap in the literature. I share O'Donnell's concern with engaging with the public's ideas about journalism, but this book's focus is on how the journalists go about writing their award-winning long-form stories and whether or not these stories perform the cultural work of helping us to live well together. This question will be addressed through an examination of the entry criteria of journalism prizes and deepened through the specific case studies of the award-winning articles in Part II.

Like O'Donnell, fellow Australian researcher Andrea Carson chose the Walkley Awards for her study into the prevalence of investigative journalism (Carson 2019). The Walkley investigative journalism category is judged on 'well-researched and presented investigations' that demonstrate 'accuracy, ethics, tenacity and public benefit' (Walkley Foundation 2020a), and Carson's research found that, despite a widespread belief it was otherwise, the standard and amount of investigative reporting had not been declining from the perceived 'golden age' of the 1980s (Carson 2019, 111.). Like Carson, who included only articles that won an award in the 'investigative journalism' category, I too limited the selection of articles for my study to those Walkley magazine-style features that won in either the 'Best Feature' (providing they were published in the magazine section of the newspaper), 'Best Feature in a Magazine', 'Best Feature in a Newspaper', 'Best Feature published in either a newspaper or a magazine' or 'Feature Writing Long (over 4000 words)' categories. In this book, I move beyond the restrictions of a limited definition of quality to ask what the writers of award-winning long-form journalism are saying *to* and *about* the society that they are a part of, and how these journalists employ literary and reporting devices in the construction of these articles. But first, a concerted theoretical effort must be made to deconstruct what is meant by the premise that a piece of work is 'excellent' or 'quality'. Although there has been limited study on prize-winning journalism and less than a handful of studies on Australia's Walkley Awards, the field of journalism has engaged, to varying degrees with the question of how to measure quality (English 2008; Street 2005).

A 1976 study surveyed 746 daily newspaper editors, later making a point that still has relevance today: 'Judgements of how well information, thoughts, emotions and experiences are expressed and communicated are rooted in a particular time and place. This applies to peer judgements of excellence or achievement' (Bogart 2004, 44). This model was still considered strong enough for Lacy and Fico (1990) to use as a baseline for their own study. They built on Bogart's list, which included: the high ratio of staff-written copy to wire service copy; total amount of non-advertising copy; high ratio of news interpretations and backgrounders to news reports; high ratio of illustrations to text; number of wire services carried; length of average news story; and high ratio of non-advertising content to advertising; and added an eighth criterion: square inches of copy divided by the number of reporters listed with by-lines (Lacy and Fico 1990, 45). All of Bogart's criteria emphasize the importance attached to the close involvement of the journalist with the article. If the article was important enough for the reporter to be given a by-line and for it to take away precious space from advertisements or eye-catching images, then it was judged by Bogart to be high-quality journalism.

When journalists construct feature articles, they are engaging in what Maras refers to as a 'language game', by using written language to convince readers of their credibility and the power of their stories (Maras 2013, 9; Scheer 2012, 202). This written work is in turn judged—in the case of the Walkley Awards by their media peers—as to whether it is 'quality'. Maras's work also reminds us that, in terms of objectivity, reading a magazine-style feature article on a Saturday morning in the original paper publication or even online is a different experience from visiting the Walkley website (which publishes a full list of winners each year) or reading a news item telling us who the Walkley winners are for the year, and then reading the winning article with that *paratextual* knowledge in mind (Genette 1997; Maras 2013, xii, 260). In the case of print, the news article announcing the winners is most often placed not on the front page but in the body of the newspaper. Or, in the case of the magazine feature itself, it is a part of the newspaper's separate weekend magazine. Online it is also given more space, not crowded onto the screen with other news articles. I collected original hard copies of the Walkley articles in my larger study of feature winners from 1988 to 2014, that had appeared in print to gain a sense of the layout of each story on the page.

Australia's Walkley Awards—An Example of a Prize Culture

An understanding of the culture surrounding prize-giving in the media is imperative in order for us to fully appreciate the extent to which exemplary narrative journalism can be considered to nourish civic life in a modern democracy. This is because the awarding of prizes is a very public declaration of what the organization bestowing the honour considers valuable and worthy of celebration. As Ida Willig observed in her study of the judges' comments for the Danish Cavling Awards:

> In material terms, the Cavling Prize is a bronze statuette not much bigger than an Oscar presented together with a sum of money … As a symbol, the Cavling represents one of the most—if not *the* most prestigious journalistic prizes in Denmark, and one of the highest achievements a Danish journalist can dream of obtaining. (Willig 2019, 5)

The following discussion on the culture of prize-giving is framed, in common with Willig's study, by the sociology of Pierre Bourdieu, specifically his field theory and the concept of symbolic capital. Bourdieu's hypothesis that 'the journalistic field produces and imposes on the public a very particular vision of the political field' (1996, 2) is particularly salient in relation to journalism awards, which are judged by fellow journalists and media professionals and become, as O'Donnell contended, 'the profession's own way of encouraging high standards of work and promoting quality' (2009, 48). As Willig explains, Bourdieu understood journalism as 'a semi-autonomous field with its own logic of practice', which, like all fields, was 'dynamic' and changed 'as the result of constant internal battles about prestigious positions in the field and ongoing external battles with other fields such as the economic and political field over positions in the overall social space' (Willig 2019, 2–3). Awards such as the US Pulitzers, the Ellie Awards, the Peabody Awards, Canada's National Newspaper and Magazine Awards, Australia's Walkleys, and Denmark's Cavling Prize are therefore part of, and exert pressure upon, the field of journalism by setting a 'benchmark of excellence', and the journalists themselves have a strong influence on the awards by entering and, crucially, by taking part in the judging process (Cray 2012; Walkley Foundation 2020a). Awards demonstrate Bourdieu's concepts of 'symbolic power' and 'cultural capital' (Benson, in Benson and Neveu 2005, 4, 21), since awards, by their very nature, lead us to draw distinctions and make boundaries between those who win and those who don't. Awards are not a perfect measure of what constitutes excellent journalism, long-form or otherwise. What a critical examination of prize-winning journalism may reveal is what Bourdieu described as the 'invisible structures and mechanisms' of the journalistic field, specifically, those factors that may influence a journalist's pursuit of excellence and, by doing so, 'create space for a more open, engaged and accountable conversation with the public', thus nourishing the public sphere (Bourdieu 1996, 1–2).

As mentioned earlier, despite the high number of prizes for the act of writing, there is relatively limited scholarship on the culture of prize-giving in general, let alone specifically for journalism (Street 2005; English 2008). Willig's study of the judges' comments for the Cavling Prize between 1945 and 2016 provides some welcome illumination of how journalistic prizes impact media practice and professional norms over time. Willig's use of Bourdieu's field theory provides a strong framework to 'study the changing symbolic capital of the journalistic field by examining the consecration of values in prestigious awards' (Willig 2019, 14). An earlier study of the Pulitzer Prize by Forde (2007) reveals the tremendous effort the media invests in winning, from writing stories that specifically addressed the criteria to employing staff to work 12-hour days in order to garner top journalism prizes. Indeed, Forde suggested the Pulitzers 'may be pulling content into American newspapers that might not otherwise be there, such as narrative and more robust and complete explanations of scientific and medical phenomena as well as worldwide financial crises' (240). Although such in-depth coverage can be seen as a positive consequence of a prize-winning culture, a study by Shepard in 2000 also found evidence of negative factors such as the demoralizing effect on those who don't win, and the inflated egos of those who do win. Shepard also discovered 'journalism's dirty little secret', which she argued was the fact that 'many contests are not fairly, thoroughly or scrupulously judged' (26). Shepard's study is a salient reminder that prizes must not be uncritically accepted as being infallible arbiters of excellence. In Australia, the Walkley Awards have attracted criticism in the past on issues such as the dropping of the International journalism category in 2017 (Meade 2017) and the choice of winners (Burrowes 2009), and there have even been instances of fights breaking out at the annual award nights (Harrison 2006; Mayne 2001). The Walkley Foundation has also been criticized for its entry fees; in 2019, the organization cut the entry fee for non-union members (union members could enter for free) from A$295 to A$150 (Walkley Foundation 2019). What a considered investigation of prize-winning journalism can provide is insight into what professional values are consecrated in awards (Willig 2019, 14).

Interviews with journalists and editors provide evidence of a 'prize culture' in Australia, also demonstrated in the way that the press celebrates its Walkley winners (ABC News Online 2013; Cray 2012; Landy 2013; Millar 2013; *Sydney Morning Herald* 2013). Further evidence of the value of this prize culture in revealing shifts in the journalistic field is the Walkley Foundation's ongoing reviews of its own processes in an attempt to keep pace with community expectations. In 2009, for example, an award was introduced for 'Best Online Journalism' in an effort to 'make sure they [the Walkleys] remain relevant' (Dempster 2009, 25; Oakes 2013; O'Donnell et al. 2012). In 2015, the Walkley Foundation introduced the 'Our Watch' awards 'to recognise and reward exemplary reporting to end violence against women' (Walkley Foundation 2020b).

By applying Bourdieu's field theory as a critical framework, we are better able to, as Willig (2019, 4) argues, 'de-naturalise what seems to be "natural" or "evident" categories of cultural practices, in this case, "good journalism"'. Integral to achieving this aim is the ability of the journalist to reinforce what Bourdieu described as 'the democratic goal of informing or educating people by *interesting* them' (1996, 3; emphasis added), as demonstrated by the judging criteria for the best long-form journalism category:

> Based on a single entry this award recognises long-form journalism that shines a light, tells a compelling story or provides in-depth analysis and investigation. It also recognises reporting excellence, accuracy, storytelling, originality and high standards of ethics and research. (Walkley Categories Explained 2020c)

The Walkley judging criteria, with their emphasis on the journalist's phronetic mission of encouraging readers to consider issues that concern civic life, is evidence of how feature writing can address Couldry's question of how we should live well, with and through the media, or how to strive for a state of eudemonia, or flourishing (Couldry et al. 2013, 1). This is made clearer through Bourdieu's insights into the power relations that exist between different 'fields' within a society (Benson 2006).

2 NAVIGATING NARRATIVE JOURNALISM: BLURRED BOUNDARIES... 37

It is more helpful again to turn, as we have seen Willig argue and as Couldry himself directs us (2003), to Bourdieu's field theory where Bourdieu expands on his theories of symbolic power and meta-capital. To summarize briefly, Bourdieu argues that to exist socially is to take part in 'an ongoing process that is enacted for the most part unconsciously without strategic intention' (Bourdieu 1996, 4). It is unhelpful to consider 'fields', such as the public, the journalists, the media owners or the Walkley Foundation in isolation; rather, they all exist in relation to each other to varying degrees. Field theory can then become a very useful frame for analysing the impact of individual Walkley features and a means of beginning to 'understand the media both as an internal production process and as a general frame for categorizing the social world' (Couldry 2003, 653). This theoretical framework is particularly useful when we are faced with the ongoing upheavals being experienced in the media world, which have rightly concerned many media theorists (McChesney 2013; Schudson 2013; Couldry et al. 2013). McChesney (2013, 3) argues we have reached 'a base camp of sorts' where we are in a position to 'better understand the decisions that society can make about what type of Internet we will have and, accordingly, what type of humans we will be and will not be in future generations'.

But whether writing appears on the printed page or on one or other of the many electronic devices we use, what is clear is, in terms of Bourdieu's field theory, that the act of writing is the seed of the journalist's cultural or symbolic 'capital' (Bourdieu and Johnson 1993). To reiterate an earlier point, without words there *is* no power, and in terms of the narrative journalism discussed in this book, the power of these stories can be found not only within the text but also in the added prestige of being award winners. Writing is a deliberate act and as feature writers commit 'acts of journalism' (Stearns 2013; Simons 2011, 10) they make choices about what to include, what to leave out, and how to engage the reader's attention. Feature writers, informed by the journalistic ideals of objectivity and fairness, also use emotions (those of the interview subject and, to varying degrees, their own) to convey the message of the story and create impact with readers. Joseph argues that emotion is key to understanding the power of long-form and what 'makes one piece sing off the page into your mind forever, and another dribble away into nothing' (2016, 17). She writes:

I believe it is writing that envelopes intellect, analysis, empathy and grace. An open mind that is able to analyse impartially; empathy of the author. Empathy with grace, leaving judgement behind. Empathy is often seen as antithetical to good journalism but I have argued for some years now that it can be the missing key to clever and evocative nonfiction writing. But it must be met with rigorous fact checking and analysis to make it verifiable and credible. (Joseph 2016, 17)

Like Joseph I also view empathetic writing as the key to understanding the alchemy of long-form that provides readers with the gift of prose that can 'sing off the page into your mind forever. As my upcoming chapters will demonstrate, it is my conviction of the power of emotion that inspired me to develop my Virtue Paradigm and my Virtue map.

REFERENCES

ABC News Online. 2013. Walkley Awards: Joanne McCarthy Wins Gold, Caroline Jones among ABC Journalists Honoured. http://www.abc.net.au/news/2013-11-29/2013-walkleys-awards-night/5123822.

Aristotle. 2019. *Nicomachean Ethics*, 3rd ed. Translated by T. Irwin. Indianapolis: Hackett Publishing.

Bak, J.S., and B. Reynolds. 2011. *Literary Journalism across the Globe: Journalistic Traditions and Transnational Influences.* Amherst, MA: University of Massachusetts Press.

Barry, D., D. Barstow, J.D. Glater, A. Liptak and J. Steinberg. 2003. 'Times Reporter Who Resigned Leaves Long Trail of Deception'. *New York Times*, 11 May. Accessed 19 June 2020. https://www.nytimes.com/2003/05/11/us/correcting-the-record-times-reporter-who-resigned-leaves-long-trail-of-deception.html.

Benson, R. 2006. News Media as a 'Journalistic Field': What Bourdieu Adds to New Institutionalism, and Vice Versa. *Political Communication* 23 (2): 187–202.

Benson, R.D., and E. Neveu. 2005. *Bourdieu and the Journalistic Field.* Cambridge: Polity.

Blume, M.M. 2020. *Fallout, the Hiroshima cover-up and the reporter who revealed it to the world.* New York: Simon and Schuster.

Bly, N. (1887) 2018. 'Ten Days in a Madhouse'. *New York World*: New York. Reprint, *Nellie Bly: Ten Days in a Madhouse.* Rockland, Maryland: Wildside Press.

Bogart, L. 2004. Reflections on Content Quality in Newspapers. *Newspaper Research Journal* 25: 40–53.

Bourdieu, P. 1996. *On Television and Journalism.* London: Pluto Press.

Bourdieu, P., and R. Johnson. 1993. *The Field of Cultural Production: Essays on Art and Literature*. Cambridge: Polity Press.

Boynton, R.S., ed. 2005. *The New New Journalism: Conversations with America's Best Nonfiction Writers on Their Craft, 2*. New York: Random House.

Burrowes, T. 2009. Opinion: Big Three's Domination of the Walkleys Says It All about Media Diversity. *Mumbrella*, October 16. https://mumbrella.com.au/big-threes-domination-of-the-walkeys-says-it-all-about-media-diversity-10454.

Butler, S., ed. 2017. *Macquarie Dictionary*, 7th ed. Sydney: Macquarie Dictionary Publishers.

Calvi, P. 2010. Latin America's Own 'New Journalism'. *Literary Journalism Studies* 2 (2, Fall): 63–83.

———. 2019. *Latin American Adventures in Literary Journalism*. Pittsburgh: University of Pittsburgh Press.

Capote, T. 1966. *In Cold Blood: A True Account of a Multiple Murder and its Consequences*. London: H. Hamilton.

Carson, A. 2019. *Investigative Journalism, Democracy and the Digital Age*. New York: Routledge.

Carson, A., D. Muller, J. Martin, and M. Simons. 2016. A New Symbiosis? Opportunity and Challenges to Hyperlocal Journalism in the Digital Age. *Media International Australia* 161 (1): 132–146.

Cawthon, D. 2012. Some Things Never Change: Myth and Structure in Pulitzer Prize Winning Stories, 1997–2012. MA thesis, University of Missouri-Columbia. Accessed June 19, 2020. https://mospace.umsystem.edu/xmlui/bitstream/handle/10355/33132/research.pdf?sequence=2andisAllowed=y.

Connery, T.B. 2011. *Journalism and Realism: Rendering American Life*. Evanston: Northwestern University Press.

Couldry, N. 2003. Media Meta-Capital: Extending the Range of Bourdieu's Field Theory. *Theory and Society* 32 (5–6): 653–677.

Couldry, N., M. Madianou, and A. Pinchevski. 2013. *Ethics of Media*. New York: Palgrave Macmillan.

Cray, S. 2012. ABC Wins 8 Walkley Awards. *ABC website/Media Centre*, December 1. http://about.abc.net.au/press-releases/abc-wins-8-walkley-awards/.

Dempster, Q. 2009. The Walkleys Are Changing. *Walkley Magazine* no. 57, 25.

Didion, J. 1979. *Slouching Towards Bethlehem*. New York: Simon and Schuster, Touchstone Books.

Dow, W. 2016. 'Reading Otherwise: Literary Journalism as an Aesthetic Narrative Cosmopolitanism' (Keynote address to the International Association of Literary Journalism Studies 11th Conference, 19 May 2016, Porto Alegre, Brazil). *Literary Journalism Studies* 8 (2): 118–137. Accessed June 19, 2020. https://ialjs.org/wp-content/uploads/2017/03/11-Keynote_118-137.pdf.

English, J.F. 2008. *The Economy of Prestige: Prizes, Awards, and the Circulation of Cultural Value*. 2nd ed. Cambridge, MA: Harvard University Press.

Ettema, J.S. 2005. Crafting Cultural Resonance: Imaginative Power in Everyday Journalism. *Journalism* 6 (2): 131–152.

Fichtner, U. 2018. Reporter Forgery: DER SPIEGEL Reveals Internal Fraud. December 20. *Der Spiegel International*. https://www.spiegel.de/international/zeitgeist/claas-relotius-reporter-forgery-scandal-a-1244755.html Accessed January 15, 2021.

Forde, K.R. 2007. Discovering the Explanatory Report in American Newspapers. *Journalism Practice* 1 (2): 227–244.

Franklin, J. 1986. *Writing for Story*. New York: Plume.

Garner, H. 1993. Did Daniel Have to Die?. *Time Australia Magazine*, March 8: 22–27.

———. 1995. *The First Stone*. Sydney: Picador.

———. 1996. *True Stories: Selected Non-fiction*. Melbourne: Text Publishing.

———. 2017. Why She Broke: The Woman, Her Children and the Lake: Akon Guode's Tragic Story. *Monthly: Australian Politics, Society and Culture*, June 22. Accessed June 3, 2020. https://www.themonthly.com.au/issue/2017/june/1496239200/helen-garner/why-she-broke#mtr.

Genette, G. 1997. *Paratexts: Thresholds of Interpretation*. Translated by J. Lewin. Cambridge: Cambridge University Press.

Harrison, D. 2006. Milne Sorry for 'shocking' Behaviour. *Age*, December 2. https://www.theage.com.au/national/milne-sorry-for-shocking-behaviour-20061202-ge3p66.html.

Hartsock, J.C. 2000. *A History of American Literary Journalism: The Emergence of a Modern Narrative Form*. Amherst: University of Massachusetts Press.

———. 2016. *Literary Journalism and the Aesthetics of Experience*. Amherst and Boston: University of Massachusetts Press.

Herr, M. 1977. *Dispatches*. New York: Knopf.

Hersey, J. 1946. 'Hiroshima'. *The New Yorker*, 31 August, 1946.

Hester, J.L. 2020. A New Monument Will Celebrate Nellie Bly's Undercover Reporting, Right Where It Happened. *Atlas Obscura*, January 8. Accessed June 3, 2020. https://www.atlasobscura.com/articles/nellie-bly-monument-new-york.

Hooper, C. 2006. The Tall Man. *Monthly*, no. 10 (March): 34–53. https://www.themonthly.com.au/monthly-essays-chloe-hooper-tall-man-inside-palm-island039s-heart-darkness-185.

Joseph, S. 2010. Telling True Stories in Australia. *Journalism Practice* 4 (1): 82–96.

———. 2016. *Behind the Text: Candid Conversations with Australian Creative Nonfiction Writers*. Melbourne: Hybrid Publishers.

Keeble, R., and J. Tulloch. 2012. *Global Literary Journalism: Exploring the Journalistic Imagination*. New York: Peter Lang.

Keeble, R.L., and J. Tulloch. 2014. *Global Literary Journalism: Exploring the Journalistic Imagination: Mass Communication and Journalism*. Vol. 15. New York: Peter Lang.

Klusmann, S., and D. Kurbjuweit. 2018. Relotius Journalistic Fraud Case: Statement from DER SPIEGEL's Editors-in-Chief. *Der Spiegel International*, December 20. https://www.spiegel.de/international/zeitgeist/der-spiegel-statement-on-relotius-fraud-case-a-1244896.html.

Kovach, B., and T. Rosenstiel. 2014. *The Elements of Journalism: What Newspeople Should Know and the Public Should Expect*. 3rd ed. New York: Three Rivers Press.

Kristjánsson, K. 2018. *Virtuous Emotions*. Oxford: Oxford University Press.

Lacy, S., and F. Fico. 1990. Newspaper Quality and Ownership: Rating the Groups. *Newspaper Research Journal* 11 (2): 42–56.

Landy, S. 2013. Your Herald Sun Team Wins Walkley Awards. *Herald Sun*. http://www.heraldsun.com.au/news/your-herald-sun-team-wins-walkley-awards/story-fni0fiyv-1226770896454.

Laughlin, C.A. 2002. *Chinese Reportage: The Aesthetics of Historical Experience*. Durham, NC: Duke University Press.

Lule, J. 1988. *Daily News, Eternal Stories*. New York: Guildford Press.

Maras, S. 2013. *Objectivity in Journalism*. Cambridge: Polity Press.

Marsh, C. 2010. Deeper than the Fictional Model: Structural Origins of Literary Journalism in Greek Mythology and Drama. *Journalism Studies* 11 (3): 295–310.

Mayne, S. 2001. Fights, Drama, Gossip, Sledging and Great Journalism. *Crikey*, November 18. https://www.crikey.com.au/2001/11/18/fights-drama-gossip-sledging-and-great-journalism/.

McChesney, R.W. 2013. *Digital Disconnect: How Capitalism Is Turning the Internet against Democracy*. New York and London: New Press.

McChesney, R.W., and V.W. Pickard. 2011. *Will the Last Reporter Please Turn Out the Lights: The Collapse of Journalism and What Can Be Done to Fix It*. New York: New Press.

———. 1998. Bodyjamming, Feminism and Public Life (Address to the Sydney Institute, 25 November 1997). *Sydney Papers* 10 (1, Summer), 69–75.

Mead, J., ed. 1997. *Bodyjamming: Sexual Harassment, Feminism and Public Life*. Sydney: Vintage.

Meade, A. 2017. Journalists Decry Move to Drop International Walkley Award. *Guardian Australia*, July 5. https://www.theguardian.com/media/2017/jul/05/journalists-decry-move-to-drop-international-walkley-award.

Michael, S. 2001. The Objectivity Norm in American Journalism. *Journalism* 2 (2): 149–170.

Millar, B. 2013. The Age wins Walkley Awards. *Age*, November 28. http://www.theage.com.au/victoria/the-age-wins-walkley-awards-20131128-2yenx.html.

Napoli, P.M. 2014. *Measuring Media Impact: An Overview of the Field*. Los Angeles: Norman Lear Center. http://www.learcenter.org/pdf/measuringmedia.pdf.

National Magazine Awards. 2020. The Ellie Awards. Accessed June 4, 2020. https://ellieawards.secure-platform.com/a/organizations/main/home.

O'Donnell, P. 2009. That's Gold! Thinking about Excellence in Australian Journalism. *Australian Journalism Review* 31 (2): 47–59.

O'Donnell, P., D. McKnight, and J. Este. 2012. *Journalism at the Speed of Bytes: Australian Newspapers in the 21st Century.* Sydney: Media, Entertainment & Arts Alliance. Accessed June 19, 2020. https://issuu.com/meaa/docs/2012_journalism_speed_of_bytes.

Oakes, L. 2013. *The Report of the 2013 Review of the Walkley Awards for Excellence in Journalism.* Walkley Foundation. http://walkleys.com/wp-content/uploads/2014/05/230516-Walkley-Review-Report-final.pdf.

Peabody Awards. 2020. Accessed 4 June 2020. http://www.peabodyawards.com/about.

Pulitzer Prize. 2020. The History of the Pulitzer Prizes. Accessed June 3, 2020. https://www.pulitzer.org/page/history-pulitzer-prizes.

Ricketson, M. 1997. Helen Garner's *The First Stone*: Hitchhiking on the Credibility of Other Writers. In *Bodyjamming: Sexual Harassment, Feminism and Public Life*, ed. J. Mead, 79–100. Sydney: Vintage.

———. 2001. True Stories: The Power and Pitfalls of Literary Journalism. In *Journalism: Theory in Practice*, ed. S. Tapsall and C. Varley, 149–165. Melbourne: Oxford University Press.

———. 2004a. 'The Awkward Truth': The Perils of Writing Journalistic Books. *Overland* 176: 51–55.

———. 2004b. *Writing Feature Stories: How to Research and Write Newspaper and Magazine Articles.* Sydney: Allen & Unwin.

———. 2010. Not Muddying, Clarifying: Towards Understanding the Boundaries between Fiction and Nonfiction. *Text* 14 (2): 1–13. http://www.textjournal.com.au/oct10/ricketson.htm.

———. 2014. From Making Front Page to Landing between Covers: An Ethical Inquiry into Contemporary Book-Length Journalism in Australia. *Ethical Space: The International Journal of Communication Ethics* 11 (4): 12–20.

———. 2019. Navigating the Challenges of Writing Book-Length Literary Journalism. *Literary Journalism Studies* 11 (2): 114–135.

Ricketson, M., and S. Joseph. 2015. Literary Journalism: Looking Beyond the Anglo-American Tradition. *Australian Journalism Review* 37 (2): 27–32.

Sarbin, T. 1995. Emotional Life, Rhetoric, and Roles. *Journal of Narrative and Life History* 5 (3): 213–220.

Scheer, M. 2012. Are Emotions a Kind of Practice (and Is That What Makes Them Have a History)? A Bourdieuian Approach to Understanding Emotion. *History and Theory* 51 (May): 193–220.

Schroeder, E.J. 1992. *Vietnam, We've All Been There: Interviews with American Writers.* Westport, CT: Praeger.

Schudson, M. 1992. A Study in Mythology. *Columbia Journalism Review*, May/June, 28–33.

———. 2003a. *The Sociology of News.* San Diego: W.W. Norton.

2 NAVIGATING NARRATIVE JOURNALISM: BLURRED BOUNDARIES... 43

———. 2003b. The Sociology of News Production. *Media, Culture and Society* 11: 263–282.

———. 2013. Reluctant Stewards: Journalism in a Democratic Society. *Daedalus* 142 (2): 159–176.

Schudson, M., and C.W. Anderson. 2008. Objectivity, Professionalism, and Truth Seeking in Journalism. In *The Handbook of Journalism Studies*, ed. K. Wahl-Jorgensen and T. Hanitzsch, 88–101. ICA Handbook Series. New York: Routledge.

Shapiro, S. 2005. *Reinventing the Feature Story: Mythic Cycles in American Literary Journalism*. Baltimore, MD: Apprentice House.

Shapiro, I., P. Albanese, and L. Doyle. 2006. What Makes Journalism 'Excellent'? Criteria Identified by Judges in Two Leading Awards Programs. *Canadian Journal of Communication* 31 (2): 1–17.

Shepard, A. 2000. Journalism's Prize Culture. *American Journalism Review* 22 (3): 22–31.

Simons, M. 2011. *Journalism at the Crossroads*. Melbourne: Scribe.

Simons, M., R. Tiffen, D. Hendrie, A. Carson, H. Sullivan, and D. Muller. 2017. Understanding the Civic Impact of Journalism. *Journalism Studies* 18 (11, Nov.): 1400–1414.

Sims, N. 1984. *The Literary Journalists*. New York: Ballantine Books.

———. 2009. The Problem and the Promise of Literary Journalism Studies. *Literary Journalism Studies* 1 (1): 7–16.

———. 2019. Degrees of Forgiveness: Why I've Changed My Mind. *International Association of Literary Journalism Newsletter* 13 (2, Oct.): 5, 10. Accessed June 19, 2020. https://ialjs.org/wp-content/uploads/2019/10/1910_IALJS_Newsletter-1.pdf

Stearns, J. 2013. *Acts of Journalism: Defining Press Freedom in the Digital Age*. New York: Free Press. Accessed May 25, 2020. https://www.freepress.net/sites/default/files/legacy-policy/Acts_of_Journalism_October_2013.pdf.

Steensen, S. 2011. The Featurization of Journalism. *Nordicom Review* 32 (2): 49–61.

Street, J. 2005. 'Show Business of a Serious Kind': A Cultural Politics of the Arts Prize. *Media, Culture and Society* 27 (6): 819–840.

Sydney Morning Herald. 2013. Fairfax Media Takes Top Honours at 2013 Walkleys. Accessed May 25, 2020. http://www.smh.com.au/national/fairfax-media-takes-top-honours-at-2013-walkleys-20131128-2yegy.html.

Taylor, J. 2005. What Makes a Good Feature? In *Print Journalism: A Critical Introduction*, ed. R. Keeble, 118–128. Abingdon, UK: Routledge.

This American Life. 2020. Our Pulitzer Winning Episode. Accessed June 4, 2020. https://www.thisamericanlife.org/704/our-pulitzer-winning-episode.

Tippet, G. 1997. Slaying the Monster. *Sunday Age: Agenda*, June 22, 1–2.

44 J. MARTIN

Tofel, R.J. 2013. *Non-Profit Journalism: Issues around Impact*. ProPublica White Paper. New York: ProPublica. https://s3.amazonaws.com/propublica/assets/about/LFA_ProPublica-white-paper_2.1.pdf.

Tulloch, J. 2014. Ethics, Trust and the First Person in the Narration of Long-Form Journalism. *Journalism* 15 (5): 629–638.

Walkley Foundation. 2019. Walkley Awards Entry Fee Halved to Improve Accessibility, Diversity, June 26. Accessed June 5, 2020. https://www.walkleys.com/walkley-awards-entry-fee-halved-to-improve-accessibility-diversity/.

———. 2020a. Terms & Conditions. Accessed June 18, 2019. https://www.walkleys.com/awards/walkleys/terms-conditions/.

———. 2020b. Our Watch Awards. Accessed June 18, 2019. https://www.walkleys.com/awards/our-watch-award/.

———. 2020c. Walkley Categories Explained. https://www.walkleys.com/awards/walkleys/categories/.

Webb, J. 2017. 'A new literary portrait of Helen Garner leaves you wanting more'. *The Conversation*, 3 May. https://theconversation.com/a-new-literary-portrait-of-helen-garner-leaves-you-wanting-to-know-more-76975.

Willig, I. 2019. Ideals of Journalism the Historical Consecration of Media Capital in Prize Awards and the Case of the Danish Cavling Award 1945–2016. *Media History*. Online May 6. https://doi.org/10.1080/13688804.2019.1608169.

Wolfe, T. 1972. The Birth of the New Journalism: Eyewitness Report by Tom Wolfe. *New York Magazine*, February 14.

Wolfe, T., and E.W. Johnson. 1973. The New Journalism. In *The New Journalism*, ed. T. Wolfe and E.W. Johnson, 3–36. New York: Harper and Row.

Zdovc, S.M. 2008. *Literary Journalism in the United States of America and Slovenia*. Lanham, MD: University Press of America.

CHAPTER 3

The Virtue Paradigm:
The Feature and Democracy

So embedded is the belief in journalism's intrinsic importance to a democratic society that often the concept is taken for granted by both practitioners and researchers (Christians et al. 2009; Couldry 2006, 2012; Couldry et al. 2013; MacIntyre 2007; Schudson 2008; Strömback 2005). There is, however, an inherent danger in the view that journalism and democracy are inseparable, and it is important to understand that 'democracy does not necessarily produce journalism nor does journalism necessarily produce democracy' (Schudson 2008, 12). It is more helpful to be aware of the ways in which journalism functions in a *representative* democracy, acknowledging that the purpose of such a democracy is *not* to include as many voices as possible but to elect those to speak on *behalf* of others (Schudson 2008, 1–10). Award-winning narrative features can be considered as salient examples of 'communication-as-culture' (Ettema 2005, 132), providing a rich archive of what James Carey describes as the most effective type of journalism, that is, writing that 'offers genuine description and explanation, compelling force and narrative detail' (Carey, in Munson and Warren 1997, 187).

Narrative Journalism and Virtue

Virtue ethics is sometimes also referred to as *aretaic* ethics, *arete* being the Greek word for virtue, which translates as 'excellence' (Preston 2007, 50). This conceptualization is helpful in understanding the role of virtues in

© The Author(s), under exclusive license to Springer Nature Switzerland AG 2021
J. Martin, *Emotions and Virtues in Feature Writing*, https://doi.org/10.1007/978-3-030-62978-6_3

45

journalism. For example, the aretaic quality—or 'excellence'—of a knife is its sharpness, its ability to cut well, whereas the aretaic quality of a racehorse, its 'excellence', is its ability to be faster than the other horses. In the case of news journalism, this excellence or aretaic quality is the story's ability to convey the facts quickly and clearly (Preston 2007, 50). In the case of award-winning features, this aretaic quality lies in the writer's ability to communicate complex issues in a way that resonates strongly with readers. Another measure of an article's aretaic quality is the degree to which it fulfils journalism's phronetic function of connecting citizens to their society by placing them in a position to contemplate questions of personal and national identity.

Beginning with Aristotle's *Nicomachean Ethics* (Aristotle 2019, 104–106 [VI.5, 1140a–1140b29]), we find the fifth-century Greek philosopher distinguished between two kinds of virtue, intellectual and moral. He defined a moral virtue as 'a confirmed disposition to act rightly, the disposition itself formed by a continuous series of right actions' (Aristotle 2019, 20–21 [II.1, 1103a14–b1]). Aristotle's list of moral virtues included courage, temperance, magnificence, pride, good temper, friendliness, truthfulness, wittiness and justice (III–IV). His intellectual virtues included scientific knowledge (*episteme*), artistic or technical knowledge (*techne*), intuitive reason (*nous*), philosophic wisdom (*sophia*) and practical wisdom (*phronesis*), which he considered the most important, or 'master virtue' (Aristotle 2019, 279–281 [VI.5–8, 1140a24–b12–1140b8–27]). I argue throughout this book, and in detail in Chaps. 4 and 6, that within narrative journalism a strong case can be made that phronesis, or 'practical wisdom', can be considered 'a master virtue'. My reconceptualization of phronesis is formed from a synergy of the 'practical' reporting and writing skills required to reach the top of the profession, and a 'wisdom' that I define as a deep commitment to educate, inform and challenge readers so that they may be better positioned to contribute to public life (Preston 2007, 50; MEAA 2019). It is this focus, not on the overall effect, or consequences, but rather on the *striving* to identify what attributes help a person live a life that achieves a 'good' end, that makes a neo-Aristotelian approach, such as outlined by media theorists Alasdair MacIntyre (2007), Noel Preston (2007) and Nick Couldry (2012, 2013), so relevant to the study of journalism. Award-winning long-form journalism is a rich source of stories that provide narrative maps for readers on what it means to be a good person living in community.

Returning to Aristotle and his concept of virtues, the Greek philosopher believed the human soul was conditioned in three ways, through feelings, capacities and dispositions (Aristotle 2019, 26–27 [II.5, 1105b2–26–1105b26–1106a20]). He differentiated between feelings (or emotions) and virtues by arguing that man was not defined by his ability to feel emotion but rather his ability to master it for a greater good: 'We are not spoken of as good or bad in respect of our feelings but of our vices and virtues ... we are praised and blamed for our virtues and vices'. If we apply this reasoning to journalism, it is evident that striking a balance between providing the reader with facts and communicating emotion is a valuable consideration for the feature writer. Just as Aristotle argued that virtues require a harnessing of emotion, journalists must also master a 'discipline of emotion', a concept that I explain in Chap. 6.

The term 'ethics' derives from the Greek word *ethos* and refers to a habit or custom. While the question of how individuals live their lives, and by extension how their behaviour contributes to how society functions, may be considered a central concern across cultures, a character trait that one community elevates to a virtue may not have the same status in a different society. As MacIntyre (2007, 182) explains: 'For Homer the paradigm of human excellence is the warrior; for Aristotle it is the Athenian gentleman'. To illustrate this point further, MacIntyre uses the example of how the thirteenth-century philosopher Aquinas modified Aristotle's virtues to include his own Christian virtues of faith, hope and charity, in order to embody the concept of a life lived for the love of God. In the eighteenth century Benjamin Franklin, one of the founding fathers of America, espoused 'cleanliness, silence and industry', and in the nineteenth century, English novelist Jane Austen wrote about the virtues of 'amiability' and 'constancy' (MacIntyre 2007, 182; Preston 2007, 50).

A neo-Aristotelian framework helps make sense of what Preston explains as 'the ethical confusion in post-modern societies where religious authority is largely absent and ethical discourse operates in a relativistic morass' (Preston 2007, 51). As Couldry notes, 'the ultimate point of ethics is not to trap us within elaborate philosophical debate but to return us critically to the necessities that shape our lives' (2012, 181–182). In line with the fundamentally practical approach that underpins Couldry's 2012 work, *Media, Society, World*, I argue that prize-winning long-form narratives may provide one path to ethical clarity. As the case studies of feature articles in Part II will demonstrate, a close reading of award-winning narrative journalism provides a means of identifying some of the character traits or virtues that are considered desirable in members of a modern democracy. While accepting that the list is by no means definitive, two of the virtues that were identified in each of the 23 Walkley Award-winning long-form feature articles included in my study were honesty and responsibility. This is not surprising, as an article that did not give an accurate account of events would fail to meet the most basic definition of reporting, let alone qualify for consideration in any reputable prize celebrating excellence in journalism. Also explicit in journalism award criteria around the world is the acknowledgement of the important responsibility journalists have to society. A salient example is Britain's National Press Award for Best Investigative Journalism. The National Press Awards are organized by the Society of Editors and are described on their website as being known as the 'Oscars' for the UK Press. The 'Best Investigative Journalism' award is in turn given for a 'body of work that reveals investigative skills of a team or individual to the full, lifting the lid and bringing to light *the* investigative news story no other news organisation has discovered' [emphasis in original] (*Society of Editors* 2020).

When identifying virtues communicated by the journalist in award-winning narrative feature articles it is helpful to also be mindful of the virtues extolled by the profession of journalism, in order to critically consider if there is a nexus between the two. In their seminal study at the beginning of the new millennium, researchers Kovach and Rosenstiel (2014) asked journalists what they saw as essential aspects of the profession and developed a list of ten principles that have been used in journalism schools as a guide for students. The first principle has since been held up as a credo for the profession: 'to provide people with the information they need to be free and self-governing'. The remaining traits include 'truthfulness, verification, loyalty to citizens, independence, monitors of power and providers of a forum for public criticism, as well as being interesting, relevant, comprehensive, proportional and to exercise freedom of conscience' (9). The ideals of truthfulness, verification and loyalty to citizens, as expressed by Kovach and Rosenstiel, are evidence of the virtues of journalism and align with Couldry's (2013, 40) virtues of 'sincerity, accuracy and truth', which he argues are 'essential, not just for the quality of democracy, but for the quality of public and social life, whether aspiring to democracy or not'. The notion of civic values (or Durkheim's 'civic morals') is central to professional journalism organizations around the globe (Durkheim 1992). Whereas Aristotle's philosophy was strongly linked to an account of human nature, MacIntyre's approach is about practice and is tradition-specific; because of this it can be said to be linked to a group's particular 'story' or what Sarbin would refer to as the group's 'emotional life' (MacIntyre 2007; Sarbin 1995, 214). Sarbin's states that 'cultural stories provide narrative guidance for actions to solve life's exigencies' (218) and I argue that prize-winning features are an important form that provides this direction.

Just as it is not enough for a modern society to rely on the virtuous disposition of an individual to ensure right action, professions such as journalists also need an overarching code of behaviour. The preamble of the code of ethics of Australia's journalism union (Media, Entertainment & Arts Alliance, MEAA) unequivocally establishes the virtues expected from its members:

> Respect for truth and the public's right to information are fundamental principles of journalism. Journalists describe society to itself. They convey information, ideas and opinions, a privileged role. They search, disclose, record, question, entertain, suggest and remember. They inform citizens and animate democracy. They give a practical form to freedom of expression. Many journalists work in private enterprise, but all have these public responsibilities. They scrutinise power, but also exercise it, and should be accountable. Accountability engenders trust. Without trust, journalists do not fulfil their public responsibilities. (MEAA 2019)

An example from the 'Accountable Journalism' website, which monitors journalism codes of ethics from around the world, is Finland's Union of Journalists' decree that their professional ethics 'involves respecting of basic human values, like human rights, democracy, peace and international understanding'. Another is the united declaration by five press unions in Greece that journalism is a 'mission', or the statement by the National Union of French Journalists that 'A journalist worthy of the name assumes responsibility for all he writes' and 'respects justice and gives it top priority' (Accountable Journalism 2020). While journalism codes of ethics, by their very nature, are idealized views of the profession, their aspiration to quality reveals how journalists see themselves and their role. As Couldry (2012, 193) argues, 'The problem is not that journalists have changed their values; they still aim to tell the truth. It is that the conditions under which they work are not ones where that value can be consistently or reliably *acted upon*' [emphasis in original].

50   J. MARTIN

As a starting point, it is helpful, as Couldry argues, to consider what the French sociologist Emile Durkheim called 'civic morals' (Couldry in Couldry et al. 2013, 39; Durkheim 1992, 48). This term refers to the duty the individual citizen owes towards the state and also includes the duty the state owes to the individual. This concept helps to provide a framework that identifies the important role the individual plays as part of a democratic society as well as the role of the media in providing the necessary information to citizens, since 'much of the power of the media comes from the simple fact that news tells us things we would otherwise not know' (Schudson 2008, 13). By examining whether any 'civic morals' (such as truthfulness and a sense of responsibility) are referenced or discursively constructed in award-winning magazine-style feature articles, it is possible to investigate the ways in which these narratives may strive to help inform readers or instruct them in how to live a 'good life'. To consider, as Preston's communitarian approach suggests, how we can navigate our lives with 'a maturing moral will and vision, despite the ambiguities and limitations' of the human condition (Preston 2007, 223).

While I appreciate a broadly communitarian approach towards virtue ethics, one which emphasizes the 'common good' and explores 'how justice finds expression in the social and associational life of human communities through community partnerships and local capacity building' (Preston 2007, 51), it is important that any analysis is informed by a critical consideration of the function of power in society. Bourdieu's concept of *habitus* is useful in understanding this connection between the individual and society as he argues that: 'To speak of habitus is to assert that the individual, and even the personal, the subjective, is social, collective. Habitus is a socialized subjectivity' (Bourdieu 1992, 126). Habitus is more specifically defined as a 'set of historical relations "deposited" within individual bodies in the form of mental and corporeal schemata of perception, appreciation and action' (Bourdieu 1992, 16). An analysis, therefore, of prize-winning articles provides a type of narrative map which can be used to navigate and interpret what virtues the journalist considers important enough to communicate throughout the text, and to argue the extent to which these virtues hold some measure of cultural capital within modern society (Benson and Neveu 2005, 4).

The skills required by journalists to construct narratives that are considered to be the paragons of their form warrants journalism's definition as a *practice*, requiring far more skill than the simple physical act of writing, in much the same way as MacIntyre distinguishes between architecture and bricklaying, arguing that architecture is a practice, but bricklaying is not (MacIntyre 2007, 188). The merit of using such criteria is captured in MacIntyre's argument that 'we cannot be initiated into a practice without accepting the authority of the best standards realized so far' (190). Couldry builds upon MacIntyre's study and reframes the Aristotelian question 'How should we live well together?' as 'How should we live well together *with and through the media?*', a problem that is essential to modern society, especially in a mature democracy (Couldry 2012, 2013, 1). Couldry is rightly critical of the effectiveness of democratic systems and argues that 'media don't integrate well into either political theory or ethics because historically, they were not intended to' (Couldry 2006, 117). This critical approach is evident in McChesney's analysis of the impact of the internet on the media when he warns against a tendency for media scholars to conflate capitalism and democracy, saying the former is taken 'as a benevolent given, almost a synonym for democracy' (McChesney 2013, xii).

Couldry's argument for a global media ethics builds upon MacIntyre's complex and nuanced analysis of the difficult task a society has in analysing itself (MacIntyre 2007, 181). Or, as succinctly explained by Neveu (2014, 534), this 'is what French liberal philosopher Benjamin Constant described two centuries ago as the paradox of the "freedom of the modern", [that] we can live in a society whilst forgetting that there is such a thing as a society'. Although the focus of this book is on western democracies, and my original study was limited to Australia, a relatively young, modern, representative democracy, this is not based upon an assumption that non-democratic societies do not have journalism that strives to convey important issues to citizens through the communication of virtues. Recent scholarship has investigated the way in which journalists in China, for example, strive to uphold professional standards and establish a meaningful autonomy from their government; a study of prize-winning journalism in non-democratic countries will be a fascinating area for future research (Simons, Nolan and Wright 2016).

Returning to Nick Couldry, Mirca Madianou and Amit Pinchevski contention in the introduction to their edited book, *Ethics of the Media* (2013, 3) that media ethics need to be brought to bear upon the standards 'by which we should judge the satisfactoriness of media institutions' own codes of ethics', it becomes clear how journalism as a profession has resisted such self-examination. They argue that it 'took malpractice across three core institutions' (media, police and government) in 2011 to force the *News of the World* 'phone hacking' scandal in the UK (Breit and

Ricketson 2012; Finkelstein and Ricketson 2012) onto the front pages and prime-time news bulletins and onto 'the agenda of government' (Couldry et al. 2013, 3). In Australia, as a response to the UK phone-hacking scandal, the federal government held the Independent Media Inquiry, which is also referred to as the 'Finkelstein Report' (Finkelstein and Ricketson 2012), to investigate the accountability of the media. The Convergence Review into media ownership in Australia had been under-way since early 2011 (Australia 2012; Lidberg 2012). The WikiLeaks controversy and whistle-blower Edward Snowden's facilitating the *Guardian* newspaper to expose US government monitoring of citizens are further examples of events that raised ethical issues of media accountability and responsibility (WikiLeaks 2015). As Couldry et al. wrote in 2013, 'we may be able to look back on the past decade as one that finally installed the ethics of media at the heart of public debate in mature democracies' (3). The media has since become embroiled in the 'fake news' debate, driven by US President Donald Trump, who took the step of banning reporters from the White House press room (De Moraes 2017). But as commentators such as Shane Owens have pointed out, in an ironic twist, Trump's war against the media has resulted in a boost to news organizations as 'consumers considered it their civic duty to pay for digital news', leading to what has become known as the 'Trump Bump', with ProPublica reporting a ten-fold increase in donations and the *New York Times* reporting a similar jump in subscriptions (Owens 2019).

Narrative Journalism and Habermas's Theory of Validity

Alongside the theoretical approaches of Bourdieu, MacIntyre, Couldry and Ettema, the work of Habermas, in particular his theory of 'communicative action', provides a valuable theoretical framework for understanding the ways in which journalists construct feature articles in order to communicate notions of virtue to readers (Edgar 2006; Habermas 1984, 1989, 1992). Habermas developed his theory—which can be understood as the 'meaningful interaction between persons'—in the 1970s and 1980s, defining three functions for communicative acts: conveying information, establishing social relationships and expressing an opinion (Edgar 2006, 21). Following on from this concept was the notion of 'communicative power', which is the influence that people may exert upon the state through public institutions, which include 'community and educational groups, churches, voluntary organisations' and, significantly, the mass media (Edgar 2006, 23). Edgar explains that Habermas's argument is that these public institutions and the mass media 'can ideally act as channels (or as a "sluice") (Habermas 1998, 250) through which public opinion is transformed by the state administration into *administrative power* [emphasis in original] so that it can be realised as enforceable laws that will constrain and direct the actions of citizens' (Edgar 2006, 23; Habermas 1996, 463–490).

Essential to this process is the concept of 'communicative reason', which refers to a 'free and open discussion upon which a final decision is made on the strength of the better argument' (Edgar 2006, 24). Although this concept was present in Habermas's earlier works, it was, according to Edgar, 'not fully articulated' until the 'mature' work of the 1970s and 1980s, in particular the 'theory of communicative action' (Edgar 2006, 24). This theory contends that in order for society to 'survive and flourish, human beings must be able both to control their natural environment (through science and technology) and communicate effectively, so as to organise themselves in viable and complex social groups' (Habermas 1971, 155–158, 1984; Edgar 2006, 24).

Award-winning narrative journalism contributes to the cultural work of effectively communicating stories to people on a wide range of important topics, which in turn empowers them with the communicative reason to engage in open debate and even take action. By considering this argument in regard to the notion of phronetic journalism—which refers specifically in this study to writing that can be considered to have the potential to impact the view of readers—it becomes clear that these stories can be seen as the writer's effort to help a society 'survive and flourish' by writing stories considered of value to what Habermas refers to as the public sphere (Green et al. 2004; Edgar 2006, 24). According to Habermas, the public sphere 'aspires to form a general will and thus inform and control the activities of the state' and is the 'steering mechanism of democracy' (Edgar 2006, 29). Habermas traces the history of the public sphere back to the eighteenth-century bourgeoisie who, as members of the rising commercial and professional classes, grew in economic interest and social power in that period. He argues that for the first time the (European) middle class could afford the cost of art and had the time to enjoy it—which was when the paradigm of eighteenth-century art, the novel, emerged from the art of letter writing in Europe (Edgar 2006, 125). From letters and pamphlets came essays, and the next crucial development was political journalism.

Whereas Habermas argued that the middle-class man of the eighteenth century was expected to 'debate his tastes, the modern consumer of culture need do nothing more than exert himself in an act of consumption' (Edgar 2006, 126). Rather than the modern-day public sphere being a place where critical debate occurs and important ideas are exchanged, it instead 'becomes the court before which public prestige can be displayed', an observation that in many ways is relevant to a critique of the internet (Habermas 1989, 201). A lacuna in Habermas's early view of the public sphere, one that he later revised, was his exclusion of many sectors of society—the working class, women and ethnic minorities. Not only were these groups excluded, that exclusion was 'not debated or even recognised' (Edgar 2006, 125; Meehan 2013; Brunkhorst et al. 2018). This blind spot attracted criticism which Habermas addressed at a conference in 1989, acknowledging that there was not just a single public sphere but rather a 'pluralistic, internally much differentiated mass public' and furthermore, that:

> The culture of the common people apparently was by no means only a backdrop ... it was also the periodically recurring violent revolt of a counter project to the hierarchical world of domination, with its official celebrations and everyday disciplines. (Habermas 1992, 427)

It is worth noting that within journalism studies Habermas is strongly associated with notions of a public good (through his concept of the public sphere) but I have returned, through his theory of communicative action, to his ideas of a shared common good. I contend that prize-winning journalism is a means to expose readers to spheres they may have been unaware of, such as a children's cancer ward, the Family Court, life on a remote island in a poverty-stricken community, or inside a prison (Linnell 1997; Legge 2002; Hooper 2006; Lucashenko 2013; Mason 1997). I argue that the best narrative journalism may provide readers with information and insight into some of these plural spheres. According to Habermas's communicative action theory, it is necessary to ask whether certain validity claims (truth, appropriateness, sincerity and comprehension) are met in order to achieve an 'ideal speech situation' (Habermas 2001, 85, 90–91). Subjecting feature articles to these claims is a means of understanding the impact of this kind of journalism. Because the questions that Habermas asks us to consider when evaluating a speech situation concern the foundational ethical veracity of the message, they are particularly valuable when applied to literary journalism, a narrative construction that strives to compel the attention of readers. Journalism prizes can be considered to represent a limited 'consensus theory of truth', as the judges have agreed on a decision, something which can only happen if 'everyone attributes the same predicate to the same object', or agrees on the meanings of shared symbols. This process was described by Habermas as a 'background consensus', sharing as it did the same symbols and meanings (Habermas 2001, 86). This theory, when applied to narrative journalism, illuminates the way in which this form has its own internal logic, one that is shared with the reader. Every aspect of the journalist's narrative is the result of a deliberate choice, from the selection of interviewees, to the questions asked, to the quotes chosen and the narrative devices employed to construct the article. This is where Habermas's four validity claims (2001, 85–86) can be a useful means of analysing feature writing. The four claims are:

1. *Truth (or knowledge)*: This applies to appropriateness, sincerity and comprehension. Truth equates with the Aristotelian concept of *logos* or logic. Put simply, does the journalist know what they are talking about and are their claims based on evidence?
2. *Appropriateness*: A measure that has interesting implications for feature writing. It addresses the question of relevance. Is the article about a matter that is considered important or in the public interest?
3. *Sincerity*: This addresses the intention of the writer. Is the piece constructed in a way that presents different viewpoints?
4. *Comprehension*: This provides the test of readability. Does the article convey information in a way that can be understood by the reader?

While I do not suggest that journalists are versed in Habermasian concepts (nor, indeed, in the philosophies of Aristotle or Bourdieu), I do argue that they are nonetheless working to a similar set of principles. This is evident in the judging criteria of the awards, which look for 'reporting excellence, accuracy, storytelling, originality and high standards of ethics and research' as well as 'creativity, impact and technique' (Walkley Foundation 2020).

Habermas's understanding of what happens when 'the functioning of the language game is disturbed and the working background consensus is undermined' is particularly helpful in the analysis of feature writing (2001,

86). For it is here, in this contested space, that questions and answers arise and, in the case of feature writing, where *readers* are engaged in a narrative that may challenge the way they view the world. For where there is disturbance, where there is conflict, there is emotion. This is how I interpret Habermas's (2001, 86) meaning of disturbing the language game and undermining the 'background consensus'. It is this aspect of feature writing that arguably performs the most valuable role in stimulating discussion in a democratic society (while of course we accept that some readers will endeavour to limit the extent of this disturbance by refusing to engage with a challenge to their particular world view, which may be comprised of certain beliefs about race, gender or religion, e.g.). Within journalism prizes around the world, a wide range of topics can be found that achieve this disturbance. Some examples include the British National Press Award won by the *Times* in 2018 for their reporting of Oxfam's sexual exploitation of Haiti earthquake victims and the US Pulitzer Prize for investigative reporting won by the *Los Angeles Times*'s investigation into a gynaecologist 'accused of violating hundreds of young women for more than a quarter of a century' (*Society of Editors* 2018, 2020; Pulitzer Prize 2019).

Perhaps one of the most helpful aspects of Habermas's validity claims—to a point—is his understanding of the notion of the 'consensus of truth' (2001, 452). He argues that we cannot decide on the truth of a set of propositions (in this case a Walkley-winning feature article) without 'reference to the competence of the judges'. This point is particularly salient for any study of award-winning journalism. And it can be helpful to our understanding of long-form features to ask in what ways a feature article meets Habermas's criteria for the 'ideal speech situation'. Although each article is written by usually only one author, a feature article contains also the reported or quoted arguments, beliefs and ideals of more than one person, often responding to claims made by others—either directly or indirectly. However, a feature is clearly a constructed text written with a specific audience or readership in mind, and these readers can often respond; letters may be written to the editor and, in the case of recent feature articles, comments posted online. In this respect, it could be seen to meet Habermas's criterion of everyone's being free to enter the debate but, on closer analysis, it is clear that the selection of letters is moderated by an editor or staff member, as are the online comments. This is a form of exclusion, and in Habermas's terms, exclusion, for whatever reason, 'is a mark of injustice' (Edgar 2006, 29). There is no doubt that the advent of social media, such as Twitter, has seen journalists engage much more closely with their readers than in the past. Although the categorization of a feature article as an ideal or distorted speech situation is complex, in Habermas's theory it is nonetheless clear that it is the process that is important. However, while I acknowledge the value of employing Habermas's validity claims to a degree in an analysis of prize-winning magazine features, it is important to note the limits of this approach. Franck Poupeau's observed that Habermas neglects the fact that language itself 'derives its authority from external sources', which is why, as outlined in Chap. 2, I also employ Bourdieu's theory of habitus, along with his views on symbolic capital, which allows a dissection of normative assumptions surrounding power (Bourdieu and Wacquant 1992; Poupeau 2000, 79–80). As Poupeau contends, the 'performative character of words requires a good deal more than the acceptance of their validity: that is, a social belief' and that communication is not exempt from relations of power (80–81).

The Imagined Virtuous Community

My idea that award-winning long-form journalists are writing for what I describe as an 'imagined virtuous community' of readers draws on the work of Benedict Anderson (1983). Briefly, Anderson framed his examination of nationalism and identity around the emergence of print capitalism and the formation of nation states. He argued that any community is *necessarily* imagined because it is simply impossible for any group larger than that of 'primordial villages of face-to-face contact' to know each member (49). I wish to extend his argument and suggest that some of the articles in my larger study, and those included as case studies in this book, have been constructed by the journalist with a particular group of readers in mind, one that I define as 'the imagined virtuous community of readers' (49). For an imagined community to achieve cohesiveness or, 'profound emotional legitimacy' (48), its members must share expectations of the behaviour required of each other. The notion of a sharing of behavioural expectations should not suggest that there is a single, homogenous imagined virtuous community, or group of readers, that are waiting to be convinced by the author's point of view. For just as there are many different public spheres or groups within a society there are also arrays of imagined virtuous communities. I contend that each of the authors of these feature articles has worked very strategically, using a range of narrative and reporting techniques, to construct a strong sense of the cohesive imaginative community that is being addressed. The journalist is urging readers to consider the ramifications of the issue being discussed, often challenging readers to ask themselves if they think what is happening is for the greater good of the community of which they are a part. I suggest that Anderson's argument is deepened when informed by Borden's claim that the principal duty of journalists is to 'take actions that bring the real community closer to the ideal community' (Borden 1993, 223).

It is a central aspect of the Virtue Paradigm to remember that journalists are a part of their own imagined community, that of the media profession and that they write for readers who, in turn, constitute a separate overlapping imagined community. These readers, along with the journalists, belong to the *overall* imagined community of the nation. I argue that an analysis of the award-winning features may provide evidence that the journalists' notion of an imagined virtuous community of readers can be considered as similar to what is considered by the community as ideal practices of citizenship. My analysis will examine if the features of this citizenship, such as fairness, *honesty* and *responsibility*, are indeed shared.

For the journalist's conceptualization of this virtuous community to be realized, for it to be considered by readers as emotionally legitimate, these readers must also consider *themselves* to be members of the wider virtuous imagined community. It is a key argument of this book that the alignment of readers with an imagined virtuous community—one that is concerned with how its members can live well together—is ultimately dependent upon the degree to which the narrative successfully communicates emotions (Anderson 1983, 48; Green et al. 2004). An understanding of that imagined virtuous community must necessarily be informed by the complex ways in which societies and communities police, protect and define their boundaries.

The practice of defining a community by naming those that are both inside and outside its boundaries has also been theorized by Ghassan Hage, whose research was prompted by his personal experience of negotiating his own belonging to both the Middle East and Australia (Hage 2015, 10). Hage asserts that in the late twentieth century the effect of globalization led to 'a new wave of paranoid white nationalism, when the anti-multicultural tide started to take hold and the politics of white nationalism grew, along with the need to affirm "American", "Australian" or "European" values' (Hage 2015, 8). Hage contended that this paranoid nationalism has had a negative impact on how Australia's Indigenous population are conceptualized by mainstream society, relegating them to the status of outsiders—or at least 'the other'—within their own country. The recognition of Aboriginal land rights changed the Australian political landscape and 'reawoke in us [Australian society] the memory of our original theft. We have begun to relate to ourselves and our land in the way that people who were thieves in the past relate to themselves and to what they have stolen and kept' (Hage 2003, 152). Hage's argument provides a valuable lens through which to consider whom the journalists imagine they are writing for. One example is Paul Toohey's 2001, Walkley award-winning feature article about an isolated Indigenous community struggling with high levels of petrol sniffing (Toohey 2001). The first Indigenous voice readers hear is not until near the end of the second page of a four-page article when they are introduced to 26-year-old mother Francie, who describes herself deprecatingly as a 'dirty, no-good rotten petrol sniffer' (Toohey 2001, 25). An awareness of the writer's subjectivity in constructing the narrative can expose assumptions and generalizations that are made about Indigenous Australians, which, as recent scholarship argues, has the danger of negating the complexity, diversity and the versatility of First Nations citizens (Latimore 2016).

Throughout this chapter, we have critically investigated the role that journalism plays in a democratic society as well as examining how participants' own cultural backgrounds and assumptions influence their position, a factor to weave into any close textual analysis of the highly structured form of the feature. By asking who is doing the speaking, what is being discussed and how it is being framed to hold the reader's attention, we can more easily make informed judgements about a society's concerns and attitudes, and ask, if stories do indeed matter, why it is that this may be the case (Edgar 2006). Just as there is no single entity that can be considered a 'public sphere', the role of the media in the different spheres that exist within a modern democratic society is neither uniformly positive nor negative (Fink and Schudson 2013). The very existence of exemplary journalism such as winners of the Walkley Features, the Pulitzer Prizes in the US or the British Press Awards provides some evidence of the dynamic and positive effect the media can play in a democratic society. More research, however, is needed on the role of the feature article in journalism and the contribution that these stories may make towards the nourishing of civic life both within and beyond democratic societies (Fink and Schudson 2013; Forde 2007; Shapiro et al. 2006; O'Donnell 2009).

REFERENCES

Accountable Journalism. 2020. Accountable Journalism: Monitoring Media Ethics across the Globe. https://accountablejournalism.org/about.

Anderson, B. 1983. *Imagined Communities: Reflections on the Origin and Spread of Nationalism*. London: Verso.

Aristotle. 2019. *Nicomachean Ethics*, 3rd ed. Translated by T. Irwin. Indianapolis: Hackett.

Australia. Department of Broadband, Communication and the Digital Economy. 2012. *Convergence Review Final Report*. Canberra: DBCDE.

Benson, R.D., and E. Neveu. 2005. *Bourdieu and the Journalistic Field*. Cambridge: Polity.

Borden, S.L. 1993. Empathic Listening: The Interviewer's Betrayal. *Journal of Mass Media Ethics* 8 (4): 219–226.

Bourdieu, P. 1992. 'Part II: The Purpose of Reflexive Sociology (The Chicago Workshop). In *An Invitation to Reflexive Sociology*, ed. P. Bourdieu and L.J.D. Wacquant, 60–215. Chicago: University of Chicago Press.

Bourdieu, P., and L.J.D. Wacquant. 1992. Part 1: Toward a Social Praxeology: the Structure and Logic of Bourdieu's Sociology. In *An Invitation to Reflexive Sociology*, ed. P. Bourdieu and L.J.D. Wacquant, 1–59. Chicago: University of Chicago Press.

Breit, R., and M. Ricketson. 2012. News' Australian Story of Ethics and Self-Regulation: A Cautionary Tale. *Television and New Media* 13 (1): 41–47.

Brunkhorst, H., R. Kreide, and C. Lafont. 2018. *The Habermas Handbook*. New York: Columbia University Press.

Carey, J. 1997. 'The Dark Continent of American Journalism'. In *James Carey: A Critical Reader*, ed. E. Munson and C. Warren, 144–188. Minnesota: Minnesota Press.

Christians, C.G., T.L. Glasser, D. McQuail, K. Nordenstreng, and R.A. White. 2009. *Normative Theories of the Media: Journalism in Democratic Societies*. Chicago: University of Illinois Press.

Couldry, N. 2006. *Listening Beyond the Echoes: Media, Ethics, and Agency in an Uncertain World*. London: Paradigm.

———. 2012. *Media, Society World: Social Theory and Digital Media Practice*. Cambridge: Polity Press.

———. 2013. Living Well with and through Media. In *Ethics of Media*, ed. N. Couldry, M. Madianou, and A. Pinchevski, 39–56. New York: Palgrave Macmillan.

Couldry, N., M. Madianou, and A. Pinchevski. 2013. Ethics of Media: An Introduction. In *Ethics of Media*, ed. N. Couldry, M. Madianou, and A. Pinchevski, 1–20. New York: Palgrave Macmillan.

3 THE VIRTUE PARADIGM: THE FEATURE AND DEMOCRACY   61

De Moraes, L. 2017. White House Bans CNN, NYT, LAT, Politico from Briefing. Deadline Hollywood website. Accessed 31 March 2017. http://deadline. com/2017/02/donald-trump-bans-cnn-nyt-lat-politco-from-white-house-press-briefing-1201971628/.

Durkheim, E. 1992. *Professional Ethics and Civil Morals*. London: Routledge.

Edgar, A. 2006. *Habermas: The Key Concepts*. London and New York: Routledge.

Ettema, J.S. 2005. Crafting Cultural Resonance: Imaginative Power in Everyday Journalism. *Journalism* 6 (2): 131–152.

Fink, K., and M. Schudson. 2013. The Rise of Contextual Journalism, 1950s–2000s. *Journalism* 15 (1): 3–20.

Finkelstein, R., and M. Ricketson. 2012. *Report of the Independent Inquiry into the Media and Media Regulation*. Canberra: Department of Broadband, Communication and the Digital Economy.

Forde, K.R. 2007. Discovering the Explanatory Report in American Newspapers. *Journalism Practice* 1 (2): 227–244.

Green, M.C., T. Brock, and G. Kaufman. 2004. Understanding Media Enjoyment: The Role of Transportation into Narrative Worlds. *Communication Theory* 14 (4): 311–327.

Habermas, J. 1971. {1968–69} *Towards a Rational Society*. Translated by J. Shapiro. London: Heinemann.

———. 1984. {1981} *The Theory of Communicative Action*. Vol. 1, *Reason and the Rationalization of Society*. Translated by T. McCarthy. Cambridge: Polity Press.

———. 1989. {1962} *The Structural Transformation of the Public Sphere: An Inquiry into a Category of Bourgeois Society*. Translated by Thomas Burger and Frederick Lawrence. Cambridge, MA: Polity Press.

———. 1992. Further Reflections on the Public Sphere. Translated by T. Burger. In *Habermas and the Public Sphere*, edited by C. Calhoun, 421–461. Cambridge, MA: MIT Press.

———. 1996. *Between Facts and Norms: Contributions to a Discourse Theory of Law and Democracy*. Translated by W. Rehg. Cambridge: Polity.

———. 1998. *The Inclusion of the Other: Studies in Political Theory*. Edited by C. Cronin and P. de Greiff. Cambridge, MA: MIT Press.

———. 2001. Truth and Society: The Discursive Redemption of Factual Claims to Validity. In *On the Pragmatics of Social Interaction: Preliminary Studies in the Theory of Communicative Action*, trans. B. Fultner, 85–103. Cambridge, MA: MIT Press.

Hage, G. 2003. *Against Paranoid Nationalism: Searching for Hope in a Shrinking Society*. Sydney: Pluto Press.

———. 2015. *Alter-Politics: Critical Anthropology and the Radical Imagination*. Melbourne: Melbourne University Press.

Hooper, C. 2006. The Tall Man. *Monthly* 10 (Mar.): 34–53.

Kovach, B., and T. Rosenstiel. 2014. *The Elements of Journalism: What Newspeople Should Know and the Public Should Expect*. 3rd ed. New York: Three Rivers Press.

Latimore, J. 2016. Not an Event but a Structure. *Overland*, April 15. https://overland.org.au/2016/04/not-an-event-but-a-structure/.

Legge, K. 2002. Patrick: A Case in the Life of a Family Court Judge. *Weekend Australian Magazine*, December 7, 34–37.

Lidberg, J. 2012. 'If It Ain't Broke, Don't Fix It'—Australian Media Industry Attitudes to Regulation and Accountability Reforms. *Pacific Journalism Review* 18 (2): 68–88.

Linnell, G. 1997. Hope Lives Here. *Sunday Age, Sunday Life Supplement*, October 5, 8–16.

Lucashenko, M. 2013. Sinking Below Sight: Down and Out in Brisbane and Logan. *Griffith Review* 41: 53–67.

MacIntyre, A. 2007. *After Virtue: A Study in Moral Theory*. 3rd ed. Notre Dame, IN: Notre Dame Press.

Mason, B. 1997. The Girl in Cell 4. *HQ Magazine*, March/April, 56–61.

McChesney, R.W. 2013. *Digital Disconnect: How Capitalism Is Turning the Internet against Democracy*. New York and London: New Press.

Media, Entertainment, & Arts Alliance [MEAA]. 2019. *Registered Rules of the Media, Entertainment & Arts Alliance*. Accessed June 1, 2020. https://www.meaa.org/resource-package/registered-rules-of-the-media-entertainment-and-arts-alliance/.

Meehan, J.J., ed. 2013. *Feminists Read Habermas: Gendering the Subject of Discourse*. Abingdon, UK: Routledge.

Neveu, E. 2014. Revisiting Narrative Journalism as One of the Futures of Journalism. *Journalism Studies* 15 (5): 533–542.

O'Donnell, P. 2009. That's Gold! Thinking about Excellence in Australian Journalism'. *Australian Journalism Review* 31 (2): 47–59.

Owens, S. 2019. Why the 'Trump Bump' Didn't Deliver Much Revenue to Voters. *Medium*, May 30. Accessed June 1, 2020. https://medium.com/the-business-of-content/why-the-trump-bump-didnt-deliver-much-revenue-to-news-publishers-40e536a92439.

Poupeau, F. 2000. Reasons for Domination, Bourdieu Versus Habermas. *Sociological Review Monograph* 48 (2): 69–87.

Preston, N. 2007. *Understanding Ethics*. Sydney: Federation Press.

Pulitzer Prize. 2019. 2019 Pulitzer Prizes: Prize Winners by Category. Accessed May 20, 2020. https://pulitzer.org/prize-winners-by-category/211/.

Sarbin, T. 1995. Emotional Life, Rhetoric, and Roles. *Journal of Narrative and Life History* 5 (3): 213–220.

Schudson, M. 2008. *Why Democracies Need an Unlovable Press*. Malden, MA: Polity.

Shapiro, I., P. Albanese, and L. Doyle. 2006. What Makes Journalism 'Excellent'? Criteria Identified by Judges in Two Leading Awards Programs. *Canadian Journal of Communication* 31 (2): 1–17.

Simons, M., D. Nolan, and S. Wright. 2016. 'We Are Not North Korea': Propaganda and Professionalism in the People's Republic of China. *Media, Culture and Society* 39 (2): 1–19.

Society of Editors. 2018. 'National Press Awards Winners: Daily Newspaper of the Year, *The Times*'. https://www.societyofeditors.org/events/national-press-awards/national-press-awardswinners/.

———. 2020. Society of Editors: Fighting for Media Freedom: Award Categories. https://www.societyofeditors.org/events/national-press-awards-2019/categories/.

Strömback, J. 2005. In Search of a Standard: Four Models of Democracy and Their Normative Implications for Journalism. *Journalism Studies* 6 (3): 331–345.

Toohey, P. 2001. Highly Inflammable. *Weekend Australian Magazine*, November 24, 24–28.

Walkley Foundation. 2020. The Walkley Awards for Excellence in Journalism. Accessed May 11, 2020. https://www.walkleys.com/awards/walkleys/.

WikiLeaks. 2015. What Is WikiLeaks. WikiLeaks Website, November 3. https://wikileaks.org/What-is-WikiLeaks.html.

CHAPTER 4

The Virtue Paradigm: A New Framework

Having established the complex role that narrative long-form journalism can reasonably be expected to perform in a modern and representative democracy we now turn our attention to the research approaches that inform this book. When first deciding upon the parameters of my original study of Walkley Award-winning feature articles—a process that will be explained in Chap. 5—I needed to undertake a quantitative approach in order to sort and manage the extensive archival material. But once I had decided which stories to include in my corpus, given that this book's central concern is with the 'ideological and cultural assumptions' present in award-winning long-form, I then relied primarily upon qualitative methods, which allow both a close reading of the text, and the identifying of the framework that places that text within a wider social context (Fursich 2009, 240). I have used the method of discourse analysis, with a specific focus on rigorous textual analysis. The term 'discourse' in this context refers to 'the capacity of meaning-making resources to constitute social reality' (Chouliaraki 2008).

No single method, however, was able to successfully grapple with the rich complexity of meaning encompassed within each piece of journalistic writing, making it necessary for me to develop my own method of classifying the range of articles in a way that distinguished between the subject matter, the overall theme and the individual virtues evident in the text. In Chap. 3 I discussed how the theories of Habermas (1989) and Bourdieu (Bourdieu and Wacquant 1992; Shusterman 1999), and neo-Aristotelian

---

© The Author(s), under exclusive license to Springer Nature
Switzerland AG 2021
J. Martin, *Emotions and Virtues in Feature Writing*,
https://doi.org/10.1007/978-3-030-62978-6_4

virtue ethics (Preston 2007; Borden 2007; Couldry 2012; Couldry et al. 2013), provide a framework for a more nuanced analysis of both the narrative devices and the overarching social context in which these features are written and read. This chapter consolidates the Virtue Paradigm as a means for the researcher to construct an interconnected theoretical scaffold, with each facet of my integrated approach contributing to the overall structure on which to base an interpretation of the text.

DISCOURSE ANALYSIS AND TEXTUAL ANALYSIS

Although there is an ongoing and lively debate among theorists about the merits of discourse analysis and critical discourse analysis, including their many variants, such as rhetorical and textual linguistic analysis, I have decided to employ discourse analysis alongside the theories of social theorists such as Habermas and Bourdieu (Billig 2008; Calhoun 1992; Fairclough 2008; Fursich 2009; Poole 2010; Molina 2009; Philo 2007). Linguist Molina explains that in order to carry out either discourse analysis or critical discourse analysis, the researcher needs to accept the opacity of language and make a 'scientific' assumption to then go 'beyond the text'. He draws the distinction that although discourse analysis does not necessarily have to focus on the text, it is able to look at 'persuasion or politeness strategies', while at no time can critical discourse analysis 'evade contents' (Molina 2009, 187). As narrative journalism is inextricably anchored to its content—these are stories written about real events and people—our analysis is at little risk of evading content. All journalism is bound to a particular place and a specific time, and it is through the journalist's meticulously constructed narrative that readers are given 'the courage to confront the frailties of our cultural totalizations' (Hartsock 2016, 5). The close textual analysis of award-winning feature articles in the second half of this book will ensure that both content and context are considered. Integral to my Virtue Paradigm model is avoiding the application of any mode of linguistic or conceptual analysis as if there was a simple formula for unravelling how the journalist communicates emotion to the reader of long-form. What the Virtue Paradigm and the Virtue Map model provide is a framework to guide investigation, not a rigid prescription of a set theoretical approach. Linguistics scholar Teun A. van Dijk points out, critical discourse analysis is often described by scholars as 'DA [discourse analysis] with attitude' because of its 'rebellious attitude of dissent against the symbolic power elites that dominate public discourse, especially in

4 THE VIRTUE PARADIGM: A NEW FRAMEWORK   67

politics, media and education' (van Dijk 2013). But van Dijk asserts that although CDA is often cited as a method of analysis, this is a widely held misconception, and that 'CDA is (any) DA of critical scholars, and hence CDA is rather a social or political movement than a method'. He further deconstructs the term by asking:

> what would be the systematic, explicit, detailed, replicable procedure for doing 'critical' analysis? There is no such method. Being critical, first of all, is a state of mind, an attitude, a way of dissenting, and many more things, but not an explicit method for the description for the structure or strategies of text and talk. (van Dijk 2013)

Instead of researchers declaring 'I am going to apply CDA', van Dijk advocates the term 'critical discourse studies' be used to refer to 'the theories, methods, analyses, applications and other practices of critical discourse analysts and to forget about the confusing term "CDA"'. In line with his argument, this book will draw upon a discourse analysis approach, one that is also informed by Habermas's theory on public spheres (Habermas 1989). In this way, I will be able to consider the way in which the language is being used to persuade or convince readers of a particular message and to construct the particular social conditions that are operating within the narrative.

Also helpful in the consideration of the influence of the journalists' choice of narrative construction in prize-winning long-form is Fursich's model of textual analysis. Fursich wants to 'salvage' textual analysis as a viable form for media study, as media texts present a 'distinctive discursive moment between encoding and decoding that justifies special scholarly engagement' (Fursich 2009, 238). Drawing upon my own experience as a teacher of media curricula, in particular feature writing, I would argue that close textual analysis is an important and regularly used approach to understand how narrative journalism works. An example of this is 'the x-ray technique' taught by Roy Peter Clark at the Poynter Institute who has written a book on the topic, which encourages a forensic examination of feature articles (Clark 2010, 2016).

It is this practice of analysing how journalists encode meaning and how readers—in this instance the Walkley judges, who are themselves journalists—may decode that meaning that is of value for my approach. Fursich points out that there are several distinct ways of doing context studies, such as taking a cultural anthropology position, or the literary studies approach with its focus on criticism and rhetoric (Fursich 2009;

Clifford and Marcus 1986; Burke 1966; Fish 1980). Further to this are semiotics and post-structuralism, which stress the importance of language in building social relations (Barthes 1972; Derrida 1976; Foucault 1972, 1983). The important contribution of semiotics and post-structuralism to media studies has meant that analysing media content can no longer be understood as an objective exercise; rather, the text is 'read' taking into consideration the social context in which it was written as well as an acknowledgement of the subjectivity of the reader (Fursich 2009, 240). The rising awareness of context has led to a deconstructionist approach, examining the 'internal inconsistencies' in the text (Derrida 1976). Fursich's argument that independent textual analysis is able to 'elucidate the narrative structure, symbolic arrangements and ideological potential of media content' (Fursich 2009, 239) is the synergistic approach that I apply in my analysis of the articles included in Part II of this book. It is my hope that this analysis will go some way towards bridging the gap between the cultural anthropology position and the literary studies approach.

TRANSPORTATION THEORY

When a journalist is able to successfully employ narrative and reporting devices to construct a feature article, allowing readers to become immersed in the story to the extent that they are permitted to vicariously experience the emotions of those involved in the narrative, then a powerful act of 'transportation' has occurred. A brief example is the opening sentence of Hannah Dreier's 2019 Pulitzer prize-winning feature, 'A Betrayal', which I discuss in detail in Chap. 9: 'If Henry is killed, his death can be traced to a quiet moment in the fall of 2016, when he sat slouched in his usual seat by the door in 11th-grade English class' (Dreier 2018). When I read this line, I am first alerted to the danger facing Henry, and then Dreier's description allows me to be transported in my imagination to a high school classroom. The transportation of readers is directly dependent upon the skill of the journalist in communicating emotions and virtues to readers. Transportation has been studied in relation to fiction (Nell 1988; Green et al. 2004, 312–313; Lee 2011), but how the journalist also achieves this transportation in a feature article is an often neglected topic within the study of narrative journalism. The journalist's efforts to transport readers into a carefully constructed narrative world are essential in giving those readers the opportunity to invest heavily enough in the story to consider and perhaps even to change the way in which they view themselves and their communities. A simple focus on the text that is limited to an analysis of language could miss the rich line of investigation into how a journalist imbues a narrative with emotions and virtues and whether this can be considered as contributing to the flourishing of a society.

The foundation for transportation theory can be found in the work of researchers such as Victor Nell (1988), who investigated how and why readers of fiction could become 'lost' in a story, and Schank and Abelson (Schank and Abelson 1995), who went as far as to argue that narratives, or stories, are the most natural mode of thought, or Csikszentmihalyi (1990), who identified reading as the most frequent example of this kind of 'flow' activity (where readers become immersed or 'lost' in a story) partaken by individuals worldwide. While early theorists such as Raney strove to develop a conceptualization of enjoyment that included both cognitive and affective factors (Raney 2002, cited by Green et al. 2004, 311), researchers such as Green et al. (2004) extended this discussion to include our wider engagement with the media and pushed the debate beyond the notion of pleasure. The researchers also explored the notion of what they termed 'transportation', which they defined as 'a distinct mental process, an integrative melding of attention, imagery, and feelings' which is 'thought to leave the experiencer's beliefs and perceptions changed in some measurable way, whereas enjoyment does not imply measurable change' (Green et al. 2004, 312–313).

Key to the notion of transportation is that although the experience may not be an 'enjoyable' one for the reader, nonetheless the consequences of being absorbed in different narrative worlds may include 'connections with characters and self-transformations' (Green et al. 2004, 311). When this reasoning is applied to the analysis of journalistic feature articles, it becomes evident that stories about real people and real events have the potential to have lasting impact on the reader. Indeed, studies by Green and Brock, showing stories that were labelled as either 'fact' or 'fiction', suggested that readers may be transported equally well into factual and fictional worlds (Green et al. 2004, 322). The quality of the writing is of course integral to this process, for 'Just as a leaky boat does a poor job of transporting people across the water, poorly constructed narratives do not help readers enter the story world. Most readers know good craftsmanship when they encounter it' (Green et al. 2004, 320).

Transportation theory is an integral component in the Virtue Paradigm methodology. Narrative journalism, by exposing readers to an event they

70   J. MARTIN

may never have experienced, may allow them to 'appreciate truths about themselves and their world', thus bringing about 'transformations that endure in some way once individuals return from the narrative world to their everyday reality' (Green et al. 2004, 317). While Raney (2002) strove to develop a 'complete conceptualization of enjoyment', I use transportation theory to construct a conceptualization of emotion and virtue, not in regard to fiction but in regard to journalistic features. Journalism's focus on real events intensifies the possibility that transportation 'draws upon, and perhaps helps develop, individuals' natural tendency toward empathy and perspective taking' (Green et al. 2004, 316–317).

A brief consideration of award-winning journalism about tragic events demonstrates how the process of transportation need not even be an enjoyable experience. Being transported can allow people to explore and experiment with other possible selves that 'individuals might become, wish to become, or fear becoming' (Markus and Nurius 1986, cited by Green et al. 2004, 318). Reading an article about people risking their lives to save sleeping toddlers from a burning day-care centre, for example, can prompt readers to ask how they would have coped in the same situation (Whittaker 2005). The feature provides a 'safe' means of exploring different selves, for although readers may return from the constructed narrative world altered in some way, they are not in any direct harm or danger. The feature articles are therefore 'a way of experiencing our world without necessarily seeing ourselves implicated in it'; for example, people may read about a couple who lose their child to cancer without suffering that loss themselves, but they may also imagine what the impact of the death of their own children would have upon them (Telotte 2001; Linnell 1997).

Phronetic Journalism: The Virtue of Practical Wisdom Within Feature Writing

A consideration of the theoretical implications of how journalists use emotion to construct award-winning feature narratives is deepened when informed by an understanding of Aristotle's notion of the intellectual virtue of phronesis (*NE* VI.5) and how this concept has been re-imagined by scholars over the past 50 years (Gadamar 1980; MacIntyre 1981; Schön 1983, 1987; Stout 1988; Dunne 1997, 1999; Flyvbjerg 2001; Roseneil and Frosh 2012; Kinsella and Pitman 2012b). Aristotle's virtue of phronesis is generally defined as 'practical wisdom or knowledge of the proper ends of life', and the philosopher considered phronesis as superior to his other two intellectual virtues of *techne* and *episteme*. In their 2012 book, *Phronesis as Professional Knowledge*, Elizabeth Kinsella and Alan Pitman defined 'episteme' as 'scientific, universal, invariable, context-independent knowledge' and 'techne' as context-dependent, pragmatic, variable, craft knowledge that is orientated towards practical instrumental rationality governed by a conscious goal. The defining quality of phronesis is that it is 'an intellectual virtue that implies ethics' (Kinsella and Pitman 2012a, 2). If we attempt to apply this set of virtues to journalism, the 'techne' would be the ability to construct sentences, to write in particular journalistic styles and to have mastered the basics of reporting. The 'episteme' could be best understood as the body of knowledge surrounding the profession of journalism which would encompass the foundational belief that it is the responsibility of journalists to accurately inform the public about important issues. The journalistic 'episteme' would also include the study of journalism, including theories from the field of media and communications, but also across a wide range of disciplines such as literature, psychology, sociology, history and philosophy. And finally, phronesis is the journalist's striving to educate and inform readers on complex issues that impact their lives.

The term 'phronetic social science' was introduced in 2001 by Bent Flyvbjerg in his influential book, *Making Social Science Matter* (Flyvbjerg 2001). His book came to be regarded as a 'manifesto' for those who sought to open up political sciences to new ways of examining power relations between individuals, governments, corporations and society as a whole (Flyvbjerg et al. 2012, 28). Flyvbjerg, who came from the field of planning and environment studies, argued that phronesis was what the social sciences, with their emphasis on episteme and techne, had to offer that the natural sciences could not. Flyvbjerg understood phronesis as something that 'grows out of intimate familiarity with practice in contextualized settings', that sets it aside from these other more traditional approaches (Flyvbjerg et al. 2012, 28). He proposed (2001, 60) that a phronetic approach should ask four key questions:

1. Where are we going?
2. Is this desirable?
3. What should be done?
4. Who gains and who loses and by which mechanisms of power?

As will be demonstrated in the case studies in the second half of this book, Flyvbjerg's four phronetic questions provide an instructive framework to investigate how journalists construct award-winning narratives. Applying Flyvbjerg's questions to an analysis of prize-winning long-form features brings much-needed attention to the way in which stories can address issues of power—and powerlessness—for readers. My four questions, reframed to apply to long-form journalism, ask:

1 Where is this story going? Or, where does this story take readers? How does it inform and educate readers?
2 Is this a desirable direction? What are the ramifications of the issues discussed for living well in a community?
3 Is the journalist, through their textual construction, suggesting or advocating what 'should' be done? Does their construction invite readers to consider what the best actions are to benefit the community as a whole? Does the journalist's writing prompt readers to consider what injustices should be addressed and how?
4 Does the journalist's writing prompt readers to consider the question of who gains and who loses and by which mechanisms of power? Or to ask who is responsible and how a community best protects its most vulnerable?

In Flyvbjerg's model, phronetic social science may involve in-depth case studies that provide forensic detail about power interactions between all parties in an attempt to understand and convey the complexity of the relationships of those involved (Flyvbjerg et al. 2012, 29).

Writing just over a decade after Flyvbjerg in 2012, Kinsella and Pitman began a conversation about phronesis with scholars from education, health, philosophy and sociology who shared 'concerns that something of fundamental importance—or moral significance—was missing in the vision of what it means to be a professional' (Kinsella and Pitman 2012a, 1). They noted that they were part of a long line of scholars who had been advocating the value of phronesis to professions and even 'a reconceptualization of social science itself' since the 1980s (Kinsella and Pitman 2012b; Flyvbjerg et al. 2012; MacIntyre 1981; Nussbaum 2001; Schön 1983, 1987). Kinsella and Pitman asked what the implications for professional education and practice might be if practitioners took 'phronesis seriously as an organising framework for professional knowledge' (2012a, 1). The authors acknowledged that there was a diverse range of understandings among interdisciplinary scholars about what phronesis is and 'how it might be understood, applied, and extended in a world radically different to that of the progenitor of the term, Aristotle' (1). It is in keeping with Kinsella and Pitman's open invitation to consider the value of phronesis across different academic disciplines and professions that I have developed my own concept of 'phronetic journalism'. There appears to be very little scholarship on how Aristotle's master virtue can be applied to journalism; for example, there is not one reference to journalism in the index of Flyvbjerg et al.' 2012 manifesto on phronesis, *Real Social Science*. While the mass media is clearly understood throughout the book as influential, the media is mentioned more specifically in relation to particular case studies, or as an effective means of scholars conveying their message to a wider audience, for 'phronetic social scientists are explicitly concerned about public exposure, because they see it as one of the main vehicles for the type of social and political action that is at the heart of phronesis' (Flyvbjerg et al. 2012, 108–109).

Sociologist and gender studies researcher Sasha Roseneil (2012) has also argued that a phronetic approach had much to offer the field of feminist social studies. She said that it was unfortunate that Flyvbjerg's ideas had not been taken up by social scientists beyond the policy and practice-orientated fields of research, and suggested that a phronetic approach, with its concise questions about power, offered feminist social researchers such as herself 'a powerful clarification of approaches that we have been employing, and a new language for practices that we might consider adopting or strengthening' (Roseneil 2012, 25). With respect to scholars such as Roseneil and with a strong acknowledgement of the significance of Flyvbjerg's contribution to a modern interpretation of Aristotle's master virtue of phronesis, I advocate a further reconceptualization as a lens through which to better understand the social advocacy role of journalism. I ask that we consider the following question: if phronetic social science is concerned with using practical wisdom 'in ways that improve society', how can this philosophy be applied to journalism and in particular, to the understanding of how journalists draw upon narrative and reporting devices to construct narratives that communicate emotion and virtues to readers?

The specific reporting or describing of events and know-how, combined with narrative skills and devices—which constitute the *techne* of journalism—are the building blocks used by a skilled writer to construct a compelling feature article. And while the researcher can thoughtfully and effectively apply any number of theoretical frameworks, or epistemes, which might include, as this study has, the views of Habermas and Bourdieu or the theories of Preston, Couldry, Schudson and Maras, they are simply insufficient on their own to investigate the 'transportive' power of award-winning feature writing (Schudson 2003a, b, 2008; Maras 2013). It is as if the techne and the episteme, while they are both important, are separated by too big a gap between practice and theory to be convincingly bridged by any attempt to knit the two together into a cohesive theoretical whole. But the introduction of the notion of phronesis, the practical application of wisdom in journalistic writing, allows a questioning of just how and why journalists are able to construct narratives that draw upon emotion to forge connections with their readers. For it is in this way that phronetic journalism provides a vehicle to learn how to live well in a modern democracy by considering what virtues are considered worthwhile in a society.

The term phronesis has a particular usefulness in the analysis of long-form journalism as it enables the researcher to gauge whether there is a strong sense of community duty that provides readers with the opportunity to change their world view and perhaps even prompt them to action. But before considering how well Aristotle's concept of phronesis may apply to the globalized media culture of the twenty-first century it is crucial to understand the problems inherent in doing so. Aristotle's world, despite being deeply patriarchal and defined by class and race, was considered by the ruling elite to be 'stable and eternal'. As Kinsella and Pitman explain, Aristotle lived in a word where:

> the object of the intellect was to gain knowledge, and, through knowledge, wisdom (*sophia*) and to develop a love of knowledge (*philos*). Hence, philosophy was the pursuit of the elite: the object was society ruled by the wise 'philosopher king.' In current times, while we may wish for wise, thinking political leaders, we do so in a fundamentally different social and philosophical world. (Kinsella and Pitman 2012a, 3)

Any interpretation of Aristotle's phronesis must recognize the myriad of complexities and differences that define modern societies, and what the implications of those differences mean when we contemplate what is considered as the virtuous or the good. There is also a problem, as Ellett points out, with the common definition of phronesis as 'practical wisdom, or knowledge of the proper ends of conduct and of the means of attaining them; distinguished by Aristotle from theoretical knowledge or science, and from technical skill'. Ellett argues that the popular definition of phronesis is misleading as it 'fails to make clear that, for Aristotle, the *ultimate, proper end* of the good life is determined by *theoretical reason* and not by practical reason'. And, as Ellett explains, 'for Aristotle, theoretical reason holds that all things must have a form (and function), and that the form for humans enables the philosopher to show that the highest good for *all* humans is the contemplation of knowledge' (Ellett 2012, 20). Ellett rightly rejects Aristotle's moral essentialism, or what MacIntyre (1981, 88) described as the position that mankind has 'an essential nature and an essential purpose or function'. I would argue, however, that people can be helped to make sense of the complexity of the social constructions of gender, class and ethnicity that intersect our lives in a totally mediatized world via the means provided by award-winning narrative journalism.

While the wholesale rescuing of the concept of phronesis for application in a modern context is both undesirable and unrealistic, this virtue may still stake a claim for performing an important role in how society defines itself. Phronesis also aligns with Habermas's validity claims of truth, appropriateness, sincerity and comprehension, which are useful in providing a theoretical barometer of how well the article in question meets the criteria for an 'ideal speech situation' (Habermas 2001, 85–103). Phronesis also interlocks with all seven of Schudson's functions of news in a democratic society: information, investigation, analysis, social empathy, promoting a democracy, public forum and mobilization (Schudson 2008, 339). As I discuss in Chap. 5, my preliminary reading of the Walkley Features and my subsequent pilot study, which included identifying overarching themes within these narratives, revealed that Schudson's first four functions of news—information, investigation, analysis and social empathy—were common in different degrees to all of the feature articles in my corpus. Schudson's remaining functions of 'publicizing a democracy', 'providing a public forum' and 'mobilization' (339) only applied to a small number of the stories that met the criteria for phronetic journalism. I contend that the addition of an eighth function, that of 'identity', will deepen any analysis of journalistic narratives and that, when fulfilled, all of Schudson's seven functions contribute to the development of a community's identity.

Finally, as we will recall from our discussion in Chap. 3, the value of phronesis as a journalistic tool is illustrated in Kovach and Rosenstiel's 2001 study which, based upon interviews with journalists, listed ten guiding principles for the profession (Kovach and Rosenstiel 2014). The first principle is 'to provide people with the information they need to be free and self-governing' (Kovach and Rosenstiel 2014, 9). The other principles are 'truthfulness, verification, loyalty to citizens, independence, monitors of power and providers of a forum for public criticism, as well as being interesting, relevant, comprehensive, proportional and to exercise freedom of conscience' (Kovach and Rosenstiel 2014, 9).

Phronesis is considered the 'master virtue' of the Virtue Map on the grounds that phronetic journalism advocates action, and inherent in this virtue is a sense of striving towards a greater truth or understanding. Evidence of the value of the virtue of phronesis can be found, although not explicitly identified as phronesis, in the criteria of journalism awards globally. Some examples include Spain's Ortega y Gasset Awards, given to reporters whose work displays a 'remarkable defense of freedom, independence, honesty and professional rigor as essential virtues of journalism' (Premios Ortega y Gasset 2020), Canada's Michener Award, which judges entries upon 'their impact on the public and the degree of arms-length public benefit that is generated' (Michener Award 2020), and in Poland the Golden Pear Award, which

> 'celebrates publications that have a conscious desire to creatively interfere with the existing reality' and the desire to not uncritically present the phenomena, event and social processes taking place in their country. (Golden Pear 2020; my translation)

It is important to acknowledge there is a risk that a phronetic approach, with its emphasis on action, could lend itself to journalists brazenly hijacking the narrative for their own political ends simply because: 'Where the virtues are required, the vices also may flourish' (MacIntyre 2007, 193). The Virtue Map's particular focus on award-winning journalism mitigates this risk and provides the opportunity to appreciate the important function that the media performs in what Pantti described as 'the mobilization of compassion' (2010, 228). The Virtue Map also illuminates phronetic journalism's potential to effect change and shows the ways in which 'the news media provide an interpretive framework that allows subjective emotions to become public aspirations and to lead to collective moral or political action' (Pantti 2010, 223) For example, an article in the *New York Times*, aptly titled 'To Anyone Who Thinks Journalism Can't Change the World', lists three international stories in one month that led to immediate reforms, including a sanitation program in South African schools after two children drowned in pit toilets (McDermott 2018). Employing the Virtue Map to identify the presence of phronesis in a story facilitates a deeper appreciation and understanding of both the dynamics of feature writing and the potential of journalism to effect social change. It is important, however, that this book's focus on phronesis is not considered as discounting the value of what is considered episteme or techne. Just as Kinsella and Pitman advocated in their 2012 book concerning the profession of education, the aim is to highlight how episteme and techne have been privileged at the expense of phronesis in discussions about journalism. The Virtue Map is a new means to redress that imbalance.

References

Barthes, R. 1972. *Mythologies*. Translated by A. Lavers. New York: Hill and Wang.

Billig, M. 2008. The Language of Critical Discourse Analysis: The Case of Nominalization. *Discourse & Society* 19 (6): 783–800.

Borden, S. 2007. *Journalism as Practice: MacIntyre, Virtue Ethics and the Press*. Farnham, Surrey: Ashgate.

Bourdieu, P., and L.J.D. Wacquant. 1992. *An Invitation to Reflexive Sociology*. Cambridge: Polity Press.

Burke, K. 1966. *Language as Symbolic Action: Essays on Life, Literature and Method*. Berkeley: University of California Press.

Calhoun, C., ed. 1992. *Habermas and the Public Sphere*. Cambridge, MA: MIT Press.

Chouliaraki, L. 2008. Discourse Analysis. In *The SAGE Handbook of Cultural Analysis*, ed. T. Bennett and J. Frow, 674–698. London: Sage.

Clark, R.P. 2010. Develop X-Ray Reading Skills to Improve Your Writing. *Poynter*, January 27. https://www.poynter.org/reporting-editing/2010/develop-x-ray-reading-skills-to-improve-your-writing/.

———. 2016. *The Art of X-Ray Reading*. New York: Little, Brown and Company.

Clifford, J., and G.E. Marcus, eds. 1986. *Writing Culture: The Poetics and Politics of Ethnography*. Berkeley: University of California Press.

Couldry, N. 2012. *Media, Society, World: Social Theory and Digital Media Practice*. Malden, MA: Polity Press.

Couldry, N., M. Madianou, and A. Pinchevski. 2013. *Ethics of Media*. New York: Palgrave Macmillan.

Csikszentmihalyi, M. 1990. *Flow: The Psychology of Optimal Experience*. New York: Harper & Row.

Derrida, J. 1976. *Of Grammatology*. Translated by G.C. Spivak. Baltimore, MD: Johns Hopkins University Press.

Dreier, H. 2018. A Betrayal. *ProPublica*, April 2. Accessed February 6, 2020. https://features.propublica.org/ms-13/a-betrayal-ms13-gang-police-fbi-ice-deportation/.

Dunne, J. 1997. *Back to the Rough Ground: 'Phronesis' and 'Techne' in Modern Philosophy and in Aristotle*. Notre Dame, IN: University of Notre Dame Press.

———. 1999. Virtue, *Phronesis* and Learning. In *Virtue Ethics and Moral Education*, ed. D. Carr and J. Steutel, 49–63. London: Routledge.

Ellett, F.S. 2012. Practical Rationality and a Recovery of Aristotle's 'Phronesis' for the Professions. In *Phronesis as Professional Knowledge: Practical Wisdom in the Professions*, ed. E.A. Kinsella and A. Pitman, 13–34. Rotterdam: Sense Publishers.

Fairclough, N. 2008. The Language of Critical Discourse Analysis: Reply to Michael Billig. *Discourse and Society* 19 (6): 811–819.

Fish, S. 1980. *Is There a Text in This Class? The Authority of Interpretive Communities*. Cambridge, MA: Harvard University Press.

Flyvbjerg, B. 2001. *Making Social Science Matter: Why Social Inquiry Fails and How It Can Succeed Again*. Translated by S. Sampson. Cambridge: Cambridge University Press.

Flyvbjerg, B., T. Landman, and S.F. Schram, eds. 2012. *Real Social Science: Applied Phronesis*. Cambridge: Cambridge University Press.

Foucault, M. 1972. *The Archaeology of Knowledge and the Discourse on Language*. Translated by A.M. Sheridan Smith. New York: Pantheon Books.

———. 1983. The Subject and Power. In *Beyond Structuralism and Hermeneutics*, ed. H. Dreyfuss and P. Rabinow. Chicago: University of Chicago Press.

Fursich, E. 2009. In Defense of Textual Analysis. *Journalism Studies* 10 (2. Jan.): 238–252.

Gadamar, H.G. 1980. Practical Philosophy as a Model of the Human Sciences. *Research in Phenomenology* 9: 74–85.

Golden Pear. 2020. Złota Gruszka i Zielona Gruszka (website). Accessed May 31, 2020. http://www.stowarzyszeniedziennikarzyrp.krakow.pl/prices.html.

Green, M.C., T. Brock, and G. Kaufman. 2004. Understanding Media Enjoyment: The Role of Transportation into Narrative Worlds. *Communication Theory* 14 (4): 311–327.

Habermas, J. 1989. *The Structural Transformation of the Public Sphere: An Inquiry into a Category of Bourgeois Society*. Translated by Thomas Burger and Frederick Lawrence. Cambridge, MA: MIT Press.

———. 2001. Truth and Society: The Discursive Redemption of Factual Claims to Validity. In *On the Pragmatics of Social Interaction: Preliminary Studies in the Theory of Communicative Action*, trans. B. Fultner, 85–103. Cambridge, MA: MIT Press.

Hartsock, J.C. 2016. *Literary Journalism and the Aesthetics of Experience*. Amherst and Boston: University of Massachusetts Press.

4 THE VIRTUE PARADIGM: A NEW FRAMEWORK   79

Kinsella, E.A., and A. Pitman. 2012a. Engaging Phronesis in Professional Practice and Education. In *Phronesis as Professional Knowledge. Professional Practice and Education: A Diversity of Voices*, ed. E.A. Kinsella and A. Pitman, vol. 1, 1–11. Rotterdam: Sense Publishers.

———, eds. 2012b. *Phronesis as Professional Knowledge. Professional Practice and Education: A Diversity of Voices*. Vol. 1. Rotterdam: Sense Publishers.

Kovach, B., and T. Rosenstiel. 2014. *The Elements of Journalism: What Newspeople Should Know and the Public Should Expect*. 3rd ed. New York: Three Rivers Press.

Lee, C. 2011. *Our Very Own Adventure: Towards a Poetics of the Short Story*. Melbourne: Melbourne University Press.

Linnell, G. 1997. Hope Lives Here. *Sunday Age, Sunday Life Supplement*, October 5, 8–16.

MacIntyre, A. 1981. *After Virtue: A Study in Moral Theory*. Notre Dame, IN: Notre Dame Press.

———. 2007. *After Virtue: A Study in Moral Theory*. 3rd ed. Notre Dame, IN: Notre Dame Press.

Maras, S. 2013. *Objectivity in Journalism*. Cambridge: Polity Press.

McDermott, M.T. 2018. To Anyone Who Thinks Journalists Can't Change the World. *New York Times*, September 5. Accessed March 19, 2019. https://www.nytimes.com/2018/09/05/insider/isis-thailand-south-africa-reforms.html.

Michener Award. 2020. Michener Awards Foundation. Accessed June 18, 2020. http://www.michenerawards.ca/english/.

Molina, P. 2009. Critical Analysis of Discourse and of the Media: Challenges and Shortcomings. *Critical Discourse Studies* 6 (3): 185–198.

Nell, V. 1988. The Psychology of Reading for Pleasure: Needs and Gratifications. *Reading Research Quarterly* 23 (1, Winter): 6–50.

Nussbaum, M. 2001. *The Fragility of Goodness: Luck and Ethics in Greek Tragedy and Philosophy*. Cambridge: Cambridge University Press.

Pantti, M. 2010. Disaster News and Public Emotions. In *The Routledge Handbook of Emotions and Mass Media*, ed. K. Doveling, C. von Scheve, and E.A. Konjin, 221–236. London: Routledge.

Philo, G. 2007. Can Discourse Analysis Successfully Explain the Content of Media and Journalistic Practice? *Journalism Studies* 8 (2): 175–196.

Poole, B. 2010. Commitment and Criticality: Fairclough's Critical Discourse Analysis Evaluated. *International Journal of Applied Linguistics* 20 (2): 137–155.

Premios Ortega y Gasset. 2020. Works Published in 2019. Cerrada: The Call. https://elpais.com/elpais/premios_ortega_y_gasset.html.

Preston, N. 2007. *Understanding Ethics*. Sydney: Federation Press.

80   J. MARTIN

Raney, A.A. 2002. Moral Judgement as a Predictor of Enjoyment. In *Communication and Emotion: Essays in Honor of Dolf Zilmann*, ed. J. Bryant, D. Roskos-Ewoldson, and J. Cantor, 61–84. Mahwah, NJ: Erlbaum.

Roseneil, S. 2012. Doing Social Research after the Cultural Turn: Research with Practical Intention. In *Social Research after the Cultural Turn: A (Self-)Critical Introduction*, ed. S. Roseneil and S. Frosh, 16–35. London: Palgrave Macmillan.

Roseneil, S., and S. Frosh, eds. 2012. *Social Research after the Cultural Turn*. London: Palgrave Macmillan.

Schank, R.C., and R.P. Abelson. 1995. Knowledge and Memory: The Real Story. In *Knowledge and Memory: The Real Story*, ed. R.S. Wyer Jr., 1–85. Hillsdale, NJ: Lawrence Erlbaum Associates. http://cogprints.org/636/1/KnowledgeMemory_SchankAbelson_d.html.

Schön, D.A. 1983. *The Reflective Practitioner*. New York: Basic Books.

———. 1987. *Educating the Reflective Practitioner*. San Francisco: Jossey-Base.

Schudson, M. 2003a. *The Sociology of News*. San Diego, CA: W.W. Norton.

———. 2003b. The Sociology of News Production. *Media, Culture and Society* 11: 263–282.

———. 2008. *Why Democracies Need an Unlovable Press*. Malden, MA: Polity Press.

Shusterman, R. 1999. *Bourdieu: A Critical Reader*. Malden, MA: Blackwell.

Stout, J. 1988. *Ethics after Babel*. Boston, MA: Beacon Press.

Telotte, J.P. 2001. Introduction: Film and/as Technology: Assessing a Bargain. *Journal of Popular Film and Television* 28 (4): 146–149.

van Dijk, T.A. 2013. CDA Is NOT a Method of Critical Discourse Analysis. Association of Studies on Discourse and Society (EDISO) Website. Accessed May 31, 2020. https://www.edisoportal.org/debate/115-cda-not-method-critical-discourse-analysis.

Whittaker, M. 2005. Ordinary Heroes. *Weekend Australian Magazine*, June 18, 26–31.

CHAPTER 5

The Virtue Map: The Walkley Project

INTRODUCTION

Before I introduce the Virtue Map in detail in Chap. 6 and proceed to the case studies of feature articles in Part II, it is necessary for me to provide some context of my larger research project that is the foundation of my model. An important part of this background is an understanding of the history of the Walkley Awards and the development of long-form feature writing in Australia. In my discussion of prize culture in Chap. 2, I emphasized that journalism prizes 'are not only rewards for individual achievements, but also provide a barometer of the prominent journalistic ideals of a given journalistic field at a given time' (Willig 2019, 15). As Willig's insightful application of Bourdieu's field theory (Benson and Neveu 2005) to her study of the Danish Cavling prize for journalism demonstrates:

> Every time a prize is awarded for journalism, a collective action of consecration takes place, in addition to the recognition of the individual achievement. In this way, journalism prizes symbolize journalistic ideals and offer a historical barometer showing the construction of symbolic capital over time. (Willig 2019, 15)

Taking the time to establish the historical context of the Walkley Awards will allow me to contextualize how and why the prize is used as a 'metonym for extraordinary journalistic practice', in the same way that

---

© The Author(s), under exclusive license to Springer Nature
Switzerland AG 2021
J. Martin, *Emotions and Virtues in Feature Writing*,
https://doi.org/10.1007/978-3-030-62978-6_5

81

Willig (2019, 5) asserts the Cavling prize enjoys such high status in Denmark. My discussion will proceed to a description of the initial pilot study for the Walkley Project, which framed the scope of this larger study. We will then examine the construction of the Virtue Map in detail, including how the original story categories were chosen, and how these themes were subsequently changed for this book in order to better demonstrate the international application of the model. The focus will then shift to a discussion of the virtues that comprise the Virtue Map before concluding with an elaboration of the rationale that underpins the selection of feature articles for case studies of Part II.

A Brief History of Feature Writing in Early Australia

Although it is not possible to do justice within the limits of one book to the complex and fascinating topic of how the feature article, and indeed journalism, developed in Australia, I will in this chapter signpost some of the unique ways in which narrative journalism, as we appreciate it today, emerged from its colonial beginnings. Australia, for the first 40 years of its existence as a colony, did not have anything that even remotely resembled what we would consider a 'free press'. Although a wooden printing press came out on the First Fleet in 1788, 'total government censorship was in place until the 1820s', with the first trained printer, George Howe, taking over from a convict, George Hughes, in 1800 (McDonald and Avieson 2019, 38). When the first newspapers, the *Sydney Gazette* and the *New South Wales Advertiser*, were published in 1803, they were little more than vehicles of government propaganda. But, as Willa McDonald and Bunty Avieson (who, along with Kerrie Davies, are the developers of the Australian Colonial Narrative Journalism database) explain, it is 'the journals of the explorers, published mostly in book form in England, letters written home by convicts and settlers, works of memoir, and sketches published once a local free press began to surface' that provide a glimpse into the germination of what would become recognizable as narrative journalism in early settler culture (38).

By 1888, more than 60 daily newspapers were being published in Australia and, over the course of the nineteenth century, almost 600 periodicals were published, with the first literary periodical printed in 1821

(Young 2019; McDonald and Avieson 2019, 42). The ACNJ database, which covers the period from 1788 to 1901, is the first serious attempt to investigate 'the history of the craft of narrative journalism from the early days of the colony' and focuses on 'factual writing and memoir that crosses the boundary from being primarily reportage to an exploration for the writer's own consciousness' (ACNJ 2020a). The database provides examples of Australia's earliest journalists, including Thomas Carrington's first-person account of the capture of the infamous bushranger, Ned Kelly (ACNJ 2020b). While the story of Ned Kelly looms large in the Australian imagination, as researchers McDonald, Avieson and Davies point out, very few people know the name of the journalist who wrote the story upon which the legend was built (McDonald and Avieson 2019, 37; McDonald and Davies 2015). The work of John Stanley James—who was known as 'the Vagabond' and used undercover, immersive reporting to write enormously popular stories for the *Argus* newspaper in 1876 and 1877—is included, as well as journalism by the celebrated poet A.B. (Banjo) Paterson, who wrote about the experiences of soldiers in the Boer War (McDonald and Avieson 2019, 43). The founders of the ACNJ database rightly assert that this ongoing project provides much-needed recognition of the history of literary journalism, including the work of women such as Hay Thomson, whose undercover article into conditions into the Kew Asylum in Melbourne was published in March and April 1886, predating Nellie Bly's deservedly famous 'Ten Days in a Madhouse' written for Joseph Pulitzer's *New York World* (Davies and McDonald 2020; Bly 1887). The database also contributes to growing international recognition of a form that 'communicates matters of national and international consequence in ways accessible to the reading public' (ACNJ 2020a) and raises the profile of a field of study 'that once dropped between the cracks of English and journalism/media departments in the academy' (McDonald and Avieson 2019, 35). Just as important is how the database draws attention to whose stories were *not* told in colonial Australia, making it clear that, 'From its very beginning in Australia, literary journalism has been a form belonging to settler culture, with particular voices notably absent, e.g., those of women and the First Peoples', with the writing of the previously mentioned Catherine Hay Thomson proving the exception rather than the rule (McDonald and Avieson 2019, 35).

An Early History of the Walkley Awards

The Walkley Awards were founded in 1956 by the New Zealand-born pioneer of Ampol Petroleum, Sir William Gaston Walkley, known as Bill Walkley. According to former journalist and media lecturer John Hurst, who wrote a seminal book on the history of the awards, *The Walkley Awards: Australia's Best Journalists in Action*, Bill Walkley had built up strong relations with the media over the previous two decades, with many reporters admiring him for standing up to major petrol suppliers and never wavering in his belief that there was oil to be found in the Australian desert. Hurst (1988, 9) recounted how Walkley chartered a plane to 'take a large party of pressman' to 'see the spudding in of the first oil well, confident that they at least would give him a fair go despite what the sceptics were saying'. The 'food was first class, there was plenty of grog, each journalist was given a sixty-page booklet of background information and Walkley was his usual affable self and always accessible'. Walkley appeared to have genuinely liked and respected journalists because 'they had never misquoted him or betrayed any confidence he had placed in them and that occasional press criticism of him, while pungent, was fair' (10). Walkley also employed a number of former journalists, including Terry Southwell-Keely, who had been the deputy chief-of-staff at the *Sydney Morning Herald*. It was Southwell-Keely who suggested to Walkley that he create a national prize to be given to the writers of the best examples of Australian journalism. Hurst said that Walkley, who 'had often wondered why there was no Australian equivalent of the prestigious American Pulitzer prize for journalism', accepted the challenge and his offer was in turn welcomed by the Australian Journalists Association (AJA, which joined with Actors Equity Australia and the Australian Theatrical and Amusement Employees Association to form the Media, Entertainment and Arts Alliance or MEAA in 1992). The inaugural Walkley Awards were established in 1956 with a cash prize pool of £1000 and trophies for just five categories: Best Piece of Newspaper Reporting, Best Newspaper Feature Story, Best Magazine Feature Story, Best Provincial Newspaper Story and Best Photograph. The prize pool was unevenly split, with £500 awarded to the Best Newspaper story, £200 to the Best Newspaper Feature and £100 each to the Best Magazine feature, Best Provincial Newspaper Story and Best Photograph (Hurst 1988, 10). The first Walkley Award went to Eva Sommer, a 22-year-old cadet at the Sydney newspaper the *Sun* for an extraordinary story about a stowaway with amnesia (Sommer 1956). A photograph of the winners shows a diminutive Sommer surrounded by men in suits, who look not at her but at each other, reaching across her to shake hands with their male colleagues. Bill Walkley stands proudly behind Sommer with a paternal hand resting on her shoulder (Walkley Digital Archive 2019).

While media organizations today proudly boast about the achievements of their Walkley Award-winning employees, it took some time for the prize to gain the kind of cultural capital it enjoys today as 'the pinnacle of achievement for any Australian journalist' (Walkley Foundation 2020a; Landy 2013). According to Hurst, the early years of the Walkley Awards were affected by the acrimonious relationship between the AJA and newspaper proprietors over salary and working conditions that some times led to strike action. Some newspaper owners also refused to be a part of the Walkley judging panels and held the view that they *already* rewarded journalists because 'they paid them' (Hurst 1988, 11). But, year after year, the Walkley Awards continued and, upon his death in 1976, Bill Walkley bequeathed $10,000 a year to the AJA in perpetuity for the awards, ensuring the prize continued to become more accepted as a part of the media culture. Before long, newspaper proprietors had come to accept the Walkleys as the premier journalism prize in Australia and were (and still are) 'happy to proclaim the achievements of the prize-winners on their pay-roll' (Hurst 1988, 10–11). It is also worth noting that, in the early years of the Walkleys, journalists often 'had to be goaded by the AJA or their editors into entering the competition' (13). As the trustee of the Walkley Awards, Ted Harris, told Hurst in 1988: 'Journalists ... can sometimes be notoriously laissez-faire. They're very industrious in their work but can be remarkably lethargic about looking after their own affairs (13). According to the Walkley Foundation website, the Awards now receive 'more than 1300 entries across 30 categories', including the Walkley Book Award, which recognizes 'excellence in longform'. The volume of entries and the number of categories suggests a rise in prestige of the Walkley Awards over the past 30 years and a cultural shift in the media towards the value of prizes (Walkley Foundation 2020a). Just as Willig noted in her study of the Cavling Prize that the Danish award had evolved from its introduction in 1945 to become 'highly institutionalized and a part of the professional vocabulary', so too the title 'Walkley winner' is a badge of prestige that needs no explanation within Australia's media.

A Recent History of the Walkley Foundation

One of the most significant changes since Hurst's coverage of the Walkley Awards is the vote by the MEAA in 2000 to form the Walkley Foundation for Journalism (Walkley Foundation 2020b). The Foundation is a registered, not-for-profit charity whose funding comes from government, media companies, corporate Australia, philanthropists and individual donors (Walkley Yearbook 2019, 26–27). The Walkley Foundation was initially run by three nationally elected officials of the Media section of the MEAA, the federal secretary of the MEAA and the chair of the Walkley Advisory Board. The Walkley directors appointed the Walkley Advisory Board, which was made up of 10 to 12 senior media industry members who judged the Walkley Awards (Walkley Foundation 2020c). In 2020, there were five Walkley directors, including three women: Marina Go, the chair of the Walkley Foundation; Lenore Taylor, editor of *Guardian Australia*; and Karen Percy, ABC reporter and co-vice president of the Media section of the MEAA. The two male directors were Marcus Strom, the president of MEAA Media, and ABC reporter Michael Janda (Walkley Foundation 2020c). The directors then appointed the Walkley Judging Board, which in 2020 was chaired by Taylor and included 14 media professionals—9 women and 5 men. The Walkley Foundation's daily operations are overseen by chief executive officer and company secretary Louisa Graham. In addition to the directors and the Judging Board, the Walkley Public Fund Committee, made up of two senior journalists and three industry professionals, oversees the allocation of funds to promote journalism excellence, such as media scholarships, mentorships, awards and public awareness campaigns (Walkley Foundation 2020d).

Another, earlier, watershed moment for the Walkley Awards was when entries were opened to non-union members in 1997. MEAA members had always been granted free entry, but from 1997 non-members could pay a $175 entry fee 'as a contribution to the cost of the awards program' (Burton 1997, 21). Despite expanding the competition, the organizers received criticism for the new non-member charge and, as a result, there was a perception of union bias towards award winners (Smith 2012). In 2019, the entry fee for non-members was reduced to $150, with MEAA members still being able to enter for free. Non-members entering the book section are charged $260 (Walkley Foundation 2020e).

In 1997 the judging system also changed, to one 'based on the two-tier Pulitzer Prizes system which aimed to create transparency and remove the potential for bias and professional conflicts of interest' (Dempster 2009). At the time of writing, the two-tiered system remained in place, which meant the Walkley Advisory Board selected the first-tier panel of three judges from the media industry for each of the award categories. The exceptions are the book and documentary categories, introduced in 2005, which can have up to nine judges, and the photography prize, which has five judges. The first-tier panel, which includes a mix of media professionals to reflect a balance across different organizations, states, expertise and gender, is then given at least two weeks to review the entries before meeting in person or via teleconference to select three finalists in no particular order. Judges are given appraisal forms to help them evaluate entries as well as guidelines 'encouraging them to consider factors such as resources, demands on time and geographic location' (Walkley Foundation 2020e). The judges' shortlist is then given to the second-tier Walkley judging board, a rotating panel of up to 15 senior Australian media professionals, who then make the final determinations. The judging board reviews all of the finalists' entries over four weeks and then meets for a day to decide upon the winners. All judges sign conflict of interest declarations and board members who have entered and become finalists do not participate in any board judging for that year (Walkley Foundation 2020f).

All winners receive a Walkley trophy, with the winner of the Gold Walkley also receiving business class flights from Qantas up to the value of $10,000. The Copyright Agency Cultural Fund provides $5000 prize money for both the Arts Journalism Prize and the Walkley-Pascall Prize for Arts Criticism. Although based upon the Pulitzer Prizes system, the Walkley Awards judging process in practice differs fundamentally from the US awards. In 2014, there was no Pulitzer Prize awarded for feature writing, despite the category having three feature finalists, as none of the entries won the required seven votes from the 17 judges to win. A feature winner was also not awarded in 2004 (Pulitzer Prize 2020). There has never been an instance of a Walkley feature category being without a winner. First-tier panels are not required to nominate a winner, but where there is a unanimous opinion a submission can be 'suggested' to the Walkley Board as a potential winner (Walkley Foundation 2020e). The judges' identities are not revealed until the finalists are announced. The Walkley Board then reviews each of the finalists' entry material—almost 100 entries over four weeks. Members of the board meet for about half a day to discuss the merits of each entry and review the comments of the first-tier judges.

The judges are instructed by guidelines set down by the Walkley Advisory Board, which state that the Walkley Awards recognize 'creative and courageous journalism that seek out the truth and give new insight to an issue' (Walkley Foundation 2020a). The website states that the awards recognise:

> excellence, independence, innovation and originality in storytelling and distinctive reporting. This can be through research and investigations, well-crafted and innovative presentations, news breaking single stories or engaging, entertaining and/or informative reporting. (Walkley Foundation 2020a)

General criteria include how the story was initiated and followed, newsworthiness, consideration of resources available, creativity and innovation, research and investigation, balance, accuracy and ethics, consideration of production pressures, best use of the format used, excellence in written or verbal communication, including technical skill and public impact and benefit, which includes audience engagement and serving specific communities (Walkley Foundation 2020a). The judges are also expected to consider the MEAA's code of ethics which includes, among other goals, a declaration that journalists have a responsibility to inform citizens and animate democracy (MEAA 2020). All journalists who enter the awards must sign an entry form that declares the reporter has produced original work that abides by the MEAA Code of Ethics (Walkley Foundation 2020d).

A BRIEF HISTORY OF AUSTRALIA'S MAGAZINE CULTURE AND THE WALKLEY AWARDS FOR FEATURE WRITING

Although roughly the same size in area as the continental United States, Australia has a population of less than 26 million compared to the US, which has just over 330 million people. Australians have always been avid magazine readers; before the internet, in the 1990s, one study found they bought more magazines per head than any other country in the world (World Population Review 2020; Bonner 2002, 188; Ricketson 2016, 72). The realities of Australia's small population mean, however, that it has never been economically viable to publish a magazine of the calibre of the *New Yorker*, which publishes four to six long feature articles each week, many of which have taken weeks, sometimes months, of research (Ricketson 2016, 72).

Despite the small size of the Australian publishing market, the Walkley Awards can proudly claim that they recognized the value of feature writing with its own dedicated prize more than two decades before the US Pulitzer founded its prize for feature writing in 1979 (Pulitzer Prize 2020). Historically the Pulitzer Prizes were awarded only for journalism that was published in newspapers. It wasn't until 2017, after 'two years of experimentation', that the Pulitzer Prize Board opened all of their journalism categories to magazines, saying, 'The broad expansion of digital journalism has led to a growing overlap in the work and roles of newspapers, digital-only news sites and magazines' (Pulitzer Prize 2016). But from the outset Bill Walkley listened to the Australian journalists' union, the AJA, that there should be two separate awards for feature writing, one for 'best feature in a newspaper' and another for 'best magazine story', as 'they served different audiences and often had to produce a different kind of material' (Hurst 1988, 263). Less impressive, however, was the disparity in the prize money, with the top award of £500 going to 'best news story' and only £200 awarded for the 'best feature in a newspaper' prize, with the 'best magazine story' faring worst of all with only £100 (Walkley Scrapbook 1956). Hurst explained that one reason for the 'odd' disparity was that the news reporting entry 'was more likely to be a scoop' than a feature writing piece (Hurst 1988, 79). It wasn't until 1978 that the competition organizers, acting once again on advice from the AJA, voted to change the prize pool so that both the news and feature writing sections received $750. It was also decided to introduce a new $1000 prize, the Gold Walkley, for the best overall story in print, radio or television (Hurst 1988, 13). As we will recall, 1979 was also the year that the US Pulitzer Prize introduced their own feature writing prize, indicating that there was a growing recognition in both countries of the value of the more expressive long-form.

Evidence that American journalists provided at least some inspiration for their Australian counterparts is found in Hurst's account of Evan Whitton's 1967 Walkley Award for Best Feature Story for his undercover, immersive series on 'Life on the Pension' (Whitton 1967; Hurst 1988, 117–120). Hurst recounts that Whitton, while 'living poor' during the research stage of his series, would often read in the State Library Victoria. One day 'he came across some correspondence between the two American writers, Tom Wolfe and Frank Kermode, on the techniques of New

Journalism' (Hurst 1988, 117). He said that Whitton remembered the advice that his boss, Sol Chandler, had told him that mirrored the New Journalism approach: 'My dear boy, I want every detail—not just the significant details, all of them', which Whitton delivered, with sections of his story in the form of diary entries (Hurst 1988, 118).

Another impetus for Australian newspapers and magazines to print longer, more in-depth articles about current affairs in the late 1970s in Australia was to meet the challenge posed by radio and television. In the face of hourly news bulletins and current affairs and documentaries, newspapers had to do more than just recycle old news for their readers. Instead, the publications had to provide 'more of the why and how things happened' and it was the feature writers who had the necessary skills 'to seduce bug-eyed televiewers away from the box to read again' (Hurst 1988, 149). What emerged during this period, no doubt influenced by the rise of New Journalism and the impact of the new technologies, is a further blurring of the boundaries between what was considered a news story and what was considered a feature. As Hurst noted, 'it appears that at times there was some confusion in the minds of entrants and/or the judges about whether entries belonged to the news or feature section' (Hurst 1988, 149). What was beyond doubt, however, was that feature stories were as well researched and written as the news reports. In 1978, the competition organizers decided to combine the 'best magazine feature' and 'best feature in a newspaper' into a single 'best feature' category. The prize money for the best news story was also dropped from $1000 to $750, and the feature prize boosted from $400 to $750, providing clear evidence the Walkley organization recognized the journalistic value of the feature article (Hurst 1988, 79).

The boundaries between news and magazine features continued to shift during the 1980s, with some newspapers including glossy magazine inserts to entice readers away from the competition. While magazines were considered the 'showbiz' side of the print media, Hurst noted that 'amid the froth and bubble, one finds many well-written profiles of people in the news and in the more serious magazines many in-depth articles, spiced with sharp commentary, on important social and political issues' (1988, 263). The last Walkley Award for 'Best Magazine Story' was awarded in 1977 to Paula Goodyer of the women's magazine *Cleo* for an article about the sex lives of the elderly. In 1978, the competition organizers merged the 'Best Feature in a Newspaper' and 'Best Magazine Story' sections into a single prize: 'Best Feature—Either in a Newspaper or Magazine'. Hurst was critical of the change, labelling it 'a concession to those who believe that feature writing for magazines or for newspapers demands the same set of skills' (1988, 296). Concession or not, the single category remained in place, simply being renamed 'Best Feature Writing' in 1988, a title that lasted until 1998 when the prize was split once more into 'Best Feature in a Magazine' and 'Best Feature in a Newspaper' (Burton 1997). In 2013 the 'Feature Writing Long' for articles over 4000 words and 'Feature Writing Short' for articles under 4000 words were introduced and, at the time of writing this book, remained in place.

A factor in the Walkleys renaming the award to 'Best Feature Writing' in 1988 may have been a growing trend in the 1980s, as Ricketson noted in his 2004 book, *The Best Australian Profiles*, for local magazines to import the work of overseas journalists such as Lynn Barber and Barbara Amiel, who were renowned for the 'killer interview', which effectively raised the status of the profile writer and the magazine-style feature article (Ricketson 2004, 17). Ricketson observed that this trend towards importing feature writers not only resulted in less space for Australian writers but also brought out the competitive nature of journalists and meant that journalists 'got the message loud and clear that they could be as big a name as the people they wrote about'. Revisiting his topic of the long-form profile in Australia in 2016, Ricketson noted that, since 2004, it had become obvious that the job losses in newsrooms, which included among their number many experienced journalists, and the subsequent 'ratcheting-up' of the number of stories those remaining were expected to file, had led to a lot less time, money and necessary experience to write quality long-form. What the public was left with was 'a great deal more media heat but precious little light' (Ricketson 2016, 70). Jane Cadzow, who began in 1989 as a feature writer with the *Sydney Morning Herald* and the *Age* newspaper's *Good Weekend* magazine, published each Saturday, told Ricketson in an interview that both the word length and turnaround time for feature articles had contracted since the 1990s. Cadzow claimed that articles that once would have run up to 5000 words were, in 2014, 'all fewer than 4,000 words and some ran at 2,000 words'. Where Cadzow used to have a month or even five weeks to write a piece, she said the deadline was now down to three weeks (Ricketson 2016, 73).

While the opportunities to write longer, deeply researched feature articles had contracted for staff journalists like Cadzow, freelance journalist Margaret Simons found it wasn't until early in the twenty-first century that the landscape for the publishing of long-form non-fiction in Australia shifted, bridging the gap between the short feature and non-fiction book. Dr Simons, who in 1995 had written a series of essays inspired by her reading of Joan Didion and Janet Malcolm, was going to publish them in a book, as there was no other forum for long-form. As she said to me in an interview on 4 March 2015,

> These writers [Didion and Malcolm] re-introduced me to the notion that it is possible to do journalism in a different way. I remember distinctly thinking there is nowhere I can publish these because at the time the only place you could get more than a couple of thousand words was one of the weekend colour mags—the *Good Weekend*, the *Australian*—to ask them for more than two thousand words was a big ask.

But this changed in 2001 when the *Quarterly Essay,* an imprint of Black Inc. Books, founded by entrepreneur Morry Schwartz a year earlier, was launched. Each issue of the *Quarterly Essay* features a 25,000-word article by a prominent journalist or author on a single topic of public interest. This was followed by the *Griffith Review* in 2003, another quarterly publication which featured essays, reportage, fiction and poetry in each themed issue. *New Matilda* magazine began in 2004 accepting longer features, and the *Monthly,* another Black Inc. publication, opened in 2005. The *Monthly* usually published features of between 2000 and 4000 words, but also ran stories around 10,000 words on the topic of 'Australian politics, society and culture' (Ricketson 2016, 73). Amidst the success stories, there were also magazine closures, including the *Bulletin* in 2008, the *Independent Monthly* and the *Eye* (Forde 2000, 2; Ricketson 2016, 73).

Among the surviving magazines, Schwartz's *Quarterly Essay* and the *Monthly* have pegged out a particularly powerful position in the national consciousness, as evidenced by the number of Walkley Awards garnered by the Black Inc. publishing house. In 2006, Chloe Hooper's essay-style feature article of 10,062 words, published in the *Monthly,* won that year's Magazine Feature award; Annabel Crabb's 100-page *Quarterly Essay* article on Malcolm Turnbull won the 2009 award; and David Marr's article on Kevin Rudd in the *Quarterly Essay* won the following year (Hooper 2006; Crabb 2009; Marr 2010). When the categories changed in 2013, Indigenous writer Melissa Lucashenko won the long feature article section award for her *Griffith Review* article on poverty among Australia's working poor, followed by Paul Toohey's exhaustively researched 2014 article on Australia's refugee policy in the *Quarterly Essay* (Lucashenko 2013; Toohey 2014).

Ricketson argues that new publications dedicated to long-form journalism, combined with the content shift of many newspapers and magazines online, created new opportunities for writers of long-form journalism to reach a global audience (Ricketson 2016, 71). For Simons, *Guardian Australia*, launched in 2013, provided her with a bigger audience when a story she wrote on the plight of the children of sex tourists left behind in the Philippines was republished internationally in the *Guardian Weekend* magazine (Simons 2019). Her story went on to win the 2019 Foreign Press Media Association Award for travel and tourism story of the year (FPMA 2019). Speaking in a follow-up interview with me on 18 March 2020, Simons said that having her story published on the *Guardian*'s international site meant her article 'gained a big audience and … won an award. So, it opens Australian long-form to an international audience which, for me at least, has been quite significant'. In addition to the opportunity for long-form to be published on platforms with international reach such as the *Guardian*, online-only sites such as *Salon* and *Slate* started up in 1995 and 1996 respectively, and in 2009 the site *Longreads* began, followed by *Longform* in 2010, which aggregated long-form articles for readers (Giles 2014, 8–11). Conversely, as noted by Fiona Giles, the aggregating sites revealed a market for individual articles to be published and purchased online, such as Amazon's *Kindle Singles*, which was launched in 2012 (Giles 2014, 8–11.)

Speaking with me in March 2020, Simons said that she thought that book publishing in Australia continued to go 'from strength to strength', with 'more and more journalists writing about an issue for conventional journalism then stretching their wings into long-form through the book'. The Walkley Foundation introduced its Book Award in 2005 and in 2020, the Longform Journalism Award has a book and a documentary section. The book award:

> celebrates the value and importance of long-form journalism, acknowledging the proud line-up of Australian writers who have taken subjects of enduring topicality and consequence from news bulletins, eye-witness reporting, investigations and historical records and provided readers with expanded factual detail, revelation and greater clarity of analysis in book form. (Walkley Foundation 2020g)

For Simons, another important development in long-form has been the rise of the podcast, with the breakthrough National Public Radio podcast,

Serial, hitting the public consciousness in 2014. The podcast, which was co-created and co-produced by Sarah Koenig (who also hosted the series) and Julie Snyder, and developed by the long-running NPR *This American Life* team, tells one story over the course of a season (Koenig and Snyder 2014). Simons said she remembered how everybody was talking about how 'new and special' the podcast form was, but how she was herself not seduced by the argument that the form was somehow a more 'intimate' medium: 'It's not fairy dust; just because you put something on a podcast doesn't mean it is great journalism; but the best of it is a new frontier for long-form journalism, I think'. A significant shift for Simons was the way in which the journalist would 'take you into their process' and 'that process then becomes a part of the story'. As she said to me in a phone interview on 18 March 2020,

> I think the on-demand nature of it [podcasting] brings it closer to the printed form than traditional broadcasting. And yes, I now think it has become a bit clichéd and a bit fetishized, that: 'I am a real person, I am a real journalist, doing journalism here and look at me doing it'.

An unexpected but welcome additional avenue for Simons's long-form journalism has been the *Quarterly Essay's* policy to have each author record an audio book of their essay. At the time of our interview Simons had just completed recording her *Quarterly Essay* long-form feature, 'Cry Me a River', about the plight of Australia's Murray–Darling Basin river system, extending the reach of her writing once more (Simons 2020).

The Walkley Project

My research was motivated by the question: 'How do journalists make us—the readers—feel emotion through the textual construction of their stories?' I began by reviewing the Walkley feature articles published from 1956, which I sourced from the organization's official archive, held in the State Library of New South Wales and cross-referenced with Hurst's helpful list (1988). While I had hoped to include all of the winning feature articles from 1956, it quickly became apparent that I would need to narrow my corpus if I were to do justice to the close reading and analysis I wanted to devote to each article. As we will recall, from 1956 to 1977 there were two sections dedicated to feature writing: 'Best Story Published in an Australian Magazine' and 'Best Newspaper Feature Story', resulting in more than 40 stories. In 1978, the competition organizers decided to combine the awards into the single category of 'Best Feature either in a Newspaper or Magazine'. This prize section lasted until 1988 when the title was changed to 'Best Feature Writing', adding another ten stories. My selection of the 1988 starting date is an acknowledgement of two key factors. First, the competition organizers' decision in 1988 to re-name the news and magazine feature categories was a culmination and consolidation of their decade-long belief that well-written, forensically researched features on important matters could be found across both magazines and newspapers. Secondly, John Hurst's excellent book on the history of the Walkley Awards ended in 1988, so it seemed a logical decision to continue my research from this point.

THE WALKLEY PILOT PROJECT

Having established 1988 as the starting point of my Walkley Project, I began by reading the nine winning stories up until 1997. It was during this stage that I experienced at first hand what we will recall Hurst referred to as a gradual blurring of boundaries that had occurred between news and feature writing over the years. For example, between 1991 and 1996 I judged only one Walkley-winning feature, Helen Garner's 1993 story, 'Did Daniel Have to Die?', about the murder of a toddler, to have the hallmarks of a magazine-style feature. The other five stories included Ellingsen's 1991 series of articles on human rights violations in China, Button's 1992 feature 'Brand New Day' on Australia's search for an international identity, Neill's 1994 article about family violence in Aboriginal communities, Robson's 1995 feature on well-known Sydney lawyer John Marsden, and Hartcher's 1996 article 'How the Enemy Became an Ally' about Australia's relationship with Indonesia. Based upon my own 25-year experience as a journalist, I judged that these stories (with perhaps the exception of Robson's feature on Marsden) were, on the whole, more indicative of newspaper features, relying to a greater degree on the communication of facts than on the extensive use of narrative tools that are the hallmark of narrative journalism.

In 1997, the Walkleys underwent a major review and the award was yet again split into two sections. This time there was, once more, a prize for 'Newspaper Feature Writing' and another for 'Magazine Feature Writing'. I read all of the articles in both of these sections and then made the reluctant decision to restrict the analysis to the Walkley magazine-style features.

One of the main reasons for my decision was the practicalities of just how much close textual analysis I could encompass in my project. The second reason was because, as was the case with the stories from the decade earlier, I judged that most of the Walkley winning magazine features had a stronger emphasis overall on narrative techniques such as scene setting, characterization and the communication of the emotions of those written about than the articles in the news feature section.

The continued push of journalists to blur the line between magazine and news features challenged me as a researcher, forcing me to clarify with each article what it was that I considered 'literary journalism'. My decisions were, in some cases, a harsh compromise between including a worthy news feature and the lack of space. Within the winning newspaper features section, for example, there were some powerful examples of long-form journalism that I excluded from my study. These included two first-person accounts, Jack Marx's 2006 confession about his seduction by fame in his article, 'I Was Russell Crowe's Stooge' and Jill Baker's 2010 account of her battle with breast cancer following the sudden death of her husband. Patrick Carlyon's 2009 article, 'Where the Hell is Everyone?', on Victoria's Black Saturday bushfires of that year, won in the news feature category, but would certainly not have been out of place in the magazine feature section in terms of its narrative style. Overall, however, the news feature winners, while certainly including examples of strong, clear writing, nonetheless had a stronger emphasis on the 'breaking story', and, as a result, tended to focus upon the straightforward presentation of facts with an emphasis on 'objectivity' rather than the illumination of complex issues that was found in the magazine feature category (Kovach and Rosenstiel 2014, 98–106; Maras 2013, 1). These included a news feature about a tragic fire at a backpacker hotel that claimed the lives of 15 people (Harvey 2000), a crisis facing Australia's Family Court (Thomas 2002), an article on the legalization of euthanasia (Button 2007) and an exposé of an Australian-based international gambling syndicate, the 'punter's club' (Low 2012). In the interests of consistency, therefore, rather than include only one or two articles from the newspaper category, I decided to focus solely on the magazine feature winners.

I continued to follow this imperfect yet necessary delineation between news and magazine feature articles when the Walkley Foundation, in 2012, once again changed the feature category, this time to 'Feature Writing Short (under 4,000 words)' and 'Feature Writing Long (over 4,000 words)'. The change was in response to the fair criticism that the single category created an uneven playing field as judges were 'comparing apples with oranges' in judging a 25,000-word *Quarterly Essay* article, which took months to research and write, together with a magazine-style feature of 4000 words (Oakes 2013, 7). It is interesting to note that the number of entries in the newspaper feature section dropped from 69 in 2005 to 41 in 2012, and from 2008 onwards, the category did not exceed 50 entries (Oakes 2013, 8). In the 2013 Walkley Review, Laurie Oakes points out that print news entries reached their lowest level in that year—from a high of 76 in 2004 to just 31 in 2012. Oakes speculated that this could be partly due to the shrinking traditional media and also because journalists were publishing news first online and then following up with print versions (8). In contrast, the number of magazine feature entries grew steadily from a low of 27 in 2003 to 56 in 2012 (8). In 2016 a spokesperson for the Walkley Foundation confirmed they had received 38 entries in the Feature Writing Long (over 4000 words) category and 68 in the Feature Writing Short (under 4000 words) category. In 2019, this had grown to 49 entries in the Feature Writing Long section and 107 in the Feature Writing Short section, suggesting that the decision to split the feature categories achieved the Walkley Foundation's aim of encouraging journalists to submit news features without the disincentive of being judged against a 25,000-word essay (Helen Johnstone, personal communication 2020).

Emerging Themes and Virtues

Following my preliminary reading of the Walkley articles from 1988 to 2014, I determined two separate but interrelated approaches. First, I identified the different topics of each magazine feature until I had devised broad thematic categories. Initially these were divided into stories about: the murder of children, the protection of children, Indigenous Australians, the Australian citizen and the Australian nation. I have since modified these themes to children; the disadvantaged or socially marginalized; the citizen; and the nation. I will discuss the reasoning behind my thematic categories at the close of this chapter. Having established the initial broad category themes for the Australian Walkley articles, I then conducted a close textual analysis of the first five award-winning feature articles in my corpus. I began with the 1988 Walkley for best feature, which was won by Michael Gawenda for his article 'Echoes of a Darker Age: Australia's Nazi War Crime Trials', in *Time Australia* (Gawenda 1988).

Gawenda's feature investigated the possibility of establishing a war crimes tribunal in Australia, an issue that exposes the difficulties facing a relatively young nation state struggling to define its identity as one offering opportunity and hope for a good life for all of its citizens. Janet Hawley, who had a 35-year career as a popular profile writer for the *Sydney Morning Herald*'s *Good Weekend* magazine, won the Walkley feature award in 1989 and 1990. Hawley's 1989 award was for her 1988 profile of the dying, 94-year-old 'grand old man of Australian art', Lloyd Rees (Hawley 1988). In 1990, Hawley won the feature award as well as the Gold Walkley for a remarkable double profile article about the artists William Dobell and Joshua Smith (Hawley 1990). Her story revisited the 1943 Archibald Prize for Portraiture, which became one of the biggest controversies to ever rock the Australian art world when Dobell's portrait of fellow artist, Smith, was denounced by some as a 'caricature'. For the reasons outlined earlier in this chapter, I omitted the 1991 and 1992 winners, as these articles had more characteristics of news features. The 1993 Walkley Award was won by the much-loved Australian writer Helen Garner for her article 'Did Daniel Have to Die?' about the brutal death of a toddler at the hands of his mother's de facto spouse, despite the child suffering ongoing injuries that were treated by medical staff in the lead-up to his death (Garner 1993). The fifth article in my corpus was the 1997 Walkley Award for Best Feature Writing, which was won by Gary Tippet for his article, 'Slaying the Monster', about Indigenous man Tony Lock, who was imprisoned for killing his childhood abuser with an axe (Tippet 1997).

It was during this process that I began to identify particular virtues that the journalists were constructing and communicating to readers through the use of narrative and reporting devices. To summarize briefly, in my initial close textual analysis I found the virtues of *empathy*, *honesty* and *responsibility* were evident in all five features, with four out of the five (the exception at the time of the first study being Garner's 1993 article) also displaying the virtues of *courage* and *resilience*. As the discussion of individual articles will show in Part II of this book, I have subsequently revised my assessment of Garner's feature to encompass what I now consider the tragic, innocent courage and resilience of the dead toddler, Daniel Valerio. In Gawenda's, Garner's and Tippet's features, I further identified an effort on the part of the journalist to communicate to readers a need for community action on the issue. Having performed the close textual analysis on the first five stories, I was able to continue the process with the remaining 18 stories.

It was from this study that I established six virtues to be included in my new analytical framework tool, the Virtue Map: *responsibility, honesty,* full *empathy, courage, resilience.* For the sixth virtue, I turned to Aristotle's master virtue of *phronesis,* which I explained in Chap. 3, is commonly defined as practical wisdom, as a starting point to encapsulate the journalist's call for community action that I had identified. As will be elaborated on in the next chapter, I have reconceptualized Aristotle's virtue of phronesis to fulfil the role of 'master virtue' in my Virtue Map, a powerful tool for identifying when, where and how award-winning long-form journalists utilized their considerable reporting and writing skills to textually communicate emotions to readers. In addition to identifying the six virtues from my Walkley study I also found that each of the 23 stories could be categorized under the story themes of 'children', 'Aboriginal Australians', 'citizens' and 'the nation', with nine articles including at least three of the themes. The 'nation' theme applied to 20 stories, the 'citizen' theme to 16, the 'children' theme to 12, and six stories specifically concerned Australia's Aboriginal population. I had originally considered a 'social justice' theme but I decided the term, although relevant, was too broad within the context of a national study to recognize the unique historical and ongoing discrimination experienced by Indigenous Australians. As I discussed in Chap. 1, the most recent publicly available data shows that 31 per cent of Indigenous people are living in poverty, compared to 13 per cent of the whole population (Markham & Biddle 2018; ACOSS 2020). Lisa Waller and Kerry McCallum, have found, based upon their research into more than 30 years of Australian media coverage on Indigenous issues, that Indigenous people are regularly portrayed as victims of discrimination, and that this portrayal is a source of shame for the nation (Waller and McCallum forthcoming 2021). Waller and McCallum argue that what they refer to as a Social Justice narrative embodies the belief that it is 'a matter of social justice for governments to help those most unfortunate in the society and it was the whole community's responsibility to solve the problems Indigenous people experienced'. I employ the Social Justice narrative to internationalize the Virtue Map for a broader audience by replacing the 'Aboriginal Australian' category with the theme of 'marginalized or disadvantaged people'. Expanding the category consolidated the sense that, as global citizens, we all bear a collective responsibility for the care of all members of society.

Table 5.1 The Virtue Map: a study of Walkley Award-winning features 1988–2014

Year	Walkley Award-winning feature	Original publication	Date or issue	Page numbers	Categories/Chapter titles						Virtues					
					Murder of children	Protection of children	Indigenous Australians	The Australian citizen: dishonesty	The Australian citizen: amorality	The Australian nation	Phronesis	Responsibility	Honesty	Full empathy	Courage	Resilience
1988	Michael Gawenda 'Echoes of a Darker Age: Australias Nazi War Crime Trials'	*Time Australia*	23 May 1988	12–19		●		●	●	●	●	●	●	●	●	●
1989	Janet Hawley 'Lloyd Rees: The Final Interview'	*Sydney Morning Herald, Good Weekend*	15 Oct 1988	39–48					●			●		●		●
1990	Janet Hawley A Portrait in Pain'	*Sydney Morning Herald, Good Weekend*	18 August 1990	18–29					●			●		●	●	●
1993	Helen Garner 'Did Daniel Have to Die?'	*Time (Australia)*	8 March 1993	22–27	●	●		●	●	●		●		●	●	
1997	Gary Tippet 'Slaying the Monster'	*Sunday Age, Agenda*	22 June 1997	1–2		●	●	●	●			●		●		●
1997	Bonita Mason 'The Girl in Cell 4'	*HQ*	Mar/Apr 1997	56–61			●	●	●			●	●	●		●
1998	Garry Linnell 'Hope Lives Here'	*Sunday Age, Sunday Life!*	5 Oct 1997	8–16		●			●			●	●	●	●	●

Year	Author / Title	Publication	Date	Pages
1999	David Leser 'Who's Afraid of Alan Jones?'	*Age, Good Weekend*	14 Nov 1998	26–37
2000	Richard Guilliatt 'The Lost Children versus the Commonwealth'	*Sydney Morning Herald, Good Weekend*	20 Nov 1999	18–23
2001	Greg Bearup 'Death Surrounds Her'	*Sydney Morning Herald, Good Weekend*	19 May 2001	26–31
2002	Paul Toohey 'Highly Inflammable'	*Australian, Weekend Australian Magazine*	24 Nov 2001	24–28
2003	Kate Legge 'Patrick: A case in the life of a family court judge'	*Australian, Weekend Australian Magazine*	7 Dec 2002	34–37
2004	Jane Cadzow 'The Right Thing'	*Age, Good Weekend*	14 Aug 2004	32–36
2005	Mark Whittaker 'Ordinary Heroes'	*Australian, Weekend Australian Magazine*	18 Jun 2005	26–31
2006	Chloe Hooper 'The Tall Man'	*Monthly*	Mar 2006	34–53
2007	Malcolm Knox 'Cruising'	*Monthly*	Sep 2006	26–36

(*continued*)

Table 5.1 (continued)

Year	Walkley Award-winning feature	Original publication	Date or issue	Page numbers	Categories/Chapter titles						Virtues					
					Murder of children	Protection of children	Indigenous Australians	The Australian citizen: dishonesty	The Australian citizen: amorality	The Australian nation	Phronesis	Responsibility	Honesty	Full empathy	Courage	Resilience
2008	Billy Rule 'Crusade for Kaitlin'	*Sunday Times, STM Magazine*	2 Mar 2008	14–18	●				●	●	●	●	●	●	●	●
2009	Annabel Crabb 'Stop at Nothing: The Life and Adventures of Malcolm Turnbull'	*Quarterly Essay*	Issue 34	1–100						●		●	●			●
2010	David Marr 'Power Trip: The Political Journey of Kevin Rudd'	*Quarterly Essay*	Issue 38	1–91					●	●		●	●			●
2011	Mike Colman 'Tree of Life'	*Courier Mail, QWeekend*	23 Apr 2011	10–14						●		●		●	●	●
2012	Jane Cadzow 'The World According to Bryce'	*Sydney Morning Herald, Good Weekend*	17 Mar 2012	14–19	●				●			●	●			
2013	Melissa Lucashenko 'Sinking below Sight: Down and out in Brisbane and Logan'	*Griffith Review*	Edition 41	53–67			●			●	●	●	●	●	●	●
2014	Paul Toohey 'That Sinking Feeling'	*Quarterly Essay*	Issue 53	1–94						●	●	●	●	●	●	●
				Total	2	10	6	4	12	20	14	23	23	19	15	20

Conclusion

In this chapter, I have explained how the Virtue Map emerged as a result of my earlier study into the role of emotion in a selection of magazine features from Australia's premier journalism prize, the Walkley Awards. I began with a brief history of the Walkley Awards and an overview of the development of journalism from the time of European colonization. After a description of how the landscape of feature writing in Australia has changed since the Walkleys began, I then proceeded to outline my pilot study and to explain how I selected the stories included in my final project. Finally, I concluded the chapter with an explanation for how I decided upon my thematic categories for the Virtue Map, including my rationale to change these themes to better prepare the model for use internationally. This chapter closes with a table that shows how the Virtue Map was operationalized in my original Walkley study (see Table 5.1). The Virtue Map lists, along the vertical axis, the four thematic categories of children, marginalized or disadvantaged people, citizens and the nation. Alongside the themes are listed the virtues of *courage, empathy, honesty, resilience, responsibility*, and the master virtue of *phronesis*.

References

[ACNJ] Australian Colonial Narrative Journalism. 2020a. About. *AustLit*. Brisbane: University of Queensland. https://www.austlit.edu.au/austlit/page/12870667. Accessed 18 May 2020.

———. 2020b. Carrington, Francis Thomas Dean. *AustLit*. Brisbane: University of Queensland. https://www.auslitjourn.info/writers/a-e/carrington-francis-thomas-dean/. Accessed 19 May 2020.

[ACOSS] Australian Council of Social Services and the University of New South Wales. 2020. *Poverty in Australia 2020*. Sydney: ACOSS and UNSW http://povertyandinequality.acoss.org.au/wp-content/uploads/2020/02/Poverty-in-Australia-2020_Part-1_Overview.pdf. Accessed 21 May 2020.

[MEAA] Media, Entertainment & Arts Alliance. 2020. *MEAA Journalist Code of Ethics.* https://www.meaa.org/meaa-media/code-of-ethics/. Accessed 20 May 2020.

Baker, J. 2010. The Big C and Me. *Herald Sun, Weekend Magazine*, October 23, 4–10.

Benson, R.D., and E. Neveu. 2005. *Bourdieu and the Journalistic Field*. Cambridge: Polity.

Bly, N. (1887) 2018. 'Ten Days in a Madhouse'. *New York World*, New York. Reprint 2018. *Nellie Bly: Ten Days in a Madhouse*. Rockland, Maryland: Wildside Press.

Bonner, F. 2002. Magazines. In *Media and Communications in Australia*, ed. S. Cunningham and G. Turner, 3rd ed., 188–199. Sydney: Allen & Unwin.

Burton, T. 1997. Walkley Review. *Walkley Magazine* (Special Edition), 18–27.

Button, J. 1992. Brand New Day. *Time Australia*. April 6, no. 14, 12 –18.

———. 2007. *A Death in Zurich: Dealing in the Desire for Death*. Sydney Morning Herald, February 3. https://www.smh.com.au/national/dealing-in-the-desire-for-death-20130524-2k5b2.html. Accessed 21 May 2020.

Carlyon, P. 2009. Where the Hell is Everyone? *Herald Sun*, February 14. http://www.news.com.au/news/where-the-hell-is-everyone/story-fna7dq6e-1111118849619. Accessed 21 May 2020.

Crabb, A. 2009. Stop at Nothing: The Life and Adventures of Malcolm Turnbull. *Quarterly Essay, no.* 34: 1–100.

Davies, K., and W. McDonald. 2020. Hidden Women of History: Catherine Hay Thomson, the Australian Undercover Journalist Who Went inside Asylums and Hospitals. *The Conversation*, January 17.

Dempster, Q. 2009. The Walkleys Are Changing. *Walkley Magazine* 57: 25.

Ellingsen, P. 1991. 'Rock around the Wok', February 23, 46; 'Chinese Torture Scars the Truth', February 26, 11; 'A Vain Search for Human Rights', April 1, 11; 'Portrait of Human Bondage', June 5, 11. Human Rights in China series. *Sydney Morning Herald*.

Forde, S. 2000. Closing the Eye: Looking Overseas for Australian Newspaper Policy Options. *Asia Pacific Media Educator*, no. 9, 192–201. http://ro.uow.edu.au/apme/vol1/iss9/15. Accessed 20 May 2020.

[FPMA] Foreign Press Media Awards. 2019. 2019 FPA Awards Winners and Shortlists for Each Category. https://www.fpalondonawards.org/#shortlist. Accessed 1 June 2020.

Garner, H. 1993. Did Daniel Have to Die? *Time Australia Magazine* 10: 22–27.

Gawenda, M. 1988. Echoes of a Darker Age. *Time Australia Magazine*, May 23, 12–19.

Giles, F. 2014. The Magazine That Isn't: The Future of Features Online, *Text* Special Issue 25. http://www.textjournal.com.au/speciss/issue25/Giles.pdf. Accessed 21 May 2020.

Hartcher, P. 1996. How the Enemy Became an Ally. *Australian Financial Review*, July 4, 18–19.

Harvey, A. 2000. Heartbreak Hotel: Eight Days in Childers. *Daily Telegraph*, *Weekend Extra*, July 1, 42–43.

Hawley, J. 1988. Lloyd Rees: The Final Interview. *Sydney Morning Herald, Good Weekend Magazine*, October 15, 39–48. http://www.smh.com.au/good-weekend/gw-classics/lloyd-rees-the-final-interview-20140917-10bd9n.html. Accessed 23 June 2020.

5 THE VIRTUE MAP: THE WALKLEY PROJECT   105

———. 1990. A Portrait in Pain. *Sydney Morning Herald, Good Weekend Magazine*, August 18, 18–29. http://www.smh.com.au/good-weekend/gw-classics/a-portrait-in-pain-20140903-10c76n.html. Accessed 23 June 2020.

Hooper, C. 2006. The Tall Man. *Monthly* 10 (March): 34–53.

Hurst, J. 1988. *The Walkley Awards: Australia's Best Journalists in Action*. Melbourne: John Kerr.

Koenig, S., and J. Snyder. 2014–2020. Season 1, Episode 1: The Alibi. *Serial* podcast. Serial Productions, produced by NPR Radio and WBEZ Chicago, podcast, MP3 audio, 53:26, October 21. https://serialpodcast.org/about. Accessed 21 May 2020.

Kovach, B., and T. Rosenstiel. 2014. *The Elements of Journalism: What Newspeople Should Know and the Public Should Expect*. 3rd ed. New York: Three Rivers Press.

Landy, S. 2013. Your Herald Sun Team Wins Walkley Awards. *Herald Sun*. http://www.heraldsun.com.au/news/your-herald-sun-team-wins-walkley-awards/story-fni0fiyv-1226770896454.

Low, H. 2012. Punters Club Made Millions "Disappear". *Australian Financial Review*, September 1. https://www.examiner.com.au/story/293656/punters-club-made-millions-disappear/. Accessed 21 May 2020.

Lucashenko, M. 2013. Sinking Below Sight: Down and Out in Brisbane and Logan. *Griffith Review*, no. 41: 53–67.

Maras, S. 2013. *Objectivity in Journalism*. Cambridge: Polity Press.

Markham, F., and N. Biddle. 2018. *Income, Poverty and Inequality*. CAEPR 2016 Census Paper No. 2. Canberra: Centre for Aboriginal Economic Policy Research. https://caepr.cass.anu.edu.au/research/publications/income-poverty-and-inequality. Accessed 23 June 2020.

Marr, D. 2010. Power Trip: The Political Journey of Kevin Rudd. *Quarterly Essay* 38 (June): 1–91. Melbourne: Black Inc.

Marx, J. 2006. I Was Russell Crowe's Stooge. *Sydney Morning Herald*, June 7. http://www.smh.com.au/news/national/when-i-was-russell-crowes-stooge/2006/06/06/1149359738242.html. Accessed 21 May 2020.

McDonald, W., and B. Avieson. 2019. Having Your Story and Data Too: The Australian Colonial Narrative Journalism Database. *Literary Journalism Studies* 11 (2): 33–55.

McDonald, W., and K. Davies. 2015. Creating History: Literary Journalism and Ned Kelly's Last Stand. *Australian Journalism Review* 37 (2): 33–49.

Neill, R. 1994. 'Our Shame'. Review section. *Weekend Australian Magazine* 18 (June): 1–2.

Oakes, L. 2013. *The Report of the 2013 Review of the Walkley Awards for Excellence in Journalism*. Walkley Foundation. http://walkleys.com/wp-content/uploads/2014/05/230516-Walkley-Review-Report-final.pdf.

106   J. MARTIN

Pulitzer Prize. 2016. Pulitzer Prizes Open All Journalism Categories to Magazines. Press release. Pulitzer Prize, October 19. https://www.pulitzer.org/news/pulitzer-prizes-open-all-journalism-categories-magazines. Accessed 20 May 2020.

———. 2020. Feature Writing. https://www.pulitzer.org/prize-winners-by-category/211%20Accessed%2020%20May%202020. Accessed 20 May 2020.

Ricketson, M. 2004. *The Best Australian Profiles*. Melbourne: Black Inc. Books.

———. 2016. The Return of the Long-Form Profile: A Case Study of the Quarterly Essay and the Monthly in Australia. In *Profile Pieces: Journalism and the New 'Human Interest' Bias*, ed. S. Joseph and R.L. Keeble. London: Routledge.

Robson, F. 1995. Standing Accused. *Sydney Morning Herald*, March 15, 13.

Simons, M. 2019. Do You Ever Think about Me? The Children Sex Tourists Leave Behind. *Guardian*, March 20. Accessed 21 May 2020.

———. 2020. Cry Me a River: The Tragedy of the Murray–Darling Basin. *Quarterly Essay* 77 (March): 1–114. https://www.quarterlyessay.com.au/essay/2020/03/cry-me-a-river. Accessed 24 June 2020.

Smith, M. 2012. Did You Know the Walkleys Are Run by a Labor Union? *Michael Smith News.com*. http://www.michaelsmithnews.com/2012/12/did-you-know-the-walkley-awards-are-run-by-a-labor-union.html. Accessed 13 July 2016.

Sommer, E. 1956. Outcast!, *Sun Herald*, July 2, 1.

Thomas, H. 2002. Court in Crisis. *Courier Mail*, September 21, 29.

Tippet, G. 1997. 'Slaying the Monster'. *Sunday Age: Agenda*, June 22, 1–2.

Toohey, P. 2014. That Sinking Feeling. *Quarterly Essay* 53: 1–94.

Walkley Digital Archive. 2019. Women and the Walkleys. http://omeka-s.deakin.edu.au/s/walkleyarchive/page/walkleyswomen. Accessed 19 May 2020.

Walkley Foundation. 2020a. The Walkley Awards for Excellence in Journalism: Encouraging Excellence. https://www.walkleys.com/encouraging-excellence/.

———. 2020b. Walkley Foundation Limited Governance Policy. https://www.walkleys.com/about/governance/.

———. 2020c. The Walkley Directors. https://www.walkleys.com/about/directors/.

———. 2020d. Walkley Public Fund: What Price Would You Pay? https://www.walkleys.com/what-price/. Accessed 20 May 2020.

———. 2020e. Terms and Conditions. https://www.walkleys.com/awards/walkleys/terms-conditions/. Accessed 9 April 2020.

———. 2020f. The Walkley Judging Process. www.walkleys.com/awards/walkleys/the-walkley-judging. Accessed 20 May 2020.

———. 2020g. The Walkley Book Award. https://www.walkleys.com/awards/walkleys/walkley-book-award/. Accessed 24 April 2020.

Walkley Scrapbook. 1956. *The W.G. Walkley National Award for Australian Journalism: Annual Awards*. Walkley Archive, Mitchell Library, Library of New South Wales, Call No: MLMSS6898 26X (44). Accessed 10 February 2018

Walkley Yearbook. 2019. Our Values: Independence and Good Governance. *Walkley Magazine Yearbook* 2. https://cdn5.walkleys.com/wp-content/uploads/2019/12/2019-Walkley-Yearbook.pdf. Accessed 20 May 2020.

Waller, L., and K. McCallum. Forthcoming 2021. Settler Colonial Representations of Indigenous Disadvantage. In *The Routledge Companion to Media and Poverty*, ed. S. Borden. London: Routledge.

Whitton, E. 1967. Life on the Pension. *Truth*, June 24 and July 15.

Willig, I. 2019. Ideals of Journalism the Historical Consecration of Media Capital in Prize Awards and the Case of the Danish Cavling Award 1945–2016. *Media History*. Online May 6. https://doi.org/10.1080/13688804.2019.1608169.

World Population Review. 2020. United States Population 2020 (Live). https://worldpopulationreview.com/countries/united-states-population/. Accessed 20 May 2020.

Young, S. 2019. *Paper Emperors: The Rise of Australia's Newspaper Empires*. Sydney: New South Publishing, University of New South Wales.

CHAPTER 6

The Virtue Map: Emotions and Virtues

INTRODUCTION

In order to appreciate journalists' intricate construction of their creatively produced award-winning feature articles, it is imperative to understand the integral function of emotion in narrative. But before we proceed to the case studies of award-winning journalism in Part II, we must first explore some of the complex answers to the following foundational questions: What is an emotion? What is a virtue? And what is the relationship between the two? As we will recall from Chap. 1, my Virtue Paradigm and the Virtue Map are predicated upon MacIntyre's observation that human beings are essentially 'story-telling animals' who convey the meaning of their experience through the expression of emotion (MacIntyre 2007; Sarbin 1995). Evidence of the degree to which emotion informs narrative is found in an informal study of 70 people by American psychologist and criminologist, Ted Sarbin. When Sarbin (1995, 214) asked the participants to define an emotion he noted that they were only able to explain what sadness or anger meant to them by narrating an experience to illustrate the feeling. Sarbin's experiment demonstrated the importance of understanding that a person's 'emotional life', a term that Sarbin uses to 'capture the fullness of human experience', is essentially 'storied'. One of the key tasks for journalists writing features is to find the most effective means of conveying the emotional life of their subjects—and in some cases themselves—to readers through the construction of powerful stories.

© The Author(s), under exclusive license to Springer Nature Switzerland AG 2021
J. Martin, *Emotions and Virtues in Feature Writing*,
https://doi.org/10.1007/978-3-030-62978-6_6

EMOTIONS

Fundamental to my model is the understanding that how 'we feel about others is what aligns us with a collective' (Ahmed 2004, 27). It is our emotions that enable us to see ourselves as existing in relation to others and this in turn enables us to live in a community through our construction of a shared set of virtues. Independent feminist scholar Sara Ahmed explains that emotions are not considered simply as something felt 'within' or 'without' us but rather as defining 'the contours of the multiple worlds that are inhabited by different subjects' (25). The word emotion, from the Latin *emovere*, means 'to move, to move out' (27). To expand upon this definition, emotions have the ability to *move* us and it is this quality that perhaps best articulates their integral function in the construction of long-form journalism. Ahmed's conceptualization supports French sociologist Emile Durkheim's view that emotions concern our attachments to others and are essentially 'what holds or binds the social body together' (Durkheim 1976, 209). It is important to distinguish emotional experiences as more than simply 'perceived perturbations within the body' or 'feelings' (Sarbin 1995, 214). In the simplest of terms, emotions are not just something a person experiences or 'has', they are also something that a person 'does', and it is this process that connects individuals to each other. In her seminal 2001 work, *Upheavals of Thought: The Intelligence of Emotions*, Martha Nussbaum declared:

> Emotions shape the landscape of our mental and social lives. Like the 'geographical upheavals' a traveller might discover in a landscape where recently only a flat plain could be seen, they mark our lives as uneven, uncertain and prone to reversal. (Nussbaum 2001, 1)

Nussbaum recognizes the importance of narrative to our understanding and expression of emotions and suggests that in order to 'talk well' about love, fear or anger 'we will need to turn to texts that contain a narrative dimension, thus deepening and refining our grasp of ourselves as beings with a complicated temporal history' (2). Whereas Nussbaum suggests that perhaps readers should turn towards the fiction of Marcel Proust as a means to 'encourage us in such imaginings, deepening and refining our grasp of upheavals as though in our own lives', I contend that exemplary long-form journalism is another medium through which we can be

6 THE VIRTUE MAP: EMOTIONS AND VIRTUES

also encouraged to contemplate our contemporary emotional lives. By describing emotions as far more than 'just the fuel that powers the psychological mechanism of a reasoning creature', but as 'parts, highly complex and messy parts, of this creature's reasoning itself', Nussbaum provides a more nuanced definition than what we will recall was Dillard's description, writing a decade earlier, of emotions as 'very coarse computer programs' or as the 'simple-minded servants of behaviour' (Dillard 1998, xix, xxxi). Dillard's comparison between our flesh-and-blood emotions and a machine that is a system of circuits, and, by definition, utterly devoid of emotion, is a workable starting point, but for the purposes of our discussion, we must probe further. Nussbaum embraces the 'peculiar depth and the potentially terrifying character of the human emotions', understanding that our emotions are far more than 'bodily tugs or stabs or flashes' (Nussbaum 2001, 16). She argues, 'How simple life would be, if grief were only a pain in the leg, or jealousy but a very bad backache. Jealousy and grief torment us mentally; it is the thoughts we have about objects that are the source of our agony—and, in other cases, delight' (16). To continue Nussbaum's analogy, there would be no need to try and make sense of our feelings through the creation of our own narrative or by immersing ourselves in the story of someone else; we could swallow a pill instead. But as emotions are *not* simply physical sensations, a pill may temporarily soothe but it will never banish the source of the pain. But, to push the medical metaphor to its limits, masterfully constructed long-form articles may function as a form of 'medicine', or perhaps even as a 'vaccine' that injects the reader with a carefully controlled 'dose' of a narrative that stimulates our emotional system and opens pathways for the consideration of virtues which allows us to live well together as a community. Or, less fancifully, as Nussbaum proposes:

> If we think of emotions as essential elements of human intelligence, rather than just as supports or props for intelligence, this gives us especially strong reasons to promote the conditions of emotional well-being in a political culture: for this view entails that without emotional development, a part of our reasoning capacity as political creatures will be missing. (Nussbaum 2001, 3)

Nussbaum's argument that emotions are not simply sensations that are felt in the body but they also 'perform some cognitive function and convey content' has its roots in the ancient philosophy of Stoicism. In brief, Nussbaum's 'neo-Stoic' account of emotions rejects the Stoics' claim that animals and babies were incapable of emotion because they were not capable of independent thought. Like Nussbaum, Fitterer views emotions as a 'vital part of apprehending and judging the world of value' but he pushes back against her proclamation that emotions 'are *immediate* judgements of personal and eudaimonic [flourishing] values' (Fitterer 2008, 67, my emphasis). For Fitterer, Nussbaum's definition only holds if, by the use of the word 'judgement', Nussbaum is referring to 'a kind of tentative assertion that still awaits a *critically reflective* [my emphasis] act to become judgment proper' (80). Instead, Fitterer views emotion as a 'kind of proto-judgment':

> coming before and being a necessary condition for personal concrete judgements of value, but emotion is not itself such a judgment. Rather, emotion is an immediate apprehension of a possible value, something that may turn out, in fact, to be a genuine good (or bad) for my flourishing. (Fitterer 2008, 80)

Fitterer's insightful description of emotions as 'proto-judgements' serves as a suitable definition for us as we attempt to navigate the connection between emotions and virtues. Fitterer acknowledges the substantial contribution Nussbaum has made to the study of emotions, particularly her insight that 'emotions always involves an appraisal of something's close yet vulnerable connectedness to our eudaimonic sense of well-being' or, as Fitterer neatly summarizes: 'We don't get emotional unless we "take things personally" ' (86). I share with Fitterer and Nussbaum the view that emotions, despite being felt by all of us, every day, defy easy categorization and provide a fascinating area of study.

VIRTUES

Having established some broad guiding principles to define 'the highly complex and messy parts' of ourselves that are our emotions, I will now expand upon the links between emotion and virtue. A welcome guide on this journey is scholar Kristján Kristjánsson, whose 2018 book *Virtuous Emotions* helps navigate the path from Aristotle's view of what it means to achieve a state of eudemonia, to our modern-day conceptualization of what it means to live a 'good life'. In common with Nussbaum and Fitterer, Kristjánsson agrees that Aristotelian emotions have a cognitive core:

> and it is this cognitive core that underlies the assumption of responsibility for emotions, for we can typically be held accountable for, and evaluated morally with respect to, the content of our cognitions—unless those are the results of indoctrination or brainwashing. (Kristjánsson 2018, 1)

As will be expanded upon in the case studies in Part II, the Aristotelian belief in the 'cognitive core' of emotions allows fresh insight into the emotional labour of journalism, particularly long-form. Journalism involves a series of interlinked cognitive acts that are, at the same time, deeply value-laden and informed by emotion. In order for writers to transfer their thoughts into text, it takes an act of creativity which necessarily draws upon the imagination, to varying degrees, depending upon the writer, the topic and the journalistic genre (Ricketson 2017; Morton 2018). Inherent in the act of journalism is the notion of physically creating a piece of writing: there is a striving towards a goal, a striving that we will also find in the pursuit of virtues.

Let us now extend our understanding of the distinction between emotions and virtues for, as we will recall in our earlier discussion on neo-Aristotelian theory, 'where the virtues are required, the vices also may flourish' (MacIntyre 2007, 193). As Fitterer (2008, 67) explains, 'As many emotions as can be evoked to incite change, say by Aristotelian rhetoric, can also be used to maintain the status quo'. Beyond this, Kristjánsson (2018, 2) articulates the value of an Aristotelian account of virtuous emotions, noting 'that many people are drawn towards virtue ethics primarily because of its facility to make sense of the moral salience of our emotional lives', an observation that applies to my own choice of a neo-Aristotelian framework and its application to long-form journalism. It is helpful at this juncture to heed Kristjánsson's caveat that one should not adopt a completely deferential interpretation of Aristotle's virtue ethics 'as there is often no specific text to be deferential to', reminding us that the Greek philosopher's 'account of individual emotions is at times truncated and flawed—even by his own lights—if not simply missing' (3). Many of Aristotle's works have been lost and the modern English translations amount to around 2,450 pages. We cannot tell which of Aristotle's surviving treatises are 'finished'; rather they 'may be "files" that he revised, expanded, summarized, or combined, either for teaching or when new ideas struck him' (Aristotle 2019, xiv). Despite the limitation of Aristotle's theory, if we can proceed as Kristjánsson urged (2018, 2), 'armed with conceptual and moral weaponry from Aristotle's arsenal' it is possible that 'we can make advances in the understanding of people's emotional lives that would be otherwise closed to us—or at least constitute arduous uphill battles'.

Central to Aristotle's virtue theory 'is the assumption that emotional reactions constitute essential ingredients in virtues' and that emotional dispositions can have 'an intermediate and best condition', which happens when the emotions are felt 'at the right times, about the right things and in the right way' (Aristotle 2019, 28–29 [1106b17–35]). For Aristotle, virtues and vices were considered settled character states, or *hexeis* in Greek, which were 'concerned with morally praiseworthy or blameworthy responses in significant and distinguishable spheres of life' (Kristjánsson 2018, 15–16). In my own reconceptualization of Aristotle's virtue theory, I view the *striving* of a person towards the internalization of virtues such as honesty *honesty* and compassion as an ongoing process, one that is tested over time and under different circumstances. Fitterer succinctly explains this link between people's internal, personal sense of virtue and the values they uphold:

> For just as every group embodies a set of common sense insights that have survived the attrition of time and pragmatism, so too each group's set of acquired and tested practical insight inversely reflects a body of rejected concerns, unasked questions, scorned sentiments, and ignored presentations that are transmitted between members and generations. Thus, each individual never does start life with a clean slate but with a block of pre-critical assumptions of what is worth asking or worth feeling. (Fitterer 2008, 65)

It is a person's emotional life that informs their unique habitus, in Bourdieu's terms, and in turn, it is this emotional life that will influence the way in which they interact with different fields (Bourdieu and Wacquant 1992, 96–97). As I will explain in more detail in the forthcoming discussion of Aristotle's intellectual virtue of phronesis, prize-winning long-form journalism can provide a kind of 'virtue compass' to guide us in what

6 THE VIRTUE MAP: EMOTIONS AND VIRTUES   115

virtues are valued in our community. As Kristjánsson summarizes, emotions form an integral part of virtues and, in turn, virtues inform our character:

> Character is viewed by the general public as fundamental to identity, with loss of moral conscience seen as greater loss to identity even than loss of autobiographical memoire—but it is still regarded as essentially controllable and changeable. (Kristjánsson 2018, 26)

The intimate and complex connections that are possible between emotions becomes further evident when we compare Oatley's five basic emotional states of happiness, sadness, fear, anger and disgust with Aristotle's list of desire, daring, envy, gratification, friendliness, hatred, longing, jealousy and pity (Oatley 1992; Aristotle 2019, 26 [II.V, 1105b20–30]). For example, sadness could prompt a desire or longing for happiness which, depending upon the individual, could be expressed as envy or jealousy for another person's life and could feasibly change to or include hatred or anger. In contrast to the basic nature of emotions or feelings, the virtues require a deliberate choice, a decision to behave in a way that is for the greater good—that is, a way that is of benefit to other individuals and to society as a whole (Aristotle 2019, 26–27 [1105b2–1106a14]). To summarize, the Virtue Map model facilitates a new way to answer the question: how do journalists, when we read their work, provide us with the opportunity to experience emotion and through that process, open the way for us to consider virtues? Exemplars of long-form narrative journalism transcend the news cycle and are a reflection of journalism's higher purpose, helping citizens to grapple with what it means to be human and to live together in community, aligning with Kovach and Rosenstiel's argument that journalists' first duty is to citizens (Kovach and Rosenstiel 2014, 9).

VIRTUE ETHICS

Aristotle's virtue theory poses the question: 'Is there a goal or purpose for human living, a master virtue, which provides a benchmark for a good life?' (Aristotle 2019, 14 [I.X–II, VI.13 1144b1–1145b10]; Preston 2007, 49). In preparation for my introduction to the six virtues that comprise the Virtue Map, which are *phronesis, courage, empathy, honesty, resilience* and *responsibility*, it is valuable to expand on our foundational

116   J. MARTIN

conceptualization of phronesis, or 'practical wisdom'. Let us begin by differentiating between common sense and phronesis. As Fitterer (2008, 57) explains, 'One can ask, "Should I, in fact, do X?"' and 'Would X really be worthwhile?' but a person *could* answer this question based on their own self-interest, which 'would seem more like shrewdness (*deinotes*) than phronesis'. In order for common sense to be elevated to the intellectual virtue of phronesis:

> the subject must rely upon inner states and dispositions, such as feelings of preference, memories of shame and praise, responsibilities and obligations to family and friends, tribe, corporation, and so on. One hears the voices of conflicting desires and is forced to adjudicate them within an unsettled conscience. (Fitterer 2008, 57–58)

It is helpful to remember that 'in phronesis we are talking about human action, not the selection of theory' and that the 'human action in question is the functioning of virtue as the primary means to eudaimonia' [the Greek term for flourishing] (Fitterer 2008, 72). In his 2008 book *Love and Objectivity in Virtue Ethics*, Fitterer aimed to show, by drawing upon Aristotle and Nussbaum as well as the work of the less well-known Canadian Jesuit philosopher and theologian, Bernard Lonergan, the connection between emotions and moral insight, or, in his words, to demonstrate 'that living well requires loving aright' (3). Lonergan, who viewed knowledge as 'an ongoing developmental structure, involving the whole person and including the intersubjective and collaborative social world', provides a foundation for our own exploration into virtues (Lonergan 1990, 264–265). His succinct claim that 'genuine objectivity is the achievement of authentic subjectivity' has a particular salience for journalism as it encapsulates the importance of listening and researching all the facts and circumstances of an issue so that it is possible to present the situation with as little bias as humanly possible. But there may also be cases, as Fitterer argues, where:

> in direct conflict with a pure desire to know, there is operative a deep desire *not* to know, a desire to flee from unwanted or threatening insights. Such bias against well-ordered cognition can exist within the individual, the group, and the entire culture. (Fitterer 2008, 65) [emphasis in original].

6 THE VIRTUE MAP: EMOTIONS AND VIRTUES   117

But as we will recall from our earlier chapter on Australia's premier journalism prize, the Walkley Awards, the feature writing prize is given to a story that '*shines a light*, tells a compelling story or provides in-depth analysis and investigation' (Walkley Foundation 2020, my emphasis). Writers of award-winning long-form phronetic journalism whose stories expose wrongdoing or injustice—such as the sexual abuse of children by institutions—are a powerful means of breaking through a person, group or culture's 'deep desire not to know'. Another insight from Lonergan that resonates with this discussion is his notion of each of us having a 'horizon of concern', which means we are not aware of, and therefore cannot care about, things that we do not know, things that lie beyond our 'horizon' (Lonergan 1990, 31; Fitterer 2008, 88). Reading long-form journalism is one effective means of expanding our horizon of concern, and the Virtue Map provides direction into how the journalist guides this broadening of our perspective. While the fiction writer Franz Kafka declared that a 'book must be the axe that breaks the frozen sea inside us' (1904), the best of long-form journalism may also be such a weapon.

VIRTUE ETHICS IN JOURNALISM

My theoretical framework, the Virtue Paradigm, is based upon the argument that the power of narrative journalism depends upon the journalist's skill in bringing narrative and reporting devices into a synergy for the purpose of communicating emotion and, in specific instances, virtues, to readers. For, as discussed in Chaps. 3 and 4, it is through transporting readers into a narrative world which exposes them to the textual representation of the emotional lives of others. This transportation then puts them in a position to consider their own concepts of what it means to live with others in a community and to fulfil the Aristotelian notion of a 'good life' (Green et al. 2004). As Kristjánsson explains:

> In Aristotelianism, virtue education (or 'character education', as it is usually called nowadays) is not an extraneous addition to an understanding of morality or the study of moral philosophy—it is, rather, what such understanding and study are all about. So, if possessing virtues is what matters most for eudaimonia, then studying the virtues must be an integral part of

any good education. For Aristotle that clearly means not only studying them dispassionately, but actually studying them in the sense of acquiring them, just like a budding violinist studies violin playing by training to play the instrument well. (Kristjánsson 2018, 26)

The Virtue Map provides a guide for the reader to identify how the journalist constructs and prioritizes the communication of emotion to readers. The model further supplies direction into how the writer forges, reinforces or challenges a group's cultural connections. While our discussion accepts the need for a broad system of media ethics, this book is focused specifically on the question of *how* the writers of award-winning long-form construct their work to communicate emotion to readers, and how, in turn, those emotions allow readers to consider moving towards developing virtues. As I noted in Chap. 3, just as it is not enough for a modern society to rely on the virtuous disposition of individuals to ensure right action, it is important that professionals such as journalists have an overarching code of behaviour, as evidenced by the many codes of ethics of journalism organizations globally. Couldry (2006, 15) has advocated applying Aristotle's model towards defining a global media ethics founded upon the virtues of 'accuracy, sincerity and care' that contribute to a society living 'well' together. His proposal for a global media ethics has, however, been criticized by scholars such as former BBC reporter Kate Wright, for failing to appreciate the particular challenges of working in modern newsrooms. Wright argues that Couldry's advocacy for a 'global media ethics' is 'a profoundly value-laden business' and that one that risks failing to value 'more local or indigenous approaches to journalism' or to appreciate the difference between news gathering in democratic and non-democratic nations (Wright 2014, 372; Couldry 2012). As a former newsroom reporter, I agree with Wright's assessment of the value of clear, workplace-specific, guidelines for journalists while acknowledging that Couldry's case for a journalists' code of ethics is only a small part of what he means by media ethics. As a media scholar and a member of the International Association for Literary Journalism Studies, I am also a passionate advocate for further study into how the form manifests across different cultures. So, while neither I nor Wright nor even Couldry himself see a neo-Aristotelian approach as definitively solving Couldry's own question of 'How should we live well together *with and through the media*?' (2012, 189; 2013, 1), it remains an important question to ask and

6 THE VIRTUE MAP: EMOTIONS AND VIRTUES 119

is one of the foundational concerns of this book. As the discussion in the next section will make clear, a key part of the answer to Couldry's question lies in a deeper appreciation of the role of emotion in journalism.

THE EMOTIONAL TURN IN JOURNALISM STUDIES

Central to an examination of the role of emotion in feature writing is the understanding that pathos has always been an integral part of storytelling. Whether on the printed page, the airwaves or the television screen, the aim is to connect with the audience and create an emotional impact. As I discussed in Chap. 2, journalistic writing that draws on emotions can be traced back to Defoe and Dickens in England and to the so-called 'yellow journalists' in the United States, in particular the writing by 'sob sister' Elizabeth Cochran, under the by-line of Nellie Bly (Bly 1887; Shapiro 2006). Bly, who worked for Joseph Pulitzer on the *World*, famously pretended to be insane and wrote about life as an inmate of an asylum (Bly 1887). This kind of writing fell out of fashion as the nineteenth century ended, with the rise of objectivity as a goal of journalism, and the dismissal of the 'yellows' by those such as Albert Ochs of the *New York Times* as newspapers with 'little breeding or dignity' (Shapiro 2006). As we noted from our discussion of the development of the feature article in Chap. 5, a strong focus on factual reporting dominated for decades until the advent of New Journalism in the 1960s, which saw the long-form narrative emerge again with formidable force as 'feature stories were released from the purgatory of the "women's pages" ' (Shapiro 2006, 53). The subsequent rise and sustained popularity of narrative journalism was rightly recognized by researcher Chris Peters when he made the salient argument that:

> By considering journalism's emotional side, even when it claims to put emotion aside, we can focus on the subtleties of style that provide the tone, feel, and potential success of the news in an increasingly fragmented, sceptical, and commercialized era. (Peters 2011, 312)

Following Peters's direction, let us now focus on some of the 'subtleties of style', the narrative devices, that journalists employ to communicate emotions to their readers. These devices include, but are not limited to: scene setting; the choice of narrative voice; dialogue; and what journalist

Tom Wolfe referred to as evidence of a person's 'status life', that is the 'recording of everyday gestures, habits, manners, customs, styles of furniture, decoration' (1973, 31–32). In addition to understanding the complex effect the particular combination of storytelling and reporting devices may have upon readers, the concept of narratorial presence should also be considered (Lee 2011, 8–9). The term 'narratorial presence' is used to describe where readers imagine themselves to be positioned, physically and/or psychically, when reading the story. It is *not* a literary device, rather it is the complex and nuanced effect of the total ensemble of devices being used at any moment in a literary narrative and refers to how readers situate themselves within the story in real time as they are reading it (Lee 2011, 8–9). A shifting narratorial presence enables readers to view the story through different perspectives, while still maintaining a sense of their own, separate self.

The manipulation of narrative perspective is another significant device employed by journalists to communicate emotions to readers in award-winning articles. As will be examined in Part II, the way in which the journalist controls the narrative voice, as well as the distance between him-or-herself and those interviewed, has a powerful influence on directing the attention of readers (Aare 2016). An appreciation of the impact of the narrative distance between the narrator and the readers can reap valuable insights, such as the inherent danger of crediting the traditional third person voice of the news story with being somehow more 'objective' than the first-person narrative (Aare 2016, 107; Tulloch 2014). Ricketson (2014, 151) argues that journalists who employ an omniscient narrative voice 'need to understand the misleading signals that an omniscient narrative voice sends in non-fiction and about when and in what ways such a narrative voice could be used'. Rather, the journalist must strike a balance between the facts of a story and the boundaries of a creative approach so that readers can enjoy one of the richest rewards of reading narrative journalism, which is to 'make sense of the chaos of life' (138–140).

Another technique used by the writers to hold the attention of readers is to 'outsource' the article's emotion onto their interviewees, rather than reveal the writer's own emotion in the story (Wahl-Jorgensen 2013a, 130, 141; 2013b, 306; 2019, 39). Wahl-Jorgensen's study of Pulitzer prize-winning articles covered what she called 'news categories' and included 'explanatory, international, national, investigative, feature and public service categories' (2013a). The notion that 'journalistic narratives are profoundly infused with emotion' was borne out in the study, which sampled the first winning entry of each category of the Pulitzer Prize-winning news feature stories from 1985 to 2011 and concluded that 94 per cent of lead paragraphs were anecdotal and, of these, 97 per cent involved 'personalized story-telling and widespread invocation of emotion' (2013a, 137–138). Wahl-Jorgensen concluded that the writers observed a 'strategic ritual of emotionality' in which they, while not expressing their own emotions directly in any of the prize-winning stories, did however use a 'neat trick' by relying on:

> the outsourcing of emotional labour to non-journalists—the story protagonists and other sources who are (a) authorized to express emotions in public and (b) whose emotions journalists can authoritatively describe without implicating themselves. (Wahl-Jorgensen 2019, 39)

While Wahl-Jorgensen's findings are significant within the broader context of the role of emotion in journalism, it is important to acknowledge that there has long been, within the small but dynamic field of literary journalism scholarship, a recognition that narrative journalists engage readers by explicitly carrying some of the 'emotional load' themselves (Pantti 2010a, b; Wahl-Jorgensen 2019; Joseph 2011; Ricketson 2014; Hartsock 2016).

Award-winning features also provide cases of journalists' utilizing what I describe as the 'emotional authority', or 'emotional load' of the first-person narrative voice for the purpose of creating interesting stories. Commenting on the rise of this style of subjective and confessional journalism, Rosalind Coward observed: 'There is no road map for this kind of writing, nor is there any critical discourse to help editors and critics differentiate between journalism which has a genuinely useful social element and that motivated by exhibitionism' (2013, 11). The Virtue Map, by providing a means to critically examining the use of first-person voice, will contribute to redressing this problem identified by Coward.

The Virtue Map's key advantage as an analytical tool for understanding long-form is the way in which it focuses on how emotion is conveyed by the journalist in the article, which in turn allows a consideration of what virtues are being constructed for readers as a result of this process. This is not to suggest that the communication of emotion is the sole preserve of feature writing, for it is evident that the very facts of the story, as captured

122 J. MARTIN

in a headline such as 'At least 26 people dead in church shooting' (*CNN* 2017), is a strong enough statement on its own to elicit an emotive response in the reader. The power of feature writing, when executed well, goes beyond relaying the shock of terrible news to urging readers towards a deeper comprehension. This is evident in Rachel Kaadzi Ghansah's 2018 Pulitzer Prize-winning article on the US gunman, Dylann Roof, who in June 2015 shot and killed nine people in a church in Charleston, South Carolina (Ghansah 2017). She wrote how she initially wanted to tell the story of Dylann Roof's victims, but she found herself instead frustrated and shocked at the young man's unwillingness or inability to explain his actions:

> I decided that if he would not tell us his story, then I would. Which is why I left Charleston, the site of his crime, and headed inland to Richland County, to Columbia, South Carolina—to find the people who knew him, to see where Roof was born and raised. To try to understand the place where he wasted 21 years of a life until he committed an act so heinous that he became the first person sentenced to die for a federal hate crime in the entire history of the United States of America. (Ghansah 2017)

The judges described her article as an 'unforgettable portrait' that used a 'unique and powerful mix of reportage, first-person reflection and analysis of the historical and cultural forces behind his killing' (Pulitzer Prize 2018). In the face of 'an act so heinous', it is Ghansah's emotional authority as a compassionate member of society struggling to comprehend a terrible crime which establishes her position as a trustworthy narrator. Emotional engagement is essential to entering into a meaningful public discussion and thus emotions should be considered as the foundation for taking political or moral action. As Pantti demonstrates in her study of disaster reporting:

> because of their role [emotions] in the forming and breaking of social soli-darities: collective identities that make communities and nations possible are built on shared emotions toward fellow insiders and perceived outsiders. (Pantti 2010a, 222)

The Virtue Map provides an analytical prism through which to better appreciate how award-winning feature writers such as Ghansah use their professional skills to contextualize significant issues such as natural disasters, tragic events, personal or political crises in ways that go beyond the statement of facts that characterize a news story. For this deep resonance to be achieved, both the journalist's reporting and writing skills must be brought into balance. If a story contains a surfeit of facts it is considered too 'dry', and if it focuses solely on the emotions of those involved it runs the risk of being dismissed as a 'sob story' (Shapiro 2006). I refer to this ability of the journalist to balance the scales between fact and feeling as 'emotional discipline'. This term addresses two distinct but highly compatible journalistic methods. The first is the understanding that journalists will not let their *own* emotions intrude upon the story they are telling; this is an implicit and accepted understanding about the methodology of journalism, one that is deeply embedded in many decades of journalistic practice that was premised upon the notion of 'objectivity'.

For some decades now there has been a growing acceptance in journalism practice and studies that pure objectivity is neither an attainable nor even a desirable goal and that 'balance, accuracy and fairness' (Kovach and Rosenstiel 2014, 63), while still problematic, are more worthwhile pursuits for the fourth estate (Maras 2013; Michael 2001; Schudson and Anderson 2008; Stenvall 2008; Tuchman 1972; Wahl-Jorgensen 2013a, b; 2019). In Chap. 2 we discussed how it is an implicit part of the contract between the reader and the feature journalist that what they write is true, and that both their facts and their quotes are verifiable Indeed, it is this 'power of the real' that is crucial to the success of the story (Ricketson 2004, 232). But for a long-form narrative to achieve the kind of impact that is remembered by readers and celebrated with awards, more than the simple gathering of facts is required. Facts are the bedrock of a feature but emotion is the fuel that ignites the prose. The interplay between how journalists marshall facts and how they use narrative devices to harness both their own emotion and the emotions of those they write about, is a complex and intricate endeavour that defies easy categorisation. Garner's 1993 story about toddler Daniel Valerio is a powerful example of a writer's ability to express her own emotion in a story (Garner 1993). When Garner won her second Walkley for long-form feature writing in 2017, for her story about a Sudanese refugee woman who drove into a suburban lake, killing the three youngest of her seven children, the Walkley judges deservedly praised her 'empathy and honesty' (Walkley Foundation 2017; Garner 2017). Emotion is at the heart of Garner's writing, a trait that has brought her both praise and criticism. In both of her Walkley feature-writing wins Garner provides a masterful demonstration of how she can harness her own emotion as a means of intensifying the impact of her story on readers. But, as cultural theorist Jan Webb argues, Garner's writing often polarises readers, and that her 'decision to place herself at the centre of the story can also become a distraction from the story itself and can leave the writer sounding didactic' (Webb 2017). As we will recall from our discussion in Chap. 2, Garner's 1995 book, *The First Stone*, in which Garner invented characters, also caused controversy for the way in which the writer expressed her own emotions to readers. Novelist Marion Halligan wrote: 'The book is not a piece of journalism, it's a novel whose main character is Garner, acting out the role of a journalist' (Halligan 1998). There is no easy answer to the question of how *much* emotion is enough in a feature story. Nor, I argue, *should* there be a simple formula to balance out the feelings with the facts, especially when we recall Nussbaum's description of 'the peculiar depth and terrifying character of the human emotion' (Nussbaum 2016, 1). What is clear is that some the best examples of long-form are by writers who are able to skilfully include their own feelings in a way that enhances rather than detracts from the transportive quality of the story. There is an additional, tantalising question which is beyond the scope of this book, which is whether the literary skill of a writer like Garner may actually magnify the ethical issues, precisely because her writing has such an impact on readers.

The second journalistic method—equally important—is the *way* in which journalists express the emotions of those involved in the story, in turn encouraging readers to experience compassion and empathy towards those written about. If we remember that writing is a deliberate act and that these narratives are a deliberate construction by journalists, the importance of every quote and every description on the page becomes evident. The Walkley judges' comments on Australian journalist Gary Tippet's 1997 article about Tony Lock, an Indigenous man who killed his childhood abuser, demonstrate the ability of a journalist to evoke compassion from readers through the use of narrative and reporting devices. The judges wrote that this article was an example of 'extraordinarily powerful writing' which gave a 'deeply affecting account of one person's experience of horrific abuse' (Tippet 1997; Walkley Magazine 1997).

Around the world, stories that are judged to have achieved a balance between information and pathos receive honours, such as *Le Monde* reporter Elise Vincent, who won the 2018 Albert Londres Prize for a series of six articles on jihadism and radicalization in France (Prix Albert

Londres 2018). The European Press Prize for the same year was won by Michael Obert for his 'distinguished reporting' on a 'dubious warlord' who had claimed to be a rescuer of African refugees, providing another example (European Press Prize 2018). In each of these articles, the journalists use the propellant of emotion to gain traction with their audience, building enough momentum to provide readers with the opportunity to be transported into the narrative.

The Virtue Map, through its neo-Aristotelian foundation of what it means to live well together, contributes to a growing body of research that supports a wider appreciation of the value of emotions to communication studies in general (Couldry et al. 2013; Boltanski 1999; Chouliaraki 2008; Nussbaum 2013, 2016; Ong 2015) and literary journalism in particular (Roberts and Giles 2014; Aare 2016; Hartsock 2016; Shapiro 2006; Joseph 2011; Wahl-Jorgensen, 2013a, b). The Virtue Map's focus on identifying virtues highlights the role that emotion performs in promoting the ideal of social cohesion (Trindade and Inacio 2017). It is timely at this juncture to return to the thoughtful observation of anthropologist and social critic Ghassan Hage who has written extensively on racism, nationalism and multiculturalism, highlighting the importance of sharing each other's stories (see Chap. 4). He argues that shared experiences:

> like family life, all social communal life is communicated to us as a gift, and like all gifts, it creates obligations when it is well given. Participating in, and 'caring for' whatever community we belong to is the common, though not necessary, mode of returning such a gift. It is through this process of gift exchange that communal affects such as pride and shame circulate. (Hage 2015, 99–100)

Award-winning long-form journalism—writing that is intimately concerned with communicating our shared humanity through an intelligent exploration of our emotions and the interpretation of controversial, complicated or traumatic topics—is such a gift.

Introducing the Virtues

Now that we have discussed the foundational theories that form the basis of the Virtue Paradigm, defined the parameters of the Virtue Map and outlined the value of a neo-Aristotelian approach to the study of emotion in journalism, we are ready to move on to a description of the six virtues that comprise the Virtue Map: *phronesis*, *courage*, *empathy*, *honesty*, *resilience* and *responsibility*.

Phronesis: The Master Virtue

Considered by Aristotle as the highest intellectual virtue, and by me as the master virtue of my Virtue Map, phronesis is often translated as 'prudence' or 'practical wisdom' (the latter of which is the definition used for this discussion), a virtue 'based on values, concerned with practical judgement and informed by reflection' (Aristotle 2019 [VI.4 1140a–V.5 1140b12]; Kinsella and Pitman 2012, 2). Phronesis enshrines the belief that 'I am not only accountable, I am one who can always ask others for an account, who can put others to the question. I am part of their story, as they are part of mine' (MacIntyre 2007, 217). Aristotle's world was deeply divided along the lines of race, gender and class, yet it was also a world that was considered 'stable and eternal', in contrast to our modern world in which the global economy, diverse nations, and the very climate seem defined by cycles of chaos (Kinsella and Pitman 2012, 3). Phronesis also functions alongside all seven of Schudson's functions of news in a democratic society: information, investigation, analysis, social empathy, promoting a democracy, providing a public forum and mobilization (Schudson 2008, 339). The value of phronesis as a journalistic tool is evident in Kovach and Rosenstiel's 'first principle' for the profession: 'to provide people with the information they need to be free and self-governing' (Kovach and Rosenstiel 2014, 9). The remaining traits include truthfulness, verification, loyalty to citizens, being independent monitors of power and providers of a forum for public criticism, as well as being interesting, relevant, comprehensive and proportional and exercising freedom of conscience (Kovach and Rosenstiel 2014, 9). Phronetic journalism makes a positive change to society, and it is this strong social justice element that elevates phronesis to the status of a master virtue. There is a risk that a phronetic approach, with its emphasis on action, could lead to journalists using their narrative power unethically, simply because: 'Where the virtues are required, the vices also may flourish' (MacIntyre 2007, 193). But as the following case studies will reinforce, the Virtue Map's particular focus on award-winning journalism goes someway towards mitigating the likelihood of maleficence, as adherence to ethical practice is central to respected media prizes (Pulitzer Prize 2020; Walkley Foundation 2020; Accountable Journalism 2020a). As discussed in Chap. 2, prizes should not be considered a perfect measure of what constitutes excellent journalism. Rather, a critical examination of prize-winning journalism provides insight into what professional values are consecrated in awards (Willig 2019, 14).

I have developed the following four criteria as a broad framework to ascertain if a feature article should be considered an example of 'phronetic journalism':

1. The article presents a narrative that 'is based on values, concerned with practical judgement and informed by reflection' (Kinsella and Pitman 2012, 2). Those values, which are defined as a person's standards and principles, may be implicit or explicit, and they may also demonstrate how emotion is used by the journalist to construct and invoke concepts of virtue to the reader. The Virtue Map is helpful as a means of identifying the emotions and virtues constructed in the feature article, as well as identifying the narrative frame or theme of the article. It is reasonable to assume that features concerned with the topic of 'justice', for example, or 'morality', would very likely reveal traits of phronetic journalism, as moral or ethical judgements require choice, and an informed choice requires the careful weighing up of facts and evidence, as presented to the reader by the journalist.

2. A phronetic article must contribute to a debate that addresses the key question of how we live well together in a community. It must be concerned with 'how justice finds expression in the social and associational life of human communities through community partnerships and local capacity building' (Preston 2007, 51).

3. In line with the professional media ethics codes of journalists around the world, of which the Australian journalists' union, the Media, Entertainment and Arts Alliance, is but one example, the article should also 'search, disclose, record, question, entertain, suggest and remember' (MEAA 2019; Accountable Journalism 2020a; Ethical Journalism Network 2019). I propose that this is what the strongest feature writing does, because such reporting emphasizes the important function of journalism as a public record (Simons and Buller 2013, 2014).

4. The feature article should transport the reader into a narrative world and, through the use of emotion, provide readers with the opportunity for transformation. Without this connection, this transportation, the potential for points 1, 2 and 3 to be met is severely curtailed (Green et al. 2004). Put quite simply, if the story is not interesting it will not hold the readers' attention and it will not be read or, if it is, it will not be remembered.
In conclusion, features that meet the definition of phronetic journalism should include as many as possible, if not all, of the above traits.

Courage

It follows that journalists charged with the responsibility of informing citizens about the society in which they live must also have the courage to hold the powerful to account and to give voice to those who are marginalized or ignored by society. The virtue of courage is enshrined in journalism codes of ethics around the globe. The first principle of the international media organization *Al Jazeera's* code of ethics is to 'Adhere to the journalistic values of honesty, courage, fairness, balance, independence, credibility and diversity, giving no priority to commercial or political over professional consideration' (*Al Jazeera* 2014; Accountable Journalism 2020b). In Australia, the Walkley Awards recognize 'creative and courageous acts of journalism that seek out the truth and give new insight to an issue' (Walkley Foundation 2020). The character trait of courage, which regulates the emotion of fear, was included among Aristotle's 'moral virtues' (Aristotle 2019, 47 [III.6–9]) and MacIntyre (2007, 192) argued that courage had its 'role in human life because of this connection with care and concern'. Defining courage as 'the capacity to risk harm or danger to oneself', MacIntyre contended it was not possible 'to resist the corrupting power of institutions without justice, courage or truthfulness' (94).

We will recall from our earlier discussion that MacIntyre's connection between courage and care and concern aligns with Couldry's advocating for a global media ethics based upon sincerity, accuracy and care (Couldry 2006, 15). A significant example of the role of courage in resisting the corrupting power of institutions is found in the global exposure by the media of sexual abuse of children by members of the Catholic Church in countries that include Argentina, Germany, the United Kingdom, Ireland, Poland, Austria, Switzerland, Canada and Australia (*Boston Globe* 2004). The 2018 Pulitzer Prize for Public Service journalism was awarded to the *New York Times* and the *New Yorker* for 'impactful journalism that exposed powerful and wealthy sexual predators … thus spurring a worldwide reckoning about sexual abuse of women' (Pulitzer Prize 2019). It is noteworthy that these abuses—by priests against children and powerful men against women—were only made public through the courage of the victims speaking out and trusting journalists such as the *Boston Globe*'s 'Spotlight' team: Walter Robinson, Sacha Pfeiffer, Matt Carroll, Phil Saviano and Michael Rezendes (*Boston Globe* 2004). Journalists must of course also possess the courage of their own convictions in holding the

6 THE VIRTUE MAP: EMOTIONS AND VIRTUES   129

powerful to account; not as well understood, however, is how they must also possess the courage to expose themselves to the traumatic stories of victims in their role of witnessing (Smith et al. 2015). The decision to take on the emotional load of the story also requires that the writer possess a strong sense of emotional discipline, in order to avoid appearing overly sentimental, turning the article into a 'sob story' (Shapiro 2006).

Empathy

The Virtue Map's potential to illuminate the foundational role of emotion in the construction of compelling journalism becomes clear when we consider the virtue of empathy. The new analytical framework of the Virtue Map highlights the value of treating empathy (which, as will be explained in detail later in this chapter, functions as both an emotion and a virtue) along with the expression of all emotion in long-form, with the same respect afforded to the discipline of verifying facts and gathering evidence, instead of being neglected, or treated, as described by Wahl-Jorgensen (2019, 37; 2020, 178) and Kotisova (2019, 1–11), as 'the elephant in the room' that is journalism. Despite it being difficult to find a compelling piece of journalism that does *not* include empathy as a central approach by the writer, the precise meaning of that emotion is contested, as evidenced by social psychologist Batson's identification of at least eight competing definitions for the term (Batson 2009). For the purposes of my argument, empathy is defined as having both cognitive and emotional dimensions, meaning that it involves recognizing feeling states and thoughts as well as empathic participation or response (Glück 2016, 894–895).

Journalism researchers such as Papacharissi understand that while technologies network us in our increasingly mediatized world, 'it is narrative that connect us to each other, making us feel close to some and distancing us from others' (Papacharissi 2014, 5). The connection with story emphasizes the value of examining not just empathy but also the overall role of affect in journalism. The Virtue Map demonstrates that empathy is, in turn, a key emotion in encouraging readers to consider the plight of others and exemplary long-form can generate impact that Papacharissi describes as being able to move 'beyond the symbolic'. In order for an impact beyond the symbolic Papacharissi argues that 'a variety of contextual factors—better described as "the longue durée" or the long haul of history—must be considered' (2014, 135). I suggest exemplars of long-form may provide some of the most powerful examples of how 'true' stories transcend the daily news cycle to become part of the warp and weft of the stories that define us.

The term empathy first appeared in English in 1909 when it was translated by Edward Bradford Titchener from the word *Einfühlung*, understanding or empathy, used by the German Romantics to describe aesthetic experience, or 'feeling into' the natural world (Glück 2016, 895). The term translates, according to Glück, as 'projecting oneself into the situation of another person or their aesthetic artwork' (2016, 894–895) and was introduced to philosophical scrutiny by German philosophers such as Robert Vischer Theodor Lipps in the early twentieth century. It is important to distinguish the difference between empathy and sympathy. Put in the simplest of terms, when someone feels sympathy there is often an element of pity, which has an implied notion of superiority, then necessarily preventing the person thinking empathically. Empathy, on the other hand, involves both the 'manifestation of concern for the other' and the extra dimension of 'being willing in principle to act in such a way that this other agent will thrive' (Koehn 1998, 52). Another helpful definition by Simmons argues:

> empathy in its *fullest* form is typically if not always essential to caring for another's well-being. When we feel concern for another's suffering, we necessarily empathize with her insofar as we share in her feelings of concern for her pain or distress. (Simmons 2014, 97, emphasis added)

To expand, when we first experience empathy, it's often an emotional reaction, an emotional empathy, which then leads on to a more cognitive expression of empathy as a desire to help, which, if acted upon, is evidence of empathy as a virtue. Scholars such as Nussbaum (2001, 302) consider empathy as 'simply an imaginative reconstruction of another person's experience' and does not, unlike compassion, include a desire to help others. But I argue that the meaning of 'sympathy', which Nussbaum notes used to be an 'emotional equivalent' for 'compassion' in the eighteenth century, has changed, so the term empathy has, in common usage, become interchangeable with 'compassion'.

As valuable as these theoretical debates on meaning are in contributing to the discipline of media scholarship, the definition of empathy as 'the manifestation of concern for the other' that is infused with a desire to help, and Simmons's term 'full empathy' (2014, 97), best encapsulates the meaning of this virtue for our purposes. The Virtue Map can enhance

6 THE VIRTUE MAP: EMOTIONS AND VIRTUES 131

appreciation of the value of full empathy, which encapsulates kindness, compassion and sympathy, to journalists' practice. For example, in one of the few specific studies of empathy in Australian narrative journalism, Sue Joseph conducts a reflexive, autoethnographic examination of six narratives she authored on trauma subjects, arguing that empathy was 'an effective and valid tool' and, furthermore, that the 'imperative' of empathy was 'an ethical necessity when dealing with subjects recounting traumatic incidents in their lives by pointing to the emotional act of this retelling' (Joseph 2011, 21, 23–24). Advocating for the journalist to reveal their own feelings in the narrative in order to more faithfully—and ethically—capture the experience of the subject is not without risk and requires that the writer conveys 'to the reader their interpretation of the interview process without embellishment' as '[m]isrepresentation of meaning at this point is a duplicitous fabricating or embellishing' (Joseph 2011, 22). But if the journalist is able to bring into synergy the reporting of facts with the communication of emotions such as empathy then this can, as Coté and Simpson advocate, 'help readers and viewers gain empathy for the suffering of victims and enrich everyone's awareness of the powerful role that trauma plays in people's collective lives' (Coté and Simpson 2006, 8).

Honesty

It is a truism that honesty is the first principle for any genuine social interaction. Media practitioners worldwide proclaim to report events with accuracy, pursuing and presenting the 'truth' to readers, as demonstrated by the Accountable Journalism website, a site that has collated and monitored ethical codes of conduct of press organizations around the globe since 2002 (Accountable Journalism 2020a). Operating on the basis that ethics are vital to good practice, the site declares that 'Truth and its presentation constitutes the main concern of a journalist'. The word 'truth' is used in the charters of at least 245 media organizations globally, including media in Germany, the UK, Ireland, Finland, Russia, Italy and Greece (Accountable Journalism 2020a). The proclamation from the National Union of French Journalists provides a salient example:

> A journalist worthy of the name considers slander, unfounded accusations, alteration of documents, distortion of facts and lying, to be the most serious professional misconduct. (Accountable Journalism 2020a)

132   J. MARTIN

The virtue of honesty, named by Aristotle as one of the moral virtues, is an essential inclusion in any Virtue Map construction. It is impossible to conceive of an award celebrating excellence in journalism that did not include honesty as an absolute requirement, as evidenced by the scandals that followed the discovery of lying by journalists such as *Der Spiegel* reporter Claas Relotius or *New York Times* reporter Jayson Blair, who, as I mentioned in Chap. 2, were both found to have faked stories (Connolly and Le Blond 2018; Mnookin 2004). The neo-Aristotelian theorist Alasdair MacIntyre argued in *After Virtue* (1981) that honesty, or truthfulness, along with the virtues of justice and *courage*, were 'genuine excellences' or virtues, 'in the light of which we have to characterize ourselves and others, whatever our private moral standpoint or our society's particular codes may be' (2007, 192). Truth is also one of Habermas's four validity claims alongside appropriateness, sincerity and comprehension (Habermas 2001, 447–456).

While any exemplar of journalism can be expected to be as honest, or as accurate an accounting of the events as possible, the Virtue Map allows a closer analysis of the value of honesty beyond simply identifying its presence and instead illuminating the complex ways in which the writer constructs a narrative that readers accept as 'speaking truth'. The virtue of honesty was found in all 23 feature articles in the Walkley study. Most crucially, the journalist's reporting skills, the integrity with which they approach the task of gathering and contextualizing the facts, from the choice of topic to the selection of interviewees and the understanding of data, reports and historical precedents, lay the foundation upon which an 'honest' story is built, convincing readers that what is written is accurate. But journalists whose writing has been celebrated as 'compelling' (one of the Walkley Awards judging criteria for excellent journalism) also invest a great deal of labour in constructing an image of themselves as trustworthy narrators dedicated to sharing information with their privileged readers. Key to communicating the virtue of honesty is the journalist's ability to encourage, and to give permission, to readers to experience emotion. And an awareness of how the writer employs narrative devices such as the first person, or the reported speech of an interviewee or the recording of specific details such as gestures, reveals the complex level of the journalism practice and the depth of writing skill that is required to present an 'honest' or 'true story' to readers (Ricketson 2014, 18).

Resilience

The power of the model to reveal assumptions of conduct through the identification of traits that are elevated to virtues is demonstrated in the frequency in which resilience emerges as a theme in award-winning long-form articles. For example, resilience was the next commonly identified virtue after honesty and responsibility, present in 20 of the 23 stories in my study of Walkley award-winning features (Martin 2017). Leaving aside the plethora of self-help books devoted to the topic of resilience, there are also many scholarly articles devoted to the topic, covering a wide range of subjects such as education, sport, engineering, politics and climate change (Kim et al. 2017; Kristjánsson 2012; Russell 2015; Blockley 2015; Ong et al. 2006). Resilience is defined as 'the human ability to adapt in the face of tragedy, trauma, adversity, hardship and ongoing significant life stressors' (Newman 2005, 227). The rhetoric of resilience is deeply embedded within the journalism profession, as is evidenced by the 'Most Resilient Journalist' award given by 'Free Press Unlimited', an Amsterdam-based foundation that oversees media projects in 42 countries and whose mission is to make 'independent news and information available to everyone' (Free Press Unlimited 2019a). The Free Press Unlimited award for resilience is given to a journalist 'who has demonstrated extraordinary strength of character, courage and perseverance in reporting the news' (Free Press Unlimited 2019b). Resilience was also a key theme for journalism scholars Anderson et al. (2015), who advocated innovation as a key to the survival of the Fourth Estate—a manifesto challenged by Creech and Nadler (2018). The importance of the virtue of resilience was recently demonstrated in the 20th anniversary edition of the journal *Journalism: Theory, Practice and Criticism*, which asked scholars to 'name the biggest challenge facing journalism today' with the 'simple' reasoning that 'with so many simultaneous provocations and questions currently cluttering the news environment, would it be possible to isolate just one so as to better articulate possible modes of resistance to it?' (Tumber and Zelizer 2018, 6). In a concluding summary for the same issue, Wasserman (2018, 229) declared that journalism must 'find ways to be *resilient* and adaptable in order to survive and flourish' and its very future will 'depend on its resilience to commercial pressures and its ability to adapt'.

It is timely at this juncture to recall that Aristotle did not include resilience as one of his moral or intellectual virtues, illustrating the way in which notions of what is considered a desirable trait can differ across time and culture (MacIntyre 2007, 181). It is therefore telling that Andrew Losowsky, in his 'predictions for journalism 2018' report for Harvard University's *Nieman Journalism Lab*, named 2018 'The Year of Resilience' (Losowsky 2017). Losowsky wrote that 'In 2018, journalists will continue to face threats from antagonists who—for political motivations, driven by a desire to create chaos, or both—are trying to disrupt and distract them for their work'. But although Losowsky said that 'we can expect the efforts of the antagonists to increase', he concluded that 2018 would also be 'the year that journalism responds by taking these threats seriously, and by learning how to protect itself'.

In the case of long-form journalism, it is always helpful to consider just who is expected to be resilient and what the consequences of that resilience are—for both the person involved and for the wider community—when this virtue is employed as an over-arching theme. Is it not in the interests of all those in power, whether that is governments, businesses, corporations or institutions, to promote a sense of resilience in those whose labour and loyalty they rely upon? Such issues are explored in Scott Blackwood's 2015 *Chicago Magazine* article, 'Here We Are', a finalist in the 2016 Longform National Magazine Awards (Longform 2016). Blackwood tells the story of Pembroke Township, an hour's drive from Chicago and one of the poorest places in America, where 'you will find a remarkable spirit of resiliency'. Another example is Andrea Elliott's 2013 feature for the *New York Times*, 'Invisible Child', which told the story of one of New York's 22,000 homeless children and won a George Polk Award, which celebrates 'intrepid, bold, and influential journalism' (George Polk Awards 2013). The virtue of resilience, when examined critically within the framework of the Virtue Map, can provide a deeper understanding about the way in which journalists write about the impact of policies imposed by the powerful upon society and how these writers communicate injustice to readers. It can also be an exploration of personal resilience, providing insight into how people such as the citizens of Pembroke, or how homeless children living in one of the biggest cities in the world, navigate lives defined by hardship.

Responsibility

The virtue of responsibility, like honesty, is considered a cornerstone value for journalists. The 'International Principles of Professional Ethics in Journalism', prepared by UNESCO between 1978 and 1983, and representing the views of 400,000 working journalists, proclaimed information in journalism as a 'social good' rather than a commodity, and described the reporter's responsibility as requiring 'he or she will act under all circumstances with a personal ethical conscience' (Accountable Journalism 2020a). In April 2019 the Ethical Journalism Network launched its international media ethics magazine with an aim to 'fight for the future of journalism', declaring: 'Without strong and independent journalism you can't have a free society' (Ethical Journalism Network 2019). The importance of journalists having a sense of social responsibility is further evidenced in the media awards given in countries such as Australia, Belgium and Denmark for the sensitive reporting of suicide (Dare et al. 2011).

It is not surprising that the virtue of responsibility, which plays such a fundamental role in our conception of community responsibility, emerges as a strong theme in long-form journalism. This was the case in my study of 23 award-winning feature articles, where responsibility and honesty were the only two virtues to be identified as a theme in every story (Martin 2017). The virtue of responsibility—as well as honesty— must surely be considered the basic requirements for people to live well together.

Embedded in the expectations people hold for the virtue of responsibility is an assumption that to be responsible is to care about the object of that attention and to fail to do so is considered an unfavourable trait or vice. The crucial juncture between story topic, journalist's skill and the receptivity of readers is where the alchemic nature of journalism, and in particular the long-form narrative, is at its most potent. Journalists who uncover injustice and, through a combination of reporting and writing skills present readers with a compelling narrative with which they can emotionally engage, can be powerful agents of change. A recent international example with a central theme of responsibility was the 2018 winner of Spain's Ortega y Gasset Award, 'The Master Scam' by Mexican digital media outlet *Animal Politico* (Castillo et al. 2018), which exposed the federal government's embezzlement of millions of public funds. A second example is the 2017 winner of Canada's equivalent of the US Pulitzer Prizes, the Michener Awards, to reporter Robyn Doolittle of the *Globe and Mail*, for a 'massive investigation into the systemic mismanagement of sexual assault cases by Canadian police forces' (Michener Awards 2018; Chan 2018; Doolittle 2017). While it is impossible to know exactly what is occurring in the minds of readers, the

Virtue Map is valuable in identifying precisely when, where and how journalists are framing their stories to communicate not only their responsibility to tell the stories but also their prompt for readers to consider the consequences inherent in holding a position of responsibility, such as being a government official or a police officer, sworn to protect citizens.

Conclusion

In this chapter, I explored the function of emotion in narrative, beginning with a consideration of the complex questions of what defines an emotion and a virtue and how we should strive to understand the connections between them. I then proceeded, through the theoretical lens of virtue ethics, to expand our foundational conceptualization of phronesis, or 'practical wisdom', before shifting our discussion to the recent broad emotional turn in journalism studies and the specific function of emotion in narrative journalism. Having discussed the foundational theories that form the basis of the Virtue Paradigm and established the boundaries of the Virtue Map, I then provided working definitions for the six virtues that comprise the Virtue Map: *phronesis, courage, empathy, honesty, resilience* and *responsibility*. To summarize, I have now, at the end of Part I of this book, examined the ways in which the Virtue Map allows the researcher to consider the layers of meaning inherent in the act of a journalist creating a well-researched, beautifully expressed article on a subject considered to be of significance to society. We now have a clearer understanding of how the Virtue Map can provide another lens to show the ways in which the writer expresses emotion—including their own—and, importantly, also to consider more fully the emotional labour that is required to construct stories that are venerated for their contribution to the social discourse. As I embark on the case studies that comprise Part II, it is timely to signal to readers that the Virtue Map model need not just be limited to award-winning long-form journalism in print form. Indeed, the Map could also be used to identify emotions and virtues, or a lack of them, across a range of media forms that employ narrative storytelling such as news or entertainment writing, television, podcasts or documentary. While the limits of space precluded such inclusions in this book, it is my hope that readers will feel encouraged, with a critical gaze, to 'map virtues' across different journalistic platforms and genres. The Virtue Map's contribution to the field of journalism studies is as a tool that helps us better understand the synergy that is created when forensic reporting skills are fused with inspired prose that has the potential, through the communication of emotion, to spark the imaginations of readers, encouraging them to consider what it means to be a citizen in this totally mediatized world.

REFERENCES

Aare, C. 2016. A Narratological Approach to Literary Journalism: How an Interplay between Voice and Point of View May Create Empathy with the Other. *Literary Journalism Studies* 8 (1): 106–139.

Accountable Journalism. 2020a. Accountable Journalism: Monitoring Media Ethics Across the Globe. Accessed April 20, 2020. https://accountablejournalism.org/about.

———. 2020b. *Aljazeera: Code of Ethics.* Accessed May 22, 2020. https:// accountablejournalism.org/ethics-codes/code-of-ethics.

Ahmed, S. 2004. Collective Feelings or, the Impressions Left by Others. *Theory, Culture and Society* 21 (2): 25–42.

Al Jazeera. 2014. Code of Ethics, November 1. https://www.aljazeera.com/aboutus/2006/11/2008525185733692771.html.

Anderson, C.W., E. Bell, and C. Shirky. 2015. Post-Industrial Journalism: Adapting to the Present. *Geopolitics, History, and International Relations* 7 (2): 32–123.

Aristotle. 2019. *Nicomachean Ethics*, 3rd ed. Translated by T. Irwin. Indianapolis: Hackett.

Batson, C.D. 2009. These Things Called Empathy: Eight Related Phenomena. In *The Social Neuroscience of Empathy*, ed. J. Decety and W. Ickes, 3–16. Cambridge and London: MIT Press.

Blackwood, S. 2015. Here We Are. *Chicago Magazine*, October 26. Accessed April 15, 2019. https://www.chicagomag.com/Chicago-Magazine/November-2015/Pembroke/.

Blockley, D. 2015. Finding Resilience through Practical Wisdom. *Civil Engineering and Environmental Systems* 32 (1–2): 18–30.

Bly, N. 1887. Ten Days in a Madhouse. *New York World*, November 27, 10.

Boltanski, L. 1999. *Distant Suffering: Morality, Media and Politics.* Cambridge University Press.

Boston Globe. 2004. The Boston Globe: Spotlight Investigation: Abuse in the Catholic Church. *Boston Globe.* http://archive.boston.com/globe/spotlight/abuse/extras/bishops_map2.htm.

Bourdieu, P., and L.J.D. Wacquant. 1992. *An Invitation to Reflexive Sociology.* Chicago: University of Chicago Press.

Castillo, M., N. Roldan, and M. Ureste. 2018. The Master Scam. *Animal Politico.* https://www.animalpolitico.com/estafa-maestra/.

138 J. MARTIN

Chan, D. 2018. Globe and Mail's Unfounded Investigation wins Michener Award. *Globe and Mail*, June 12. https://www.theglobeandmail.com/canada/article-globe-and-mail-wins-michener-award-for-series-on-police-handling-of-3/.

Chouliaraki, L. 2008. Discourse Analysis. In *The Sage Handbook of Cultural Analysis*, ed. T. Bennett and J. Frow, 674–698. London: Sage.

CNN. 2017. At Least 26 People Killed in Shooting at Texas Church. *CNN*, November 6. https://edition.cnn.com/2017/11/05/us/texas-church-shooting/index.html.

Connolly, K., and J. Le Blond. 2018. Der Spiegel Takes the Blame for Scandal of Reporter Who Faked Stories. *Guardian*, December 23. https://www.theguardian.com/world/2018/dec/23/anti-america-bias-der-spiegel-scandal-relotius?CMP=Share_AndroidApp_Tweet.

Coté, W., and R. Simpson. 2006. *Covering Violence: A Guide to Ethical Reporting about Victims and Trauma*. 2nd ed. New York: Columbia University Press.

Couldry, N. 2006. *Listening beyond the Echoes: Media, Ethics, and Agency in an Uncertain World*. London: Paradigm.

———. 2012. *Media, Society, World: Social Theory and Digital Media Practice*. Cambridge: Polity Press.

———. 2013. Introduction. In *Ethics of Media*, ed. N. Couldry, M. Madianou, and A. Pinchevski. New York: Palgrave Macmillan.

Couldry, N., M. Madianou, and A. Pinchevski, eds. 2013. *Ethics of Media*. New York: Palgrave Macmillan.

Coward, R. 2013. *Speaking Personally: The Rise of Subjective and Confessional Journalism*. Basingstoke, UK: Palgrave Macmillan.

Creech, B., and A.M. Nadler. 2018. Post-industrial Fog: Reconsidering Innovation in Visions of Journalism's future. *Journalism* 19 (2): 182–199.

Dare, A., K.A. Andriessen, M. Nordentoft, M. Meier, A. Huisman, and J. Pirkis. 2011. Media Awards for the Responsible Reporting of Suicide: Experiences from Australia, Belgium and Denmark. *International Journal of Mental Health Systems* 5 (1): 15–20.

Dillard, J.P. 1998. Foreword: The Role of Affect in Communication, Biology and Social Relationships. In *Handbook of Communication and Emotion*, ed. P.A. Anderson and L.K. Guerrero, xvii–xxxii. New York: Academic Press.

Doolittle, R. 2017. Unfounded: Why Police Dismiss 1 in 5 Sexual Assault Claims as Baseless. *Globe and Mail*, February 3. https://www.theglobeandmail.com/news/investigations/unfounded-sexual-assault-canada-main/article33891309/

Durkheim, E. 1976. *The Elementary Forms of Religious Life*. Translated by J. Strachey. London: International Psychoanalytical Press.

Elliott, A. 2013. Invisible Child. *New York Times*, December 9. http://www.nytimes.com/projects/2013/invisible-child/index.html#/?chapt=1

6 THE VIRTUE MAP: EMOTIONS AND VIRTUES   139

Ethical Journalism Network. 2019. Alan Rusbridger Opens New EJN Magazine with Call for Media Ethics. *Ethical Journalism Network*, April 6. https://ethicaljournalismnetwork.org/saving-the-news.

European Press Prize. 2018. Michael Obert. Accessed May 22, 2020. https://www.europeanpressprize.com/laureate/michael-obert/.

Fitterer, R.J. 2008. *Love and Objectivity in Virtue Ethics: Aristotle, Lonergan, and Nussbaum on Emotions and Moral Insight.* Toronto: University of Toronto Press.

Free Press Unlimited. 2019a. *Free Press Unlimited.* Accessed April 9, 2020. https://www.freepressunlimited.org/en.

———. 2019b. The Most Resilient Journalism Award. *Free Press Unlimited.* Accessed April 15, 2019. https://www.freepressunlimited.org/nl/most-resilient-journalist-award.

Garner, H. 1993. 'Did Daniel Have to Die?' *Time Australia* Magazine, no. 10, 8 March. 22–27.

Garner, H. 2017. 'Why She Broke: The Woman, Her Children and the Lake: Akon Guode's Tragic Story'. *Monthly*, June. https://www.themonthly.com.au/issue/2017/june/1496239200/helen-garner/why-she-broke.

George Polk Prize. 2013. Past George Polk Award Winners. https://liu.edu/George-Polk-Awards/Past-Winners#2013.

Ghansah Kaadzi, R. 2017. A Most American Terrorist: The Making of Dylann Roof. *GQ Magazine*, August 21. https://www.gq.com/story/dylann-roof-making-of-an-american-terrorist.

Glück, A. 2016. What Makes a Good Journalist? Empathy as a Central Resource in Journalistic Work Practice. *Journalism Studies* 17 (7): 893–903.

Green, M.C., T. Brock, and G. Kaufman. 2004. Understanding Media Enjoyment: The Role of Transportation into Narrative Worlds. *Communication Theory* 14 (4): 311–327.

Habermas, J. 2001. Truth and Society: The Discursive Redemption of Factual Claims to Validity. In *On the Pragmatics of Social Interaction: Preliminary Studies in the Theory of Communicative Action*, ed. B. Fultner, 85–103. Cambridge, MA: MIT Press.

Hage, G. 2015. *Alter-Politics: Critical Anthropology and the Radical Imagination.* Melbourne: Melbourne University Press.

Halligan, M. 1998. 'That's my story and I'm sticking to it: truth in fiction, lies in fact.' *Australian Humanities Review.* September 1998. http://australianhumanitiesreview.org/1998/09/01/thats-my-story-and-im-sticking-to-it-truth-in-fiction-lies-in-fact/

Hartsock, J.C. 2016. *Literary Journalism and the Aesthetics of Experience.* Amherst and Boston: University of Massachusetts Press.

Joseph, S. 2011. Recounting Traumatic Secrets: Empathy and the Literary Journalist. *Journalism Practice* 5 (1): 18–33.

Kafka, F. 1904. Letter to Oskar Pollak, 27 January 1904. In *Letters to Friends, Family, and Editors*. Translated by R. Winston and C. Winston. New York: Schocken Books.

Kim, J.H., C.E. Hawley, R. Gonzalez, A.K. Vo, L.A. Barbir, B.T. McMahon, D.H. Lee, J.H. Lee, and Y.W. Lee. 2017. Resilience from a Virtue Perspective: Rehabilitation Counselling Bulletin. *Rehabilitation Counselling Bulletin* 61 (4): 195–204.

Kinsella, E.A., and A. Pitman, eds. 2012. *Phronesis as Professional Knowledge: Practical Wisdom in the Professions*. Rotterdam: Sense Publishers.

Koehn, D. 1998. *Rethinking Feminist Ethics: Care, Trust and Empathy*. London: Routledge.

Kotisova, J. 2019. The Elephant in the Newsroom: Current Research on Journalism and Emotion. *Sociology Compass*.

Kovach, B., and T. Rosenstiel. 2014. *The Elements of Journalism: What Newspeople Should Know and the Public Should Expect*. 3rd ed. New York: Three Rivers Press.

Kristjánsson, K. 2012. Positive Psychology and Positive Education: Old Wine in New Bottles? *Educational Psychologist* 47 (2): 86–105.

———. 2018. *Virtuous Emotions*. Oxford: Oxford University Press.

Lee, C. 2011. *Our Very Own Adventure: Towards a Poetics of the Short Story*. Melbourne: Melbourne University Press.

Lonergan, B.J.F. 1990. *Method in Theology*. Reprint, Toronto: University of Toronto Press. Originally published in 1971.

Longform. 2016. The 2016 National Magazine Awards Finalists. Accessed April 15, 2019. https://longform.org/lists/2016-national-magazine-awards?slug=2016-national-magazine-awards.

Losowsky, A. 2017. The Year of Resilience. *NiemanLab*. Accessed June 1, 2020. https://www.niemanlab.org/2017/12/the-year-of-resilience/.

MacIntyre, A. 1981. *After Virtue: A Study in Moral Theory*. Notre Dame, IN: Notre Dame Press.

———. 2007. *After Virtue: A Study in Moral Theory*. 3rd ed. Notre Dame, IN: Notre Dame Press.

Maras, S. 2013. *Objectivity in Journalism*. Cambridge: Polity Press.

Martin, J. 2017. Inscribing Virtues in Australian Literary Journalism: An Investigation into How Journalists Communicate Emotions to Readers of the Magazine-style Walkley Award Winning Features, 1988–2014. PhD dissertation, University of Melbourne.

Media, Entertainment, & Arts Alliance (MEAA). 2019. *Rules of the Media, Entertainment and Arts Alliance*, March 5. https://www.meaa.org/resource-package/registered-rules-of-the-media-entertainment-and-arts-alliance/.

Michael, S. 2001. The Objectivity Norm in American Journalism. *Journalism* 2 (2): 149–170.

6 THE VIRTUE MAP: EMOTIONS AND VIRTUES 141

Michener Awards. 2018. The Michener Foundation. *Michener winners honoured at Rideau Hall.* June 12. Accessed January 10, 2021. http://www.michenerawards.ca/michenerwinners-honoured-at-rideau-hall-2/.

Mnookin, S. 2004. Scandal of Record. *Vanity Fair*, December. https://www.vanityfair.com/style/2004/12/nytimes200412.

Morton, L. 2018. The Role of Imagination in Literary Journalism. *Literary Journalism Studies* 10 (1): 92–111.

Newman, R. 2005. APA's Resilience Initiative. *Professional Psychology: Research and Practice* 36 (3): 227–229.

Nussbaum, M. 2001. *Upheavals of Thought: The Intelligence of Emotions.* New York: Cambridge University Press.

Nussbaum, M.C. 2013. *Political Emotions: Why Love Matters for Justice.* Cambridge, MA: Bellknap Press.

———. 2016. *Anger and Forgiveness: Resentment, Generosity, Justice.* New York: Oxford University Press.

Oatley, K. 1992. *Best Laid Schemes: The Psychology of Emotions.* Cambridge: Cambridge University Press.

Ong, J.C. 2015. *The Poverty of Television: The Mediation of Suffering in Class-Divided Philippines.* London and New York: Anthem Press.

Ong, A.D., C.S. Bergeman, T.L. Bisconti, and K.A. Wallace. 2006. Psychological Resilience, Positive Emotions and Successful Adaptation to Stress in Later Life. *Journal of Personality and Social Psychology* 91: 730–749.

Pantti, M. 2010a. Disaster News and Public Emotions. In *The Routledge Handbook of Emotions and Mass Media*, ed. K. Doveling, C. von Scheve, and E.A. Konjin, 221–236. London: Routledge.

———. 2010b. The Value of Emotion: An Examination of Television Journalists' Notions on Emotionality. *European Journal of Communication* 25 (2): 168–181.

Papacharissi, Z. 2014. *Affective Publics: Sentiment, Technology, and Politics.* Oxford Studies in Digital Politics. New York: Oxford University Press.

Peters, C. 2011. Emotion Aside or Emotional Side? Crafting an "Experience of Involvement" in the News. *Journalism* 12 (3), April: 297–316.

Preston, N. 2007. *Understanding Ethics.* Sydney: Federation Press.

Prix Albert Londres. 2018. 80e Prix de la presse écrite: Élise Vincent pour ses reportages publiés dans Le Monde. October 22. http://www.scam.fr/PrixAlbertLondres/Actualit%C3%A9s/Article/ArticleId/5845/Laureats2018.

Pulitzer Prize. 2018. Winners. Accessed March 19, 2019. https://www.pulitzer.org/winners/rachel-kaadzi-ghansah-freelance-reporter-gq.

———. 2019. The 2018 Pulitzer Prize Winner in Public Service. Accessed October 23, 2020. https://www.pulitzer.org/winners/new-york-times-reporting-led-jodi-kantor-and-megan-twohey-and-new-yorker-reporting-ronan.

142   J. MARTIN

———. 2020. Accessed April 20, 2020. https://www.pulitzer.org/.

Ricketson, M. 2004. *Writing Feature Stories: How to Research and Write Newspaper and Magazine Articles*. Sydney: Allen & Unwin.

———. 2014. *Telling True Stories: Navigating the Challenges of Writing Narrative Non-Fiction*. Sydney: Allen & Unwin.

———. 2017. The Underappreciated Role of Creativity in Journalism. *Text* Special Issue 40 (April): 1–13.

Roberts, W., and F. Giles. 2014. Mapping Nonfiction Narrative: A New Theoretical Approach to Analyzing Literary Journalism. *Literary Journalism Studies* 6 (2): 101–117.

Russell, J.S. 2015. Resilience—Warren P. Fraleigh Distinguished Scholar Lecture. *Journal of the Philosophy of Sport* 42 (2): 159–183.

Sarbin, T. 1995. Emotional Life, Rhetoric, and Roles. *Journal of Narrative and Life History* 5 (3): 213–220.

Schudson, M. 2008. *Why Democracies Need an Unlovable Press*. Malden, MA: Polity Press.

Schudson, M., and C.W. Anderson. 2008. Objectivity, Professionalism, and Truth Seeking in Journalism. In *The Handbook of Journalism Studies*, ICA Handbook Series, ed. K. Wahl-Jorgensen and T. Hanitzsch, 88–101. New York: Routledge.

Shapiro, S. 2006. Return of the Sob Sisters. *American Journalism Review* 28 (3): 50–57.

Simmons, A. 2014. In Defence of the Moral Significance of Empathy. *Ethical Theory and Moral Practice* 17 (1): 97–111.

Simons, M., and B. Buller. 2013. Journals of Record—Measure of Quality or Dead Concept? In *Journalism Education of Australia Association Conference*. http://jeaa.org.au/file/file/Simons%20and%20Buller%20-%20Journals%20 of%20record(1).pdf

———. 2014. Dead Trees, Live Links and Journals of Record—What Good Are Newspapers? In *ANZCA Conference, Melbourne*. http://www.anzca.net/documents/2014-conf-papers/781-anzca14-simons-buller.html.

Smith, R., E. Newman, S. Drevo, and A. Slaughter. 2015. Covering Trauma: Impact on Journalists. *Dart Center for Journalism & Trauma*. Accessed July 21, 2020. https://dartcenter.org/content/covering-trauma-impact-on-journalists.

Stenvall, M. 2008. On Emotions and the Journalistic Ideals of Factuality and Objectivity—Tools for Analysis. *Journal of Pragmatics* 40 (9): 1569–1586.

Tippet, G. 1997. Slaying the Monster. *Sunday Age: Agenda*, June 22, 1–2.

Trindade, A., and R. Inacio. 2017. Literary Journalism, Human Rights and Integration: A Portuguese Case. *Cuadernos.info* 40: 235–249. Accessed June 17, 2019. http://cuadernos.info/index.php/CDI/issue/view/40.

Tuchman, G. 1972. Objectivity as Strategic Ritual: An Examination of Newsmen's Notions of Objectivity. *American Journal of Sociology* 77: 660–679.

Tulloch, J. 2014. Ethics, Trust and the First Person in the Narration of Long-Form Journalism. *Journalism* 15 (5): 629–638.

Tumber, H., and B. Zelizer, eds. 2018. The Challenges Facing Journalism Today. *Journalism* 20 (1): 5–232.

Wahl-Jorgensen, K. 2013a. The Strategic Ritual of Emotionality: A Case Study of Pulitzer Prize-Winning Articles. *Journalism* 14 (1): 129–145.

———. 2013b. Subjectivity and Story-Telling in Journalism: Examining Expressions of Affect, Judgement and Appreciation in Pulitzer Prize-Winning Stories. *Journalism Studies* 14 (3): 305–320.

———. 2019. *Emotions, Media and Politics*. Cambridge, UK, and Medford, MA: Polity Press.

———. 2020. An Emotional Turn in Journalism Studies? *Digital Journalism* 8 (2): 175–194.

Walkley Foundation. 2020. Categories Explained. Accessed May 22, 2020. https://www.walkleys.com/awards/walkleys/categories/

Walkley Magazine. 1997. Walkley Review, no. 2: 20, 25–27.

Walkley Foundation. 2017. 'Helen Garner: "Why She Broke: The Woman, Her Children and the Lake": Feature Writing Long (Over 4000 Words)'. Accessed 21 July 2020. https://www.walkleys.com/award-winners/feature-writing-long/.

Wasserman, H. 2018. Relevance, Resistance, Resilience: Journalism's Challenges in a Global World. *Journalism* (20th Anniversary Special Issue: The Challenges Facing Journalism Today) 20 (1): 229–232.

Webb, J. 2017. 'A new literary portrait of Helen Garner leaves you wanting to know more.' The Conversation. 3 May. https://theconversation.com/a-new-literary-portrait-of-helen-garnerleaves-you-wanting-to-know-more-76975

Willig, I. 2019. 'Ideals of Journalism the Historical Consecration of Media Capital in Prize Awards and the Case of the Danish Cavling Award 1945–2016'. *Media History*. Online 6 May 2019. https://doi.org/10.1080/13688804.2019.1608169.

Wolfe, T. 1973. The New Journalism. In *The New Journalism*, ed. T. Wolfe and E.W. Johnson, 3–36. New York: Harper and Row.

Wright, K. 2014. Should Journalists Be "Virtuous"? Mainstream News, Complex Organisations and the Work of Nick Couldry. *Journalism* 15 (3): 364–381.

PART II

Case Studies

CHAPTER 7

Children: A Case Study

HELEN GARNER 'DID DANIEL HAVE TO DIE?'

Time Australia **Magazine**, 8 March 1993

Winner, 1993 Walkley Award for Print—Best Feature Writing

Judges' comments: 'Helen Garner's beautifully written story for *Time Australia* presents the sensitive issue of child abuse dispassionately and in a way which broadens perspective.' (Walkley 1994, 81)

Comments from Walkley Entry form: The following is the editor of *Time Australia* magazine, Michael Gawenda's description of Garner's work and its impact from the publication's entry form for the Walkley Awards. Gawenda's comments were published by the prize organizers in their 1994 'AMP Walkley Awards Directory and Diary', alongside a photo of the cover of her winning *Time Australia* article:

When Daniel Valerio was beaten to death by his stepfather, the murder attracted wide interest in child protection (or lack of it) systems in Victoria.

The trial and subsequent retrial lasted 26 sitting days. The idea was to report the case as a whole, rather than, as the dailies do, the cumbersome day-to-day court argument that gets bogged down and diluted over a long case. The brief was to try to get inside the family, to know some pattern to the neglect, abuse and indifference.

© The Author(s), under exclusive license to Springer Nature Switzerland AG 2021
J. Martin, *Emotions and Virtues in Feature Writing*,
https://doi.org/10.1007/978-3-030-62978-6_7

147

148   J. MARTIN

The article had an enormous response from *Time Australia* readers, and may well, with other media, have contributed to subsequent government action on compulsory reporting of child abuse. (Walkley 1994, 81)

THE VIRTUE MAP

(Individual virtues are italicized in this chapter for easy identification.)

- *Courage*: The lack of courage in adults, including Daniel's mother, Cheryl Butcher, to stand up and protect Daniel. Garner's courage in investing the emotional labour required to tell Daniel's story and to challenge a community's sense of responsibility.
- *Empathy*: The complete lack of empathy shown by Daniel's murderer, Paul Leslie Aiton. The lack of empathy of Daniel's mother, as described by Garner, in her failure to protect her son from her partner's violence. The lack of empathy of neighbours, and friends of the family, medical and healthcare professionals. Both Garner's empathy for Daniel and the degrees of empathy she expresses towards those involved in Daniel's death.
- *Honesty*: The dishonesty of Aiton. The lack of honesty of Daniel's mother, as implied by Garner. The honest testimony by witnesses in the courtroom, which paradoxically revealed their lack of honesty with themselves and others about the abuse of Daniel and his siblings. The honesty and accuracy of Garner's reporting.
- *Responsibility*: The lack of responsibility of both Aiton and Daniel's mother for the ongoing abuse. The lack of responsibility shown by the adults in Daniel's life for identifying and stopping the abuse, including social workers, police and friends and neighbours of the family. Garner's own keen sense of responsibility in telling Daniel's story as demonstrated by her attendance at both of Aiton's murder trials.
- *Resilience*: The heart-breaking and ultimately unsuccessful resilience of Daniel and his older siblings to withstand Aiton's abuse. The emotional resilience of Garner to cover 26 sitting days of two murder trials.
- *Phronesis*: The introduction of mandatory reporting of child abuse laws in Victoria (Table 7.1).

7 CHILDREN: A CASE STUDY 149

Table 7.1 Individual Virtue Map, Helen Garner 'Did Daniel Have to Die?'

Winning feature	Helen Garner 'Did Daniel Have to Die?'	
Publication	*Time Australia* no. 10, 22–27	
Date	8 March 1993	
Categories	Children	•
	Marginalised and disadvantaged	
	Citizens	•
	The nation	•
Virtues	Courage	•
	Empathy	•
	Honesty	•
	Resilience	•
	Responsibility	•
	Phronesis	•

INTRODUCTION

When Garner's article was published as *Time Australia* magazine's cover story on 8 March 1993, readers were confronted with the devastating and sadly not unfamiliar photo of a tiny, smiling, two-year-old boy with soft brown hair and lash-framed brown eyes. One of those eyes, his left, was clearly blackened, his skin mottled purple, yellow and grey with bruising. The toddler's head, with his halo of light brown hair, partially obscures the 'TIME' banner and, written in big white letters across his dirty green-blue top is the headline: 'Did Daniel Have to Die?', while underneath in square yellow font underlined in the magazine's trademark fire-engine red is the proclamation: 'HELEN GARNER at the trial that shook Australia'. That particular photograph of Daniel Valerio, 'half-smiling in spite of his bruised and battered face', was used as a centrepiece for a successful media push to introduce mandatory reporting in Victoria and became a symbol used by the media for subsequent child abuse stories (Goddard and Liddell 1995, 360). The poignant truth is that the impact of Daniel Valerio's death has resonated far beyond his short life of two years, resulting in changes to Victoria's child protection system and contributing to a greater sense of community *responsibility* for our most vulnerable members.

Daniel was born on 21 April 1988, the fourth and youngest child of Cheryl Butcher. He lived with his mother and two of his three siblings: seven-year-old Candice, and Benjamin, aged four years. On 8 September 1990, Daniel was beaten to death by his mother's de facto boyfriend, Paul

150   J. MARTIN

Leslie Aiton, who had moved into the family home with Cheryl and her three youngest children just five months earlier. The post-mortem revealed Daniel had 104 bruises, including healing fractures in both collar bones. The state coroner wrote that the 'most severe injuries were in the abdomen, akin in severity to those seen in road trauma victims' (Goddard and Liddell 1995, 359).

Deciding which articles to choose to best showcase how the Virtue Paradigm and the Virtue Map can be operationalized has proven to be a challenging but rewarding task. Despite the Walkley Foundation and other organizations honouring excellence in journalism for more than six decades, and the dedicated researching by journalism scholars Willa McDonald, Kerrie Davies and Bunty Avieson to establish a database of narrative journalism in colonial Australia (ACNJ 2015), the nation does not, unlike the United States, have a definitive canon of long-form journalism. The key aim of this book is to call for a deeper appreciation of the journalism that tells the story of who we are and who we wish to become. In 1993, Garner's story sounded just such a call that continues to resonate three decades after Daniel's death, making her article an outstanding example of the power of long-form journalism.

It can be all too easy, swept up in the vividness of Garner's prose, to forget that she is relying solely upon her own observational skills of two criminal trials, which are necessarily circumscribed by the complex and, to the lay observer, convoluted language of the courtroom, to communicate the pathos of Daniel's life and death. There are no interviews with the father, the mother, the neighbours or the many health professionals who saw Daniel's bruises and did nothing. There is no marshalling of child abuse statistics or the inclusion of any analysis of the latest research or interviews with the foremost experts in the field. Garner does not interview the electrician who finally 'broke through the force-field' and reported his concerns for Daniel's welfare to the police (Garner 1993, 26). What Garner does do, using her keen novelist's eye and her huge capacity for emotional discipline, is to draw for readers a haunting image of Daniel's last hours and the bleakness of the lives of his siblings, Candice and Benjamin. And while it is Aiton standing in the dock who is found guilty of Daniel's murder, Garner ensures that anyone reading her story comes away in no doubt that it is all of us that have been put on trial—and found wanting. Garner's article is an excellent example of how a writer constructs a narrative that addresses an imagined virtuous community of readers. Garner challenges readers to face the awful truth that a lack of

7 CHILDREN: A CASE STUDY   151

moral energy, of virtuous action on behalf of the community, meant that a toddler's life was lost to a man's terrible violence.

More than 25 years after its publication and 30 years after Daniel was murdered, Garner's courtroom narrative has the power to disturb, challenge and galvanize the emotions of readers on a topic that, unfortunately, is every bit as relevant today as it was in 1993. As Garner's fellow Walkley award winner Jess Hill (Walkley Foundation 2016) wrote in her 2019 book on family violence, *See What You Made Me Do: Power, Control and Domestic Abuse* (which Garner describes on the cover as 'a shattering book: clear-headed and meticulous, driving always at the truth'): 'the sheer magnitude of domestic abuse in this country is overwhelming our child protection system' (Hill 2019, 122). Hill explains although there is little reliable data on how many children are affected by family violence because 'it's simply not measured', the most recent Personal Safety Survey by the Australian Bureau of Statistics found that 'before the age of fifteen, nearly 2.1 million women and men witnessed violence towards their mother, and nearly 820,000 violence towards their father' and that one in six women and one in ten men report having been physically or sexually abused before the age of 15 (Hill 2019, 121).

Since the publication of Garner's feature in 1993, there has been a slowly growing awareness in the community of both the complexity and the long-term impact of child abuse. The murder in 2014 of 11-year-old Luke Batty by his father, when the boy was at cricket practice in outer suburban Melbourne, and the subsequent tireless advocacy of his mother, Rosie Batty, was a turning point in the coverage of family violence in Australia (Ross 2014; Hill 2019). The 2017 Australian Royal Commission into Institutional Responses to Child Sexual Abuse, one of many investigations into the issue around the world, also raised awareness of the long-lasting harm suffered by survivors (Royal Commission 2017, 9). Garner's 1993 story provides a fascinating lens to illuminate the discourse in Australia at the time about family violence. My discussion will demonstrate how discourse analysis can be operationalized alongside Schudson's seven news criteria and Habermas's theory of validity as part of the Virtue Paradigm (Schudson 2008; Habermas 2001, Chapter 5).

When Helen Garner was writing her article for *Time Australia*, she had not yet achieved her international reputation as one of Australia's most important and celebrated writers—what in Bourdieu's terms we would describe as her cultural or symbolic capital (Benson and Neveu 2005, 4). This is evident in the Walkley blurb accompanying her 1993 win, which

152   J. MARTIN

describes her simply as an 'author and freelance' journalist whose first novel, *Monkey Grip*, published in 1977 and made into a film in 1982, won the 1987 National Book Council Award (Walkley 1994, 81). As discussed in Chap. 2, it would be two more years until Garner's book *The First Stone* would be published, telling the controversial story of sexual harassment claims against a University of Melbourne professor, brought against him by female students (Garner 1995). And it would be another 20 years until Garner published *This House of Grief* in 2016, the true story of Robert Farquharson, who, drove his car into a dam, killing his three little boys on Father's Day in 2005, a book which proved her superb ability, once more, to capture the drama of a courtroom (Garner 2016). In another extraordinary demonstration of the virtues of *resilience* and *responsibility*, Garner spent eight years following the Farquharson case, through two trials and three appeals, the last failing in 2013, upholding his conviction for murdering his three sons.

Garner would go on to win a second Walkley Award in 2017, in the 'Feature Writing, Long (Over 4,000 Words)' category, for another tragic story about the death of children, this time writing about South Sudanese refugee Akon Guode, a woman who drove her car into a lake, drowning the three youngest of her seven children (Garner 2017a). In that instance, the judges described her article as 'gripping, wise, honest and true, bringing her novelist's eye and humanity to bear' (Walkley Foundation 2017). Once more Garner's commitment to her subject exemplified her possession of the virtues of *courage, empathy, honesty, responsibility* and *resilience*. But in 1993, it is reasonable to assume that the prestige of a Walkley Award win, along with the special commendation by the judges of the Gold Walkley Award, the prize for best journalist, would have certainly elevated Garner's growing public and professional profile as a writer of note (Walkley 1994).

It is helpful, when conducting our close textual analysis of Garner's article, to also consider the physical layout of the feature in *Time Australia* magazine and the paratextual material that accompanied it (Genette 1997). An appreciation of the overall framing of the article can provide a counterbalance to what necessarily becomes a fine-grained and at times quite technical explanation of complex narrative tools such as 'narratorial presence', which refers to where the reader imagines themselves to be in relation to the action taking place in the story (Lee 2011, iv). Garner's *Time Australia* cover story begins on page 23 and runs across three double pages. The story includes four beautifully executed watercolour illustrations

7 CHILDREN: A CASE STUDY   153

by John Spooner, now one of Australia's most renowned artists and a multi-Walkley award-winner, but who, in 1993, had not yet celebrated his first Walkley (Walkley Foundation 1994). As cameras were not permitted in the courtroom, the media had to send their own artists to capture the likenesses of those involved. The first of Spooner's illustrations is a full-page drawing of Aiton in the dock of the courtroom that is accompanied by a blurb listing his sentence of 22 years for killing Daniel and concluding with the sentence, 'Novelist Helen Garner sat through both trials' (Garner 1993, 22).

It is significant that Garner is referred to as a novelist, as by promoting Garner's fiction writing credentials, *Time Australia* was preparing readers for a more 'literary' read than they could reasonably expect from a news journalist trained in reporting facts. Garner's instructions issued by the magazine editors, to go beyond the 'cumbersome day-to-day court argument' of the 'dailies' and instead 'try to get inside the family, to know some pattern to the neglect, abuse and indifference', provides clear evidence of both the editor's motivation and the faith that was invested in Garner to deliver on such an ambitious brief. The aim of the blurb is to establish Garner from the outset as a reliable narrator, one who has attended both trials, demonstrating the virtues of *responsibility* and *resilience*. The cover and subsequent layout of the story make it clear to readers that Garner is a respected novelist worthy of the commission by the magazine to cover the 'trial that shook Australia'. Implied in the chosen wording on the cover is the assumption that Garner also possesses the virtue of *honesty* and, as we will see in the section below on the often-neglected topic of the emotional labour of the journalist, she also has the emotional intelligence to provide readers with insight into Daniel's death.

But first we will address the question of to what extent Garner was able to acquit her brief to 'report the case as a whole' (Walkley 1994, 81). Under the headline 'How we lost Daniel's life', Garner prepares readers for the unflinching answer to the question of her story's title, 'Did Daniel Have to Die?' By using the collective pronoun 'we', Garner is framing her article from the outset as an examination of the communal virtue of *responsibility* of a society to care for its more vulnerable members. Garner's feature consists of three main scenes. The first examines the final hours of Daniel's life through to the questioning and charging of Aiton for his murder. The second scene outlines Daniel's short life, including a tragic roll call of witnesses who failed to act to ensure that the two-year-old was taken out of harm's way. The third and final scene details the jury's verdict

154   J. MARTIN

and concludes with Garner's own scathing assessment of the man found guilty of murdering Daniel, the mother whose role it was to protect him and the community who failed to provide a safety net for the abused toddler. As our following discussion will demonstrate, Garner communicates how emotions such as sympathy and concern can only be transformed into virtues such as *courage*, *empathy* and *responsibility* through action—action that could have saved Daniel's life.

Garner opens her narrative with a question: 'What sort of a man would beat a little boy to death?' Remembering that readers have the benefit of Spooner's full-page illustration of Aiton on the left-hand page next to Garner's story, she describes 32-year-old Aiton as:

> a very big man, a tradesman who wears colourful shirts, thin ties and boots that have decorative chains; but at first glance, in the dock, he looked oddly like a child himself. On his heavily muscled body, with its overhanging belly and meaty hands, sat the round, hot-cheeked face of a boy who'd been sprung, who was in serious trouble, but who glared back at the world with eyes that sometimes threatened to pop out of his head with indignation and defiance. (Garner 1993, 23)

Garner's finely tuned observation of details takes the reader beyond Spooner's evocative drawings. Readers can confirm Garner's description in Spooner's illustration of Aiton's 'overhanging belly and meaty hands' and note how he has the 'hot-cheeked face of a boy'. Garner's depiction of a man we know is a convicted murderer, a man who has beaten a child to death, is rendered even more unsettling when he is presented, not as some unrecognizable monster but as 'oddly like a child himself', as '*infantile*' (emphasis in original, 23.) Her description of Aiton as someone who 'glared back at the world' with 'indignation and defiance' communicates to readers that he lacks a sense of *responsibility* for his actions.

On the right-hand side of the second double page is another watercolour illustration, this time of a neighbour, with the caption: 'Wayne Williams with the headguard he made for Daniel Valerio: a gesture of helpless kindness?' The illustration highlights Garner's observation:

> These witnesses are not 'bad people.' They are ordinary citizens who go about their daily business as best they can, trying to sleep at night. They saw the marked child, they harboured suspicions. Their instinctive response was correct. What stopped so many of them from speaking or acting? (Garner 1993, 24)

7 CHILDREN: A CASE STUDY   155

What Garner captures in her description is the *lack* of virtue exhibited by the witnesses, specifically a lack of *responsibility* for Daniel's safety, a lack of *courage* to speak up for a little boy who was unable to defend himself. She goes on to describe how Wayne Williams, who sometimes baby-sat Daniel and his siblings, made the makeshift headguard after he noticed how often Daniel had bruises on his 'temples, eyes, forehead and back of the head' (24). Once more Garner's prose takes the reader beyond Spooner's image by writing:

> When this colourful contraption was shown to the jury, onlookers sobbed. It seemed a gesture of helpless kindness by a good, gentle man—but wasn't it misdirected? Wayne Williams used to change Daniel's nappy. Hadn't he seen the bruises in places where the normal bumps and trips of toddlerhood don't reach?

Garner's decision to use the phrase, 'helpless kindness by a good, gentle man' reiterates the unbreakable link between being a person of virtue and being a person of action. Garner directs readers to consider whether Wayne Williams *can* be considered a good man if he failed to recognize Daniel's abuse and take the *right* kind of action. A more effective action that Williams could have taken would have been to alert the authorities to the abuse Daniel and his siblings were suffering. Daniel needed responsible adults to shield him from the violent man who would kill him, not a handmade helmet, which, no matter how well-meaning, could not and did not save the toddler from Aiton's relentless violence. In our discussion of Aristotle in Chap. 4, we noted that while emotions are essential ingredients in virtues they must be felt 'at the right times, about the right things, towards the right people, for the right end and in the right way' (Kristjánsson 2018, 20; Aristotle [1106b17–35]). If the emotions are too intense, such as Aiton's rage at Daniel, or too 'slack', as was Wayne's response to Daniel's 'clumsiness', then it is clear the result is not virtuous but detrimental, and in this instance, fatally so (Aristotle 2019, 26 [1105b26–28]).

Another example of too 'slack' an emotional response to be considered virtuous can be found in the testimony of Wayne's wife, Sylvia Williams. On the final double-page spread there is an illustration on the left-hand page with the caption: 'Sylvia Williams: Daniel called her "Mum"' and the pull-out quote 'Sylvia found a large scrotal swelling on Daniel. Cheryl "didn't know it was there"'. Garner, in her recounting of Sylvia Williams's testimony, raises once more the question of *responsibility* and accountability for what happened to Daniel. While readers may well ask why Sylvia Williams did not act, the larger, unanswered, question is how Cheryl Butcher could fail to see such an obvious injury on her son and, if she did see it, why she did not act to protect her son from harm. Garner's introduction to Sylvia Williams as the best friend of Daniel's mother provides some insight into how both women shared a disturbing discourse that, if not directly culpable for the toddler's death, certainly allowed the abuse to continue. Garner informs readers that Sylvia parroted the testimony of Daniel's mother, that the toddler was 'clumsy and accident prone', that 'all children bump into things' and that the boy must be suffering from a 'blood disorder' (26). Again, her inability or unwillingness to recognize the abuse that Daniel was suffering demonstrates a deficit of virtue, namely *responsibility* and *honesty*, even if, in the best-case scenario, that lack of honesty went as far as Sylvia Williams deceiving herself. Finally, on the last page of the story, on the right-hand side, mirroring the image of Aiton at the beginning of the article, is a full-length illustration of Cheryl Butcher, which spans the height of the page, with the simple caption: 'Cheryl Butcher, Daniel Valerio's mother'.

The effect of the layout is that the two women seem to be facing each other across Garner's prose. While certainly less confronting than the photo of a battered Daniel, Spooner's images are compelling in a different way: they draw the reader's gaze *because* they are illustrations, providing readers with a tangible reminder that their view of the courtroom can only come to them through intermediaries such as the artist and the journalist. In my own response as a reader, I have found that even now, reading the article 27 years after its publication for what must be the 100th time, I find myself scanning Spooner's drawing of Cheryl Butcher in a maddening search for any hint of emotion that might be hiding there. My search then draws me back to Garner's prose for insight, which, as I will discuss shortly, ultimately leaves me with the awful realization that some horrors can perhaps never truly be explained.

MAINSTREAM MEDIA COVERAGE OF DANIEL VALERIO'S DEATH

Garner was writing at the height of media attention over Daniel's death, covering the second trial that had to be convened after the first jury failed to reach a verdict on whether or not Aiton had murdered the two-year-old boy in 1990. There was no media coverage at the time of Daniel's death, a fact that is not in itself unusual, as the media are prohibited under law to publish any details once a person has been charged that may prejudice an upcoming court case. A year later, in November 1991, the internal protective services inquiry report was leaked to a newspaper, a full four months after the report was completed (Goddard and Liddell 1995, 359). As mentioned earlier, because Garner was present at the initial trial in October 1992, she was able to provide readers with the description of how, when the first jury was dismissed, 'many of its members [were] in tears of apparent frustration' (Garner 1993, 27). It was this second trial in early 1993 that received the most extensive media coverage, including the aforementioned concerted and ultimately successful campaign spearheaded by the Murdoch-owned Melbourne tabloid, the *Herald-Sun*, and picked up by other media and community groups, to introduce mandatory reporting of child abuse by professionals in Victoria. The *Herald-Sun*'s 'Save Our Children' campaign not only followed the court case but also created its own news by organizing a public forum on mandatory reporting and encouraging readers to write to the state government to change the law (Goddard and Liddell 1995, 360). Victoria's 'dual track' system of reporting to either the police or welfare staff was abolished and the new law required police and members of medical and nursing professions to be mandated to report 'where they believe on reasonable grounds that a child is in need of protection because of physical injury or sexual abuse' (Swain 1994, 88).

The *Herald-Sun*'s campaign was not without its critics who pointed out that paradoxically, it was unlikely that Daniel Valerio's life *would* have been saved by mandatory reporting as 'those people who needed to know of the case to protect Daniel' *did* know about it before his death (Goddard and Liddell 1995, 356). Also, experts questioned the effectiveness of the introduction of mandatory reporting 'at a time of extensive cuts to support and prevention services [which] arguably increased rather than lessened the possibility of further such deaths occurring' (Mendes 2000, 51). In terms of newsworthiness, researchers Goddard and Liddell noted:

158   J. MARTIN

this is the type of child abuse tragedy that the media relish ... a protective service that failed to respond but which passed messages to the police that never arrived; procedures that were not followed; 21 professionals who could not recognize abuse, even severe, apparently obvious child abuse; an electrician who immediately recognized abuse when highly trained and highly paid professionals did not; and a child who reported abuse and provided the weapon used. (Goddard and Liddell 1995, 359)

It can be argued that the facts of the Daniel Valerio case are sufficient on their own to cause anyone hearing them to feel strong emotions such as horror and outrage. It is therefore worth considering just how different is Garner's writing from that of a news story and how much that difference matters in the communication of virtues to readers. Surely the news that a child has been murdered is a shocking enough fact on its own, whether it is read in a news article, heard on the radio, seen on television, communicated by a friend, or, in the digital age, posted on any one of a myriad of social media platforms, to evoke an emotional response in the listener? The very survival of a society depends upon its ability to protect its children. The argument can be made that writing such as Garner's is little more than a continuation of a journalistic curve, providing more detail but, at its core narrative level, not markedly different from a news story or another feature story on the same topic. But such a reductionist approach robs us of the opportunity to examine how a writer of Garner's calibre operates the different narrative levers and storytelling devices she has mastered in such a way that her writing is celebrated and remembered nearly 25 years later as a 'beautifully written story' (Walkley 1994). Let us briefly compare an example of a daily newspaper report at the time with Garner's own prose. A short news article in the *Canberra Times* on 30 September 1992 recounted how the Victorian Supreme Court heard from Rink Jacob De Vries, a former painting work colleague, how Aiton:

allegedly said he had told the child to stand in a 'star' position, with his arms and legs outstretched, then kicked the child between the legs making him fly through the air. However, Mr De Vries said that after he spoke sharply to Aiton, Aiton stopped talking about Daniel and never brought the subject up again. (*Canberra Times*, 30 September 1992, 4)

Interpreting the same testimony Garner writes:

7 CHILDREN: A CASE STUDY **159**

The third workman, however, when Aiton bragged about his custom of making Daniel 'do a star':—stand with his legs and arms spread, upon which Aiton would kick him so hard between the legs that he flew across the room—finally jacked up. This workmate told the court that, distressed, he had 'spoken very sharply' to Aiton. In fact, he had sworn and said, 'People like you should be put away.' In this bleak story of moral paralysis and missed opportunities, even a few sharp words stand out like an act of goodness. (Garner 1993, 26)

The above example illustrates how Garner's writing goes beyond a simple accounting of the facts, providing additional dialogue to convey the disgust and anger felt by De Vries by using the typically Australian slang phrase 'finally jacked up', which conjures a vivid image of the men in the workplace. Garner then provides her own commentary on the proceedings, effectively delivering her own verdict when she writes that this is a 'bleak story of moral paralysis', her word choice conveying a keen sense of despair and hopelessness to readers that is not evident in the necessarily tight structure of the news brief. Garner, unlike the news article, does not use De Vries's name and while this would be considered a serious omission in a news report, in her long-form feature this narrative decision renders 'the third workman' as one among a number of witnesses who heard but did not act to help Daniel.

Garner's feature is also complemented by the inclusion of a news feature by the court reporter Karen Kissane, which informed readers that there 'were 30 Daniels last year' and that in Australia, 'the family is the epicentre of violence: 44 per cent of all homicides are family related, and babies under one year are more likely to be murdered than any other group in the community. Home is a castle for some but a dungeon for others' (Kissane 1993, 24). The inclusion of Kissane's article provides readers with a more traditional news reporting style, one that cites relevant facts and figures and outlines the key issues surrounding child protection. In a similar way to Spooner's illustrations, Kissane's article provides another counterbalance to Garner's descriptive narrative. But with or without Kissane's strong news article to read in concert with Garner's feature, I would still disagree with the Walkley judges' description of Garner's story as a one that 'presents the sensitive issue of child abuse dispassionately and in a way which broadens perspective' (Walkley 1994, 81). Garner's article is exquisitely structured, it is beautifully written, and it is forensically detailed, but it is certainly not, as the *Macquarie Dictionary*

160 J. MARTIN

defines the term 'dispassionate', 'free from or unaffected by passion; devoid of personal feeling or bias; impartial; calm' (Butler 2017). And this is not a flaw. Instead it is Garner's ability to harness her own emotion and present it to her readers with the greatest of discipline that has ultimately elevated her feature above the daily news churn to what Papacharissi (2015, 23–24) refers to as the 'longue durée' or 'long haul' of history. And, at the risk of over-analysing the judges' word choice, I describe Garner's story as one that 'deepens' rather than 'broadens' perspective (Walkley 1994, 81). Rather it is Kissane's article, with her succinct analysis of the Victorian justice system, that aims to inform, and in the process, broaden the readers' perspective. In contrast, it is Garner's ability to capture what may appear as the trivial details of those she writes about, what Wolfe referred to as evidence of a person's 'status life' (Wolfe 1973, 31–32), to communicate her own thoughts as well as those expressed by those in the courtroom, that *deepens* the reader's understanding of the microcosm of family, friends, neighbours and ultimately, professionals who failed Daniel. Garner's narrative structure that positions her as the reader's eyes and ears in the courtroom means she is challenging us to examine ourselves and our role within our communities.

The Virtue Paradigm: A Theoretical Compass

Discourse Analysis

In this section, I will demonstrate how discourse analysis can help illuminate the dominant power structures that were operating within the media's coverage of Daniel Valerio's death. As we will recall from Garner's entry into the Walkleys, her editor, Michael Gawenda, noted that her article had an 'enormous response from *Time* readers, and may well, with other media, have contributed to subsequent government action on compulsory reporting of child abuse' (Walkley 1994, 81). First, a reminder of our discussion in Chap. 4 of what discourse analysis (DA) is and what critical discourse analysis (CDA) is not. Neither approach is beholden to a close textual analysis, which we will perform in the next section. Instead, the basis of our approach is to accept 'the opacity of language' and to critically examine the dominant assumptions and judgements that inform Garner's story. To put it simply, no matter how beautiful the prose and how evocative the images created by the writer, every word, every phrase, every description is a deliberate choice, a construction for specific ends, a discourse. In Garner's case, her explicitly stated 'brief' was 'to get inside the family, to know some pattern to the neglect, abuse and indifference' (Walkley 1994, 81). Our discussion proceeds on the understanding reached in Chap. 4 that CDA, which is neatly described as 'DA with attitude', is *not* a method but a mindset; as van Dijk argues, 'being critical … is a state of mind, an attitude, a way of dissenting, and many more things, but not an explicit method for the description for the structure or strategies of text and talk' (van Dijk 2013).

With this in mind, we will consider how the mainstream media covered the Daniel Valerio case. A 1995 case study, written with the aim of helping social workers engage more constructively with the media, examined the 'successful though paradoxical' campaign by the *Herald-Sun* to introduce mandatory reporting as a response to Daniel Valerio's murder. As we will recall, the paradox was that those who had the power to protect Daniel already knew of his case and simply failed to act (Goddard and Liddell 1995, 356). Researchers Goddard and Liddell noted the 'moral panic' approach adopted by the *Herald-Sun*, which is in line with Mendes's subsequent identification of the tabloid as pursuing a socially conservative, family-orientated approach (Mendes 2000). Goddard and Liddell also pointed out how the *Herald-Sun*'s decision to pursue their 'Save Our Children' campaign and push for the introduction of mandatory reporting, created a media groundswell, making it 'extremely difficult for the other media to ignore it' (361). The key for other media such as *Time Australia* magazine was in how they approached the story, and, as our analysis will demonstrate, Garner's feature provides fascinating insight into the social discourse of the role of the family and the community in protecting children.

In a case study of two daily Melbourne newspapers, the aforementioned Murdoch-owned tabloid, the *Herald-Sun*, and the then Fairfax-owned broadsheet, the *Age*, sociologist Philip Mendes identified the different agendas of each publication. On the one hand, Mendes argued, the media coverage, as evidenced in the Daniel Valerio case, had identified 'structural deficits in child protection resourcing and practice' as well as 'inspiring socially equitable and effective reforms'. But the media reporting, particularly by the tabloid press:

> had been ill-informed and sensationalist, concerned primarily with articulating a social conservative agenda in defence of the traditional family, rather than identifying the real causes of, and possible solutions to, child abuse. (Mendes 2000, 58)

162   J. MARTIN

Mendes noted that the *Herald-Sun*'s approach was socially conservative and concerned with defending the nuclear family from 'allegedly subversive or deviant groups such as incompetent and/or authoritarian state social workers, or, alternatively, individually abusive parents' (55). This conservative agenda, in turn, 'almost certainly reflects the concern of powerful economic and ideological interests to attribute social problems to individual pathology, rather than to structural disadvantage'. Such an approach also advocates 'simplistic and immediate solutions to complex child protection problems' (56).

In contrast, the *Age* 'generally eschewed simple coverage of individual cases' to focus on 'broader structural reform agendas' (Mendes 2000, 55). Mendes concluded that the coverage of child abuse issues in the Victorian media had resulted in both positive and negative results for reform. Specifically, Victoria's 'dual-track' system of reporting to either police or child protective services was scrapped, and some professionals (police, child protection workers and medical practitioners) were mandated to report any 'reasonable grounds' they had to suspect a child was being physically abused. The impact of those changes was circumscribed by an increasingly poorly funded child protection sector. In addition to the 'moral panic' response identified by Mendes is the tendency of the media, particularly the tabloid press, to create 'folk devils'. In the *Herald-Sun*'s coverage of the Daniel Valerio case, Mendes argued it was the social workers who were labelled as the 'principal wrongdoers' as their 'professional failure to protect children is presented as far worse than the actual deeds of the criminally convicted abuser' (53). While both the 'moral panic' and 'folk devil' approach are flawed in the way that they imply the media 'independently orchestrate public opinion' (54), both frameworks do provide insight into how the media can amplify and also influence the public's perception.

Having articulated the dominant social discourses driving the media coverage of Daniel's death, the conservative discourse of the tabloid press to protect the traditional family and preserve the status quo and the more socially progressive approach to systemic change adopted by broadsheet publications such as the *Age*, we will now turn to Garner's coverage for *Time Australia* magazine (Garner 1993). Garner's portrayal does seek to hold the community to account. She does this by challenging the assumption that the checks and balances of government protective services, the police and the courts are adequate safeguards against child abuse. Garner's feature is book-ended with the assumption that Daniel's death is

7 CHILDREN: A CASE STUDY **163**

a community *responsibility*, which in itself steers readers away from the creation of 'folk devils' who can be used as scapegoats. This is evident from the title, 'How *We* Lost Daniel's Life' (emphasis added), which in Garner's anthology of her non-fiction writing is titled 'Killing Daniel', and in her excoriating pronouncement in the final paragraph that 'What happened to Daniel Valerio reflects on us all' (Garner 2017b, 185–192). In her summary Garner answers her own question, 'Why did the murder of Daniel Valerio pierce the public heart, pack the court, even bring some of the first jury back to the retrial to hear the outcome of this haunting story?' with the insight that it was because 'Daniel's fate was not confined within the pathology of the fractured family. It unravelled slowly, offering multiple entry points to at least 20 official agents of what we like to think of as our collective decency. And yet Daniel was lost.' While it is of course clear that Aiton murdered Daniel Valerio and is therefore responsible for his death, Garner's writing does not give readers the easy comfort of simply shaking their heads at how such a crime was able to happen when so many adults could and should have intervened.

Garner, in her persistent questioning of readers, captures a sense of why there was such a huge outpouring of anger and grief at Daniel's death. When Garner asks what sort of a man would beat a little boy to death, many readers would respond with 'a monster', but her subsequent description of Aiton as 'a boy who'd been sprung' deflates such an assumption, forcing readers to look beyond a simple folk devil characterization. When Garner writes 'At least there was a certain intensity in his demeanour' and subsequently provides readers with the opportunity to compare Aiton's demeanour to 'the dead boy's mother', Cheryl Butcher, who 'displayed the dull eyes and defeated posture of a woman whose path through life is joyless and without drive', the full tragedy of Daniel's death becomes clearer. Daniel's only hope against the violence of a full-grown man was the other responsible adults in his life. But his own mother is 'defeated' and 'without drive' and did not protect her son, and other adults who might have protected the toddler demonstrated a lack of moral energy. In February 1994 the deputy state coroner, Iain West, said that while there was insufficient evidence that Butcher was a party to the physical abuse, 'the evidence was overwhelming that she must have known Aiton was physically abusing her children' (*Canberra Times* 1994). Mr West said, 'It should be self-evident that every member of the community carries the onus of child protection and that to remain apathetic in the knowledge of abuse occurring is to grossly fail to discharge that onus.' Garner contrasts

164   J. MARTIN

Aiton with the doctors who presented evidence: 'What they conspicuously seemed to lack, and what Aiton perversely seemed to possess, was *energy*' (Garner 1993, 23).

It is unsettling reading Garner's story more than a quarter of a century after it was first published, primarily because the images she conjures of Daniel's life and death have lost none of their impact. One such image is his seven-year-old sister Candice's teacher, who saw Daniel at a school open day and 'sobbed in court as she described the "picture which still haunts her"': Daniel's "ghostly white face", his bruised temple, his unfocused, listless stare, his utter lack of response' (Garner 1993, 27). It is timely for me to reiterate that, in terms of reader-response criticism, I recognize the role of the reader in the creation of meaning and acknowledge myself as a reader with the specialist skills of a feminist scholar and former journalist but also with what Sarbin would call my own 'full emotional life' (Sarbin 1995, 214). As this book is intimately concerned with how writers encourage readers to experience emotion, and *honesty* is one of the six virtues of the Virtue Map, I feel it is also appropriate for me to acknowledge that my analysis is informed by my own experience of a violent father. My complex reaction to Garner's following descriptions of Daniel's mother demonstrates the power of a narrative to intersect with a reader's own emotional life.

> How could she not have known what was being done to Daniel? What deal did she make with herself to allow her child to suffer the brutality of her boyfriend Aiton in exchange for his company, his pay-packet—for the simple fact of not being manless? And how could she, the night after her little boy dies, agree to marry the man who had killed him? (Garner 1993, 23).

For those of us personally affected by family violence, whose mothers also failed to protect them, Garner's questions raise particularly difficult questions of *honesty*, accountability and *responsibility*. Garner then provides readers with further context about Butcher's own upbringing and life as a young mother:

> She [Butcher] had her first child at 17. Her relationships with men have been chaotic and soon broken. Now she has lost one child through violence and had two others ... taken from her soon afterwards and given into the custody of her previous de facto, Michael Valerio. (Garner 1993, 23)

As a feminist media scholar attuned to detecting and analysing the gendered nature of power and informed by my own childhood, I acknowledge how Butcher's own life experience may have circumscribed her ability to act. Reading Garner's writing nearly three decades after it was first published, we have the benefit of how societies worldwide have become more aware of and sensitive to the many ways in which women and children can be controlled by men financially, physically and emotionally. The #MeToo movement has also contributed to a greater recognition of how the abuse of women is a global issue, impacting women from all races and economic and social backgrounds. In a 2009 interview Butcher spoke out about what she saw as the Victorian State Government's failure to stop systemic child abuse (Pilcher 2009). But, in the final analysis, Garner's forensic accounting of the facts of the case laid bare the fatal price Daniel paid for the inaction of those adults who were meant to care for him and protect him from harm—and as Daniel's mother, Cheryl Butcher had the strongest duty of care to protect her son. My own personal reactions to Garner's description of Butcher have included a combination of outrage at Butcher for failing to protect her child, through to a desperate searching for reasons—economic, social and cultural—that may have circumscribed her duty as a mother to shield her son from Aiton's violence. I have even, at different points of reading the article over the years, been consumed with a righteous, and misplaced, anger at Garner herself for describing a woman and a mother in such harsh terms. Such is the power of Garner's prose that she is able to lay the foundation for readers like myself to wrestle with difficult themes and wrenching questions—questions that Garner makes clear have no easy answer. Garner's writing expands the 'horizon of concern' of her readers, challenging long-held, sometimes subconscious beliefs (Lonergan 1990, 31; Fitterer 2008, 88).

We see further evidence of Garner challenging prevailing community attitudes around the gendered nature of violence when she shifts the focus back to Aiton's accounting of events, writing how he 'hadn't meant to harm the boy, certainly not kill him' and how 'Everybody knows that a child's crying has the power to derange, and that some people—especially those who, like Aiton, have been mistreated as children—lack the resources to control their own violent tendencies'. Garner then writes, 'It seemed at the time a simple case of a bloke's having "lost it", as Aiton put it, gone berserk under pressure, lashed out' (Garner 1993, 24). To characterize Garner's description as reinforcing a dominant patriarchal discourse, a trap I have admittedly fallen into myself, is both a misreading and an oversimplification of her writing. Such an interpretation fails to appreciate how

Garner, by raising the point of view that a 'bloke' may have 'lost it', problematizes and ultimately destroys this flawed argument, as Aiton's abuse against Daniel was no momentary lapse but a sustained pattern of behaviour. Unfortunately, the idea that a man, if pushed hard enough, will go 'berserk' still persists, as is evident in a 2019 report by the independent, not-for-profit organization 'Our Watch' that includes media guidelines addressing 'common misconceptions' (Our Watch 2019). Among these is the view that 'Men "just snap" or violence is "sparked" by an argument or event', when the research shows that '80 per cent of men who murdered their partners had a history of abusing them' (Our Watch 2019).

When Garner goes on to recount how Daniel's death was not the result of one catastrophic act of violence but the end in a long line of beatings, the reader is directed once more to the mother who met Aiton through an introduction agency in February 1990; soon afterwards, he moved into her house. As we will recall, deputy state coroner Iain West was scathing in his condemnation of Butcher's role in her son's death:

> Tragically, not only did she abandon her children to persistent physical abuse by leaving them in that environment and remaining silent, but she also persisted in a line of conduct designed to direct attention from her de-facto. (*Canberra Times* 1994)

Garner reports that Butcher did not take Daniel to his follow-up appointment at the hospital after the doctors found that her son did not have a 'blood disorder', but he only had 'a slower than normal blood clotting time' (Garner 1993, 26). Garner does write how the police video of the unfinished Rosebud home:

> gave onlookers a pang of sympathy. Everyone can imagine the strain of moving into an unfinished house with three small kids in tow at the end of a Melbourne winter: the thronging plastic bags, the stained and sheetless mattresses, the incongruous pale pink leather lounge suite, the unconnected electrical wiring poking through holes in the plaster. (Garner 1993, 26)

In the above passage, we find evidence of Garner's ability to write an evocative scene by employing status markers that capture the chaos and lack of privilege of the home where Butcher lived with three of her four children and her partner. As Garner wrote herself, 'Cheryl Butcher has not been charged with any crime' but:

7 CHILDREN: A CASE STUDY   167

In a strange way, Aiton's conduct is easier to understand than Butcher's: we may loathe it, and believe it should be punished, but we can see what he did. Action is easier to grasp than inaction, somehow. Chery Butcher's behaviour remains enigmatic, the kind of thing that people lose sleep over, trying to puzzle out the meaning of such passivity, such apparent abdication of responsibility. (Garner 1993, 27)

Garner, through her forensic observation and the subsequent conclusions she draws about Cheryl Butcher, forces readers to confront their own complacency, their own assumptions that mothers are the greatest champions and protectors of their children. Mendes's research found that the coverage of Daniel Valerio's case by the *Herald-Sun* had a strong focus on defending the sanctity of the family (Mendes 2000, 55). But Garner confronts the danger of lionizing the notion of 'the family'. In her article she asks whether it was 'fear' that prevented those who 'saw the marked child' from 'dobbing', or 'were they captives of the resilient myth of the nuclear family, the ability of the most pathetic and vicious collection of children and parents to throw up a stockade around themselves, a force-field that repels outsiders?' (Garner 1993, 24). If Garner does deal in generalizations, she does so in order to expose the flawed thinking that informs them, not to reinforce dominant discourses that undermine community.

Emotional Labour

As seen in Chap. 6, within journalism scholarship there is a growing understanding that journalists engage readers by explicitly carrying some of the 'emotional load' themselves in their stories. Viewing Garner's feature through the fresh lens of the Virtue Map contributes to a more multifaceted perspective of emotional work within contemporary journalism. Garner conveys to readers a sense of her own emotional labour invested in Daniel's story and, through this process, establishes herself as a reliable narrator. First of all Garner was present in court for every day of Aiton's two separate murder trials. This fact alone communicates to readers that Garner feels a keen sense of *responsibility* to witness what happened to Daniel, as well as possessing a great deal of emotional *resilience* to be able to cope with the trauma of writing about the murder of a child. The Dart Center for Journalism and Trauma, established in 1999, acknowledges the emotional toll covering traumatic issues can take on writers and advises on self-care for journalists to protect themselves from any long-lasting harm,

168   J. MARTIN

such as the manifestation of post-traumatic stress symptoms (Smith et al. 2015).

Garner is the 'everywoman' through whose eyes we, the reader, must trust for our understanding of 'How we lost Daniel's life'. Her recounting of the stark facts of Daniel's case, such as the autopsy report which stated a 'pint of blood' was found in the toddler's abdominal cavity, in addition to 104 bruises that were counted on 'the tiny corpse, inside and out' are clear evidence of the courage needed to report and write on the case. In addition to the physical evidence there is the upsetting statements by witnesses, such as the work colleague of Aiton who told the court Aiton had 'boasted' about 'hitting Daniel on the penis with a wooden spoon' or the neighbour who 'used to hear screaming "over the sound [of] the television" that was so intolerable to her that she would go out driving in her car until it was over' (Garner 1993, 24). Such accounts demonstrate an astounding want of moral energy. Garner conveys a sense of both Daniel's ordeal and the burden of bearing witness to that ordeal when she writes how 'Daniel's slide towards the day of his death, it now became clear, was a long, slow process'. The weight of the terrible inevitability of Daniel's death is captured vividly in Garner's summary:

> The rest of the story reads, now, like a race between heavy-footed bureaucracy and a sleeker, livelier force. The boy was adrift. The people with the power to save him strolled, fumbled and tripped; and Aiton got there first. (Garner 1993, 27)

Garner's use of the trope of a 'race' is particularly effective to describe a case of child abuse, as it really is a 'race against time'. Tragically, in Daniel's case, no one else in the race could mobilize themselves to outstrip Aiton's violence. What is striking throughout Garner's writing is how tight a control she keeps on her own emotions, as illustrated by the previous examples. Nowhere is her ability to harness her emotion and use it to fuel her message for readers more powerful than in the last paragraph of her story. She writes:

> What happened to Daniel Valerio reflects on us all, on our private and public natures. It stirs up deep fears about us and makes us frightened and ashamed. I don't see how it is possible to contemplate Daniel's story without acknowledging the existence of evil; of something savage that persists in people despite all our enlightenment and our social engineering and our safety nets,

something that only philosophy, religion or art can handle: the worm in the heart of the rose.

In her conclusion Garner delivers a judgement on all of us and, in the case of Daniel Valerio, declares that we, as a society, as a community whose sacred *responsibility* it is to care for and raise our children to ensure our very survival, have failed. But her message is all the more effective for the way in which she wields the narrative tools at her disposal, speaking to readers directly, evoking emotions such as fear and shame and naming Aiton's actions as 'something savage', as 'evil'. In an interview marking her 75th birthday, Garner had this to say about the challenge of expressing emotion in her writing:

> If you let your emotions out at the moment when you're contemplating the thing, you lose that coolness where you can actually see what the thing is ... That's the point of it: If you can hold back your emotional response to something, just hold it in check, not destroy it or trample on it, but hold it back until you are away from the situation, then you see more. (Carey 2017)

Habermas's Theory of Validity

Garner's feature can also be viewed in terms of Habermas's validity claims, which were discussed in detail in Chap. 4. The four claims are truth, appropriateness, sincerity and comprehension.

We can reasonably claim that Garner's writing, having won a Walkley Award, passes 'the test of readability' and conveys 'information in a way that can be understood by the reader' as the judges described her story as 'beautifully written' (Walkley 1994, 81). Her choice of topic, 'the sensitive issue of child abuse' also meets the 'appropriateness' requirement as it addresses a 'question of relevance that is considered important' and is 'in the public interest' (Walkley 1994, 81). As for the question of truth, it is also reasonable to claim that Garner was informed about the topic and that her claims were based on evidence, specifically, what was presented in court. Garner was reporting on a court case and her story is based on the testimony of witnesses and the submission of evidence. Her feature can be considered sincere as it presents a different viewpoint. An analysis of Garner's 'sincerity' in Habermasian terms must be counterbalanced by her own views and the creative licence she takes in her description and characterization of witnesses. In the example of Garner, the Virtue Paradigm,

170   J. MARTIN

specifically the consideration of Habermas's theory of validity, exposes the complexity of feature writing and the issue of subjectivity. In the final analysis of Garner's feature, there is ample evidence that she is striving throughout, in a convincingly sincere manner, to present readers with an *honest*, accurate and also thought-provoking representation of the story of Daniel's short life and his tragic end.

Schudson's Functions of News in a Democratic Society

In order to decide to what extent Garner's feature article is an example of phronetic journalism it is helpful to consider Schudson's seven functions of news in a democratic society: information, investigation, analysis, social empathy, public forum, mobilization and promoting a democracy. As we discussed in Chap. 4, I have added an eighth function, 'identity', which takes into account the role the media plays in showing society to itself, for better or for worse. It is important to remember that Garner is not writing a 'straight' news story and we will recall her brief from *Time Australia* magazine was to 'go beyond the day-to-day court reporting'. As our following brief discussion will demonstrate, it is the accompanying news article by court reporter Karen Kissane that more easily fits Schudson's model. It was and is common practice in both newspaper and magazines to run 'breakout' stories or 'sidebars' to provide readers with the factual background and overview of a topic that is not included, or expected to be included, in a feature article. Rather, as is the case with Garner and Kissane, the two forms complement each other. Within the Virtue Paradigm, Schudson's functions of news are an instructive broad framework through which to view long-form narrative journalism, as long as we proceed on the understanding that we are not dealing with the shorter, inverted pyramid style news article or longer news feature.

Taking the limitations of Schudson's model for our purposes into consideration, it is Garner, through her coverage of both of Aiton's murder trials, which included her accurate reporting of the facts of Daniel's death, and her summary of the toddler's life, who provides readers, with 'fair and full information' so that the 'citizenry can make sound political choices' (Schudson 2008, 339). Garner includes information from the autopsy report, which found Daniel 'had died of internal bleeding from abdominal injuries' and that 'Many of his organs were bruised, his duodenum was ruptured, and the mesentery (the membrane that anchors the intestines to the back wall of the abdomen) was torn in several places' (Garner 1993,

23). Garner's feature does not provide the full context her readers would require in order to make a deeply informed opinion about the complex child protection services and the division of duties between childcare workers and the police. Instead, that responsibility is borne by Kissane in her accompanying article, 'No Place Like Home', which informs readers of how and why children are murdered and how, even if Daniel's beatings had been properly identified, he may still may not have been removed from his home.

In terms of Schudson's criterion of 'investigation', Garner certainly provides readers with a comprehensive timeline of Daniel's last hours, and notes in withering prose how and when the toddler could have been, but wasn't, saved by his mother, neighbours, child protection workers and police. But again, it is Kissane's news article, which includes an interview with the head of Victoria's Children's Protection Society and the president of the National Association for the Prevention of Cruelty and Neglect, that more clearly investigates 'concentrated sources of power, particularly government power'. For example, Kissane explains that the 'decades of widespread removal of children from families have shown that alternative care has big drawbacks too' (1993, 24). Garner's investigation relates more to the 'patterns' that she is trying to capture, resulting in an exploration of the psychological and emotional landscape of those at the trial. This is evident when she asks the previously discussed questions about how Daniel's mother and, to a lesser degree, the next-door neighbours, Wayne and Sylvia Williams, could have not known about the toddler's abuse.

In the final analysis Garner's writing can be described as fulfilling Schudson's criteria of 'analysis' and 'social empathy' to the extent that she does 'provide coherent frameworks of interpretation to help citizens comprehend a complex world' and she certainly 'tells people about others in a society so that they can appreciate viewpoints'. Although in terms of objective analysis, once again, Kissane's news story more strongly aligns with Schudson's criteria and Garner's feature provides more of a psychological probing and analysis of the witnesses from her subjective viewpoint—which, again, does not undermine the impact of her story. For example, she tells readers that the witnesses are not 'bad people' but 'ordinary citizens' and asks, 'What stopped them from speaking or acting?' In other words, why were these people unable to move from an internalization of their observations of Daniel to demonstrating the virtues of *honesty, courage, empathy* and *responsibility* that could have saved his life?

In order to consider whether Garner's work meets Schudson's final three criteria of 'public forum', 'mobilization' and 'promoting a democracy' it is necessary to view her feature story within its wider social context. As we will recall from what *Time Australia* editor, Michael Gawenda, wrote on the Walkley entry form, Garner's article 'had an enormous response from *Time* readers, and may well, with other media, have contributed to subsequent government action on compulsory reporting of child abuse' (Walkley 1993, 81). My reservations with the Walkley judges' wording aside, their comment that her story 'presents the sensitive issue of child abuse dispassionately and in a way which broadens perspective' demonstrates that Gawenda's claim has merit (Walkley 1993, 81). While Garner was not writing for the tabloid *Herald-Sun* and so not a part of that paper's 'Save Our Children' campaign that included holding public meetings and encouraging readers to write to politicians (clear evidence of providing a public forum, mobilization and promoting a democracy), her feature can be considered an important part of the media's overall response to the deep flaws Daniel's death exposed in the child protection system.

Finally, it is on my own criterion of identity that Garner's article shines in the way that she pushes readers to confront the stark courtroom reality of a child's murder trial. Although Garner is ostensibly covering the trial she is also putting us, the community, on trial and also subjecting the justice system itself to close scrutiny. Garner, who dedicated her 2016 book *This House of Grief* to the Victorian Supreme Court, said in an interview: 'It's a world where mighty archetypes clash and work themselves out. I can see the terrible faults there are in trials, but I had this strange feeling of love for the old building itself' (Wyndham 2015). Garner's respect for the court system is evident in the way she harnesses her own observations and knits these into her detailed descriptions of the evidence and testimonies of witnesses to show readers what the murder trial of a child looks like. It is in her efforts to transport readers into her narrative world that we are all called to bear witness to Daniel's tragic death.

OUR IMAGINED COMMUNITY

Garner challenges readers to examine any concept they may have of belonging to a virtuous Australian society, which, to use Anderson's terms is, necessarily, an imagined shared concept of identity (Garner 1993; Anderson 1983, 48). At different stages of her feature Garner chooses to increase the distance between the subject and the readers by shifting to a description of the court room, utilizing what Aare refers to as a 'touched up third person narration', meaning, in this instance, that Garner has 'been present in reality but has been edited out of the scenes' (Aare 2016, 133). This has the effect of establishing her as a reliable narrator since readers are able to imagine they are witnessing the events being described. Garner then shifts the narrative voice between the third-person style of narration to a 'dimmed first person narration' (Aare 2016, 134), in which the reporter is present but can only be glimpsed through the text, before transitioning smoothly to the overt first-person voice, demonstrating how this careful directing of the reader's gaze can encourage them to experience Simmons's definition of *full empathy*, which includes emotions of sympathy, compassion and kindness (Simmons 2014, 97). While Garner's employment of narrative voice and reporting of the court's proceedings certainly fulfils journalism's civic *responsibility* to 'strive to make the significant interesting and relevant', it is her narrative skills, her mastery of storytelling techniques, providing readers with the opportunity to be immersed and transported into her narrative world, that are responsible for the immense power of this feature (Kovach and Rosenstiel 2014, 9).

Within Garner's narrative, the imagined virtuous community is represented by the onlookers in the courtroom, including members of the jury, and readers are encouraged to align with their responses through her construction, responding to the testimony of the witnesses. In terms of the complex effect of narratorial presence, this courtroom scene is an intricate demonstration of Coplan's theory of how 'it is possible for a reader to move in and out of different perspectives, those of different characters or different perspectives on the overall narrative' (Coplan 2004, 149; Lee 2011, 8–9). Garner's opening description of Aiton in court encourages the readers to view the scene through her eyes, as if sitting next to her in the courtroom. She directs our gaze to Daniel's mother and then provides a small sketch of Cheryl Butcher's 'chaotic and broken' relationships with men. Daniel's last hours are described and then the details of the autopsy report are presented to readers. Garner's choice of scenes has the effect of pulling the reader's focus so that sometimes the narratorial presence is extremely intimate, as when Butcher tells the court that Aiton was 'very clinging' to her when he was being questioned by police. At other times the overall effect of the narratorial presence is more distant, as when Garner described the manner of the doctors who gave testimony to the court as 'limp, their language feeble and non-committal' (23–24).

174   J. MARTIN

Garner constructs a narrative that unflinchingly addresses the failure of the Australian legal system to protect children. One of the most effective ways she achieves this is by using the first-person voice to answer her own question, 'Why did the murder of little Daniel Valerio pierce the public heart?' (27). Garner's narrative, written by her for an imagined community of virtuous readers, achieves what Anderson has termed 'emotional legitimacy' by presenting readers with evidence of how Daniel's death may have been prevented if the adults surrounding him—adults that could have been any of us—had acted with the virtues of *responsibility* and *empathy* (Anderson 1983, 48). Garner's direct *questioning* of her readers about the public's shocked reaction to the murder of a child intensifies the phronetic element of this article, that is, its potential to contribute to the flourishing of a community by investigating how such a rupture in the fabric of a community—the murder of a child—occurred. Daniel Valerio died despite multiple visits from government social workers to his home, a documented medical history of physical injuries and the suspicions of neighbours.

Garner's article exemplifies phronetic journalism, narrative journalism that permits readers to experience full *empathy* and to consider how such a rupture in society's conception of virtue and civility, the expectations its members have of their own and others' behaviour, can be repaired—by punishing the offender—and prevented from occurring in the future. The first-person voice is crucial in enabling Garner to create a narrative that narrows the distance between readers and the subject of the article and also allows her to present readers with difficult issues such as society's failure to protect a child who desperately needed protection (Aare 2016, 107). A key component of Garner's narrative is the emotion of collective guilt, the belief that as a community we have failed to live up to our virtues of protecting our most vulnerable members, our children. Garner, by beginning her final paragraph with 'What happened to Daniel Valerio reflects on us all, on our private and public natures' is challenging readers to question their own behaviour and the wider role of belonging to a community; she is asking readers to consider how far we have fallen short of the ideal of who we think we are and to consider what we imagine our ideal virtuous community should look like. Moving into the first-person, Garner continues her personal and probing tone. In the following quote, which we will recall from our earlier dicussion forms part of Garner's conclusion, she uses the collective pronoun 'our' to imply a sense of community ownership over what happened to Daniel:

7 CHILDREN: A CASE STUDY   175

I don't see how it is possible to contemplate Daniel's story without acknowledging the existence of evil: of something savage that persists in people despite all *our* enlightenment and *our* social engineering and *our* safety nets. (Garner 1993, 27; emphasis added)

Words such as 'evil' and 'savage' are very likely to make readers uneasy, and also possibly even ashamed, about the society which unequivocally failed Daniel Valerio. Garner's construction, informed by the journalistic method and enriched with the skilled use of narrative devices, demonstrates Ahmed's argument that emotion 'defines the contours of the multiple worlds that are inhabited by different subjects' (Ahmed 2004, 25). Garner's inclusion of reporting elements such as forensic details of Daniel's injuries and physical descriptions of the accused and the witnesses consolidates her authority to present the events accurately. But it is her ability to communicate the smallest of moments that elevates her writing to the level of what the judges described as a 'beautifully written story'. One such moment is found in Garner's description of the reaction of a juror to the senior defence counsel when he said that Aiton could not be a sadist because he had brought flowers for his partner on their anniversary. Garner writes:

One of the older women on the jury, in unconscious rejection of this line of rhetoric, set her lips and slowly, firmly shook her head. It was clear at that moment that Aiton was a goner; that the defence's theatrical appeal to the complexity of human psychology and to our lack of right to make moral judgments, was missing its mark; that the muffled, phlegmatic summing-up by the prosecution, with its central image of the man's huge fist pounding into the sick child's tiny, aching abdomen, had entered the souls of that jury, and lodged there. (Garner 1993, 27)

Throughout her feature, Garner has pushed and prodded at her readers, forcing us to confront the tragedy of a toddler's death at the hands of a violent man who had been terrorizing the children in his care for months. Through her skilful weaving of the evidence of witness statements, doctors' reports and the final findings of the autopsy Garner would not let us look away. She asks the heart-breaking question, 'Did Daniel have to die?' and then she leads us on a brutal journey that explains 'How we lost Daniel's life' in the 2017 edited collection of her 'true stories'. Daniel's death was not sudden, it was not an accident or an aberration; and it was not inevitable. It was the result of multiple missteps and oversights and the sheer unwillingness of grown adults to admit what their eyes had shown them. Not all the misplaced emotions in the world could have saved Daniel. Only action, right, virtuous action could have stood against the violence of Aiton. And when that man, the electrician, did stand up and break through the 'force-field', the authorities were too slow to act, and a toddler died. But Daniel Valerio's killer *was* brought to justice. He stood trial, twice, before a jury of his peers and it is in the fact of Aiton's conviction that Garner gives her readers some hope that future children may be protected from abuse. It is captured in Garner's description of the older woman on the jury, in the set of her lips and the slow, firm shake of her head. For that juror, too, could be any of us. We decide. A killer was found guilty and was sentenced to 22 years' jail. The community failed to save Daniel, but that same community jailed his killer and then in the wake of the trial the community acted to change laws to ensure no other child would suffer his fate.

In conclusion, our examination of Garner's narrative construction has demonstrated how a journalist, through employing narrative devices and professional media skills, including direct quotes, the use of the first-person voice and scene setting, can urge readers to consider the consequences of what happens when a society fails in its fundamental duty to protect its own children. The universality of the need to protect our children is captured in the response of a Spanish reader who read Garner's story under the title of 'Killing Daniel' and said the story:

> shocked me so much that, in the absence of a punching ball, I jumped out of bed, put my shoes on and went for a run until my rage subsided. And I know—or thought I knew—how to control my anger. (Garner 2017b)

As our Spanish reader demonstrates, Garner has created within her narrative the conditions for readers to recognize that when a violation as serious as the murder of a child occurs, the rupture to the fabric of society is so deep the community falls not just below human standards but even below the nurturing instincts of most sentient beings.

REFERENCES

Aare, C. 2016. A Narratological Approach to Literary Journalism: How an Interplay between Voice and Point of View May Create Empathy with the Other. *Literary Journalism Studies* 8 (1): 106–139.

[ACNJ] Australian Colonial Narrative Journalism. 2015. About. *AustLit*. Brisbane: University of Queensland. Accessed May 18, 2020. https://www.austlit.edu.au/austlit/page/12870667.

Ahmed, S. 2004. Collective Feelings or, the Impressions Left by Others. *Theory, Culture and Society* 21 (2): 25–42.

Anderson, B. 1983. *Imagined Communities: Reflections on the Origin and Spread of Nationalism*. London: Verso.

Aristotle. 2019. *Nicomachean Ethics*. 3rd ed. Translated by T. Irwin. Indianapolis: Hackett.

Benson, R.D., and E. Neveu. 2005. *Bourdieu and the Journalistic Field*. Cambridge: Polity.

Butler, S., ed. 2017. *Macquarie Dictionary*. 7th ed. Sydney: Macquarie Dictionary Publishers.

Canberra Times. 1992. Man "Bragged about Kicking Boy in Air". September 30, 4.

———. 1994. Tot's Mum Aware of Abuse: Coroner. February 19, 11.

Carey, P. 2017. Helen Garner, "Surrounded by BS", Still Telling it like it is on Her 75th Birthday. ABC Radio National, November 7. https://www.abc.net.au/news/2017-11-07/author-helen-garner-tells-it-like-it-is-on-75th-birthday/9123322.

Coplan, A. 2004. Empathic Engagement with Narrative Fictions. *Journal of Aesthetics and Art Criticism* 62 (2): 141–152.

Fitterer, R.J. 2008. *Love and Objectivity in Virtue Ethics: Aristotle, Lonergan, and Nussbaum on Emotions and Moral Insight*. Toronto: University of Toronto Press.

Garner, H. 1993. Did Daniel Have to Die? *Time Australia Magazine*, March 8, no. 10, 22–27.

———. 1995. *The First Stone: Some Questions about Sex and Power*. Sydney: Picador.

———. 2016. *This House of Grief*. Melbourne: Text Publishing.

———. 2017a. Why She Broke: The Woman, Her Children and the Lake: Akon Guode's Tragic Story. *Monthly*, June. https://www.themonthly.com.au/issue/2017/june/1496239200/helen-garner/why-she-broke.

———. 2017b. Killing Daniel. In *True Stories: The Collected Short Non-Fiction*, 185–192. Melbourne: Text Publishing.

Genette, G. 1997. *Paratexts: Thresholds of Interpretation*. Translated by J. Lewin. Cambridge: Cambridge University Press.

Goddard, C., and M. Liddell. 1995. Child Abuse Fatalities and the Media: Lessons from a Case Study. *Child Abuse Review* 4: 356–364.

Habermas, J. 2001. Truth and Society: The Discursive Redemption of Factual Claims to Validity. In *On the Pragmatics of Social Interaction: Preliminary Studies in the Theory of Communicative Action*, trans. B. Fultner, Chap. 5. Cambridge: Polity Press.

Hill, J. 2019. *See What You Made Me Do: Power, Control and Domestic Abuse.* Melbourne: Black Inc.

Kissane, K. 1993. No Place Like Home. *Time Australia*, March 8, 24–25.

Kovach, B., and T. Rosenstiel. 2014. *The Elements of Journalism: What Newspeople Should Know and the Public Should Expect.* 3rd ed. New York: Three Rivers Press.

Kristjánsson, K. 2018. *Virtuous Emotions.* Oxford: Oxford University Press.

Lee, C. 2011. *Our Very Own Adventure: Towards a Poetics of the Short Story.* Melbourne: Melbourne University Press.

Lonergan, B.J.F. 1990. *Method in Theology.* Reprint. Toronto: University of Toronto Press. Originally published in 1971.

Mendes, P. 2000. Social Conservatism vs Social Justice: The Portrayal of Child Abuse in the Press in Victoria, Australia. *Child Abuse Review* 9: 49–61.

Our Watch. 2019. How to Report on Violence against Women and Their Children—2019 National Edition. Accessed July 21, 2020. https://media. ourwatch.org.au/resource/how-to-report-on-violence-against-women-and-their-children-2019-national-edition/.

Papacharissi, Z. 2015. Toward New Journalism(s). *Journalism Studies* 16 (1): 27–40.

Pilcher, G. 2009. Mother of Daniel Valerio Lashes Abuse Failure. *News.com.au*, August 16. Accessed June 19, 2020. https://www.news.com.au/news/ mother-of-daniel-valerio-lashes-abuse-failure/news-story/cba529ca5e65281d7cc36fb6f04e90a6?sv=eade8303ae738b5fab51b6ec24543543.

Ross, M. 2014. Mother in Shock after Son Killed by Father at Cricket Oval. *ABC News*, February 14. Accessed June 14, 2020. https://www.abc.net.au/ news/2014-02-13/mother-in-shock-after-son-killed-by-father-at-cricket-oval/5258252?nw=0.

Royal Commission into Institutional Responses to Child Sexual Abuse. 2017. Final Report: Impacts. Vol. 3. Accessed June 14, 2020. https://www.childabuseroyalcommission.gov.au/sites/default/files/final_report_-_volume_3_impacts.pdf.

Sarbin, T. 1995. Emotional Life, Rhetoric, and Roles. *Journal of Narrative and Life History* 5 (3): 213–220.

Schudson, M. 2008. *Why Democracies Need an Unlovable Press.* Malden, MA: Polity.

Simmons, A. 2014. In Defence of the Moral Significance of Empathy. *Ethical Theory and Moral Practice* 17 (1): 97–111.

Smith, R., E. Newman, S. Drevo, and A. Slaughter. 2015. Covering Trauma: Impact on Journalists. Dart Center for Journalism & Trauma. Accessed July 21, 2020. https://dartcenter.org/content/covering-trauma-impact-on-journalists.

Swain, P. 1994. Legal Studies: Mandatory Reporting of Child Abuse—A Step in the Right Direction? *Alternative Law Journal* 19 (2, Apr.): 88–89.

van Dijk, T.A. 2013. CDA is NOT a Method of Critical Discourse Analysis. Association of Studies on Discourse and Society (EDISO) Website. Accessed May 31, 2020. https://www.edisoportal.org/debate/115-cda-not-method-critical-discourse-analysis.

Walkley. 1994. *AMP W.G. Walkley Awards Directory and Diary*. Media Entertainment and Arts Alliance. Melbourne: Education Image.

Walkley Foundation. 1994. 'Walkley Winners Archive' Accessed January 15, 2021. https://www.walkleys.com/awards/walkley-winners-archive/

Walkley Foundation. 2016. 'Jess Hill: "Suffer the Children: Trouble in the Family Court" Feature Writing Long'. Accessed January 15, 2021. https://www.walkleys.com/award-winners/feature-writing-long/.

Walkley Foundation. 2017. Helen Garner: "Why She Broke: The Woman, Her Children and the Lake": Feature Writing Long (Over 4000 Words). Accessed July 21, 2020. https://www.walkleys.com/award-winners/feature-writing-long/.

Wolfe, T. 1973. The New Journalism. In *The New Journalism*, ed. T. Wolfe and E.W. Johnson, 3–36. New York: Harper and Row.

Wyndham, S. 2015. Robert Farquharson Case Struck Author Helen Garner with "a Terrible Gong of Horror". *Sydney Morning Herald*, August 15. https://www.smh.com.au/entertainment/books/robert-farquharson-case-struck-author-helen-garner-with-a-terrible-gong-of-horror-20140812-102jqn.html.

CHAPTER 8

Disadvantaged or Socially Marginalized: A Case Study

CHLOE HOOPER 'THE TALL MAN'

Monthly, no. 10, 6 March 2006
Winner, 2006 Walkley Award for Magazine Feature Writing
Judges' comments:

> Hooper's investigation into the coronial inquest on Palm Island was a standout. Respecting the world she visited, she created a sense of immense empathy and allowed readers to immerse themselves in the lives and minds of Palm Island's people. The description, the sense of threat and the atmospheric details were exceptional. (Walkley Magazine 2006)

THE VIRTUE MAP

(Individual virtues are italicized in this chapter for easy identification.)

- *Courage*: The survival of the Aboriginal population of Palm Island is a living testament to the courage of the people.
- *Empathy*: Hooper's own expression of empathy for the Palm Island community. The empathy expressed by Cameron Doomadgee's sister, Elizabeth Doomadgee, towards the police.
- *Honesty*: The desire of the Palm Island community for the truth about Doomadgee's death. A week after Doomadgee's death on 19

© The Author(s), under exclusive license to Springer Nature
Switzerland AG 2021
J. Martin, *Emotions and Virtues in Feature Writing*,
https://doi.org/10.1007/978-3-030-62978-6_8

181

November Palm Islanders rioted, demanding justice. Hooper's own pursuit of truth and the honesty that is evident in her own reporting. The lack of transparency and honesty in the actions of the police following Doomadgee's death.

- *Responsibility*: The Palm Islander community's fight to find who was responsible for Doomadgee's death and to have those responsible held to account. The holding of a coronial inquest to investigate the death in custody. The responsibility of officer-in-charge, Senior Sergeant Hurley to care for those in his custody. The responsibility of the Aboriginal police liaison officer to represent the Palm Island community. The responsibility of the government to protect all of its citizens equally and our own responsibility as a community.
- *Resilience*: The lived reality of the resilience of the Palm Islanders in the face of long-term, ongoing and systemic injustices.
- *Phronesis*: Hooper's article contributed to a wider media narrative that informed the public of the ongoing quest of the Palm Islanders for justice over the death in custody of Doomadgee and the wider issue of Aboriginal deaths in custody. Hooper also wrote a book on the topic, as well as a follow-up article on Palm Island after the coronial inquest (Hooper 2006b, 2008) (Table 8.1).

Table 8.1 Individual Virtue Map, Chloe Hooper 'The Tall Man'

Winning feature	Chloe Hooper 'The Tall Man'	
Publication	*Monthly*, no. 10: 34–53	
Date	6 March 2006	
Categories	Children	
	Marginalised and disadvantaged	•
	Citizens	•
	The nation	•
Virtues	Courage	•
	Empathy	•
	Honesty	•
	Resilience	•
	Responsibility	•
	Phronesis	•

INTRODUCTION

This book is about mapping virtues. Across the landscape of our narratives, the ink of long-form stories flows like rivers. It takes time for in-depth narrative journalism to fill the community wellspring and burst its banks to overflowing, carving out waterways that traverse previously dry landscapes, bringing awareness and knowledge to far-flung cities and towns. This is why, before we begin the following case study of Hooper's 2006 long-form narrative, 'The Tall Man', about the death of an Aboriginal man in custody on Australia's remote Palm Island, we will pause to position her article as one among many that helped swell the long, snaking river of past stories that have exposed injustice against Aboriginal Australians. These include past Walkley Award-winning stories such as Bonita Mason's 1997 article about the death of 30-year-old Janet Beetson, who died in prison simply for want of heart medication, or Richard Guilliatt's 1999 story about the landmark legal battle fought by Australia's Stolen Generation against a government that had forcibly removed 'half-caste' children from their Indigenous families. It is estimated that as many as one in three Indigenous children were taken between 1910 and the 1970s (Healing Foundation 2020). Another is Melissa Lucashenko's 2013 salutary reminder of the lived experience of poverty of Indigenous Australians in one of the nation's poorest suburbs, Logan, in southeast Queensland. These stories are part of the river that slowly gathered momentum until, at the time of writing this chapter in June 2020, it burst its banks and reached the international waters of the global 2020 Black Lives Matter protests (Black Lives Matter n.d.; *Guardian* 2020; Jash 2020).

It is not possible within the confines of this book to include an in-depth analysis of all of the voices that have spoken and continue to speak out against injustice for people of colour through long-form journalism narratives. But it *is* important to acknowledge that the phronetic striving of journalists to expose all social disadvantage and marginalization, whether due to colour, race, religion, gender, disability or age, is a fundamental tenet of the profession and a collective journey that has no end. It is also important to acknowledge how vital a role is played by writers and media commentators who have written and continue to fight to bring injustice against Aboriginal Australians to light. One example is the speech given in 2015 by Australian reporter and Wiradjuri man Stan Grant. The speech, which went viral when it was published online in January 2016, was described by fellow Australian journalist Mike Carlton as Australia's

184 J. MARTIN

'Martin Luther King moment' (Tolj and Huffadine 2016). In part, Grant said:

> The Australian Dream is rooted in racism. It is the very foundation of the dream. It is there at the birth of the nation. It is there in *terra nullius*. An empty land. A land for the taking. Sixty thousand years of occupation. (Grant 2015)

As Hage summarizes so poignantly, Australians 'relate to ourselves and our land in the way that people who were thieves in the past relate to themselves and to what they have stolen and kept' (2003, 152). And while this chapter focuses on a case study about Australia's First Nations people, the Virtue Map category of 'social injustice and marginalization' applies also to the experience of indigenous people around the world, as well as those discriminated against because of their race, gender, religious beliefs or economic status.

'HELP ME!'

In June 2020, tens of thousands of protestors rallied around Australia in solidarity with the international Black Lives Matter movement under the banner 'Stop black deaths in custody' (*Guardian* 2020; *ABC News* 2020a). Protestors carried placards with messages that included, 'Same story: different soil', 'Who do we call when the murderer wears the badge?', 'I can't breathe' and 'Stop killing us' (Willing 2020). The protests spread worldwide after the killing of George Floyd by police in the US (Johnson 2020; *ABC News* 2020b). In Australia, the protestors called for justice for David Dungay, an Aboriginal man who died in a Sydney prison in 2015. Dungay suffered from bipolar disorder and was diabetic. His family said that, like Floyd, his last words were, 'I can't breathe' (Martin 2020). The protests also followed the release of video footage of a policeman kicking a 17-year-old boy's legs out from under him and pinning him to the ground with the help of two other officers (Kidd 2020). A key factor in the global outpouring of anger and grief was the visual evidence of police brutality against their black victims.

For many people, clicking the computer link resulted in a powerful act of witnessing that moved many to act where before there had been silence. Although long-form journalism lacks the immediate, visceral impact of viewing an act of injustice, a writer of Hooper's calibre is nonetheless able

8 DISADVANTAGED OR SOCIALLY MARGINALIZED: A CASE STUDY 185

to provide readers with the opportunity to bear witness to terrible acts of injustice through the creation of a compelling narrative. The written word provides readers with the opportunity for a deeper, more sustained consideration of the issue, in contrast to the immediate shock of watching visual footage. The following haunting passage describing Doomadgee's last moments alive is one example of what the Walkley judges described as Hooper's 'exceptional' writing skills:

> The cell's surveillance tape shows Doomadgee writhing on a concrete floor, trying to find a comfortable position in which to die. He can be heard calling, 'Help me!' Another man, paralytic with drink, feebly pats his head. Before he dies Doomadgee rolls closer to the man, perhaps for warmth or comfort. (Hooper 2006a, 39–40)

In the above passage Hooper has created the conditions for the reader to empathize with Doomadgee's helplessness and, in his dying moments, his need for human comfort, evidence of the 'immense *empathy*' (my emphasis mine) that the Walkley judges commended her for. Hooper's citing of the visual evidence also provides readers with an *honest* account of events, framing her story with the foundational question of who will take *responsibility* for Doomadgee's death. In terms of narratorial presence, readers have the opportunity to imagine themselves viewing the cell's surveillance tape or perhaps positioned even inside the cell itself, alongside the dying man. In one succinct paragraph, Hooper provides the reader with different levels of perspective, from the intimate, awful observation of a man's death to prompting a consideration of the broader social, cultural and political context of how and why that death was allowed to happen.

A HISTORY OF OPPRESSION

The experience of disadvantage and social marginalization inflicted upon Australia's First Nations people since colonization has been brutal, systemic and sustained. A report by the *Guardian* Australia, who have developed a website documenting Aboriginal deaths in custody, found that more than Aboriginal people have died in custody since the Royal Commission into Aboriginal Deaths in Custody ended in 1991; since 2008, more than half of the Indigenous people who have died in custody had not been convicted of a crime (Allam et al. 2019, 2020; Wahlquist et al. 2018). The report found that in 39 per cent of Indigenous deaths

186   J. MARTIN

medical care was required but not given. Despite mental health or cognitive impairment being a factor in 43 per cent of all deaths of Indigenous people in custody, they received the care they needed in just 51 per cent of cases. Indigenous women were even less likely than men to have received all appropriate medical care prior to their death, and authorities were less likely to have followed all their own procedures in cases where an Indigenous woman died in custody (Wahlquist et al. 2018).

CRITICAL DISCOURSE ANALYSIS: SETTLER COMMON SENSE

As discussed in Chap. 5, the most recent publicly available data shows that 31 per cent of Indigenous people are living in poverty in Australia (Markham and Biddle 2018) compared with a poverty rate for the whole population of 13 per cent (ACOSS 2020). Hooper's decision to open her article with the following quote from the 1904 annual report of the Northern Protector of Aboriginals provides her readers with valuable historical context of an overwhelmingly paternalistic attitude: 'They are and will always remain children, and therefore must be protected, even sometimes against their will' (Hooper 2006a, 34). Her inclusion of the quote at the beginning of a story about an Aboriginal death in custody also suggests to readers that such an attitude still prevails. A more recent example of paternalism was the 2007 Northern Territory Emergency Response, also known as the Intervention, when the conservative federal government led by John Howard sent the army in to gain control of 73 remote Indigenous communities following a media storm over child sexual abuse claims. The government action disregarded human rights and imposed race-based discriminatory policy that still has implications today (Waller and McCallum forthcoming, 5).

In long-form journalism, the social justice narrative is often accessed by readers through emotions such as shock, anger or sadness in response to the stories they read. As discussed in Chap. 5, I have used the social justice narrative to include magazine features beyond the scope of stories that concern Indigenous issues by renaming the Virtue Map category of 'Aboriginal Australian' with the theme of 'disadvantaged or socially marginalized'. In common with Waller and McCallum, I draw on the work of North American scholar Mark Rifkin and his theory of 'settler common sense' as a helpful framework for a critical discourse analysis of Hooper's writing, one which looks beyond overt racist practice to ask:

8 DISADVANTAGED OR SOCIALLY MARGINALIZED: A CASE STUDY   187

When and how do projects of elimination, replacement, and possession become geographies of everyday non-native occupancy that do not understand themselves as predicated on colonial occupation, or on a history of settler–Indigenous relations (even though they are), and what are the contours and effects of such experiences of inhabitance and belonging? (Rifkin 2014, 9)

Within this context, settler colonialism is viewed as a 'persistent societal process', one that has 'meant genocide of Indigenous peoples, and the reconfiguring of Indigenous land into settler property' (Waller and McCallum forthcoming). While the news media has played and continues to play a part in the consolidation and defence of the settler viewpoint, it also, as my analysis of Hooper's article will demonstrate and as Waller and McCallum note, 'has the power to disrupt it' (Waller and McCallum forthcoming). Our discussion is premised upon the understanding that, as part of the discourse of the dominant settler culture, '*Our* wealth is only made possible by *their* poverty' (Waller and McCallum forthcoming, 4). Settler common sense which views poverty 'as just one of the many social indicators of disadvantage, not dispossession', is a major cultural blind spot that writing such as Hooper's can help illuminate (Waller and McCallum forthcoming, 8). As Waller and McCallum succinctly put it:

First Nations poverty and its manifestation on every social and economic index have been a fact since European colonizers arrived and began pillaging the Indigenous estate more than 200 years ago, appropriating all the land and waters and stealing its material wealth. The settler society's intense discomfort with this living history and refusal to make reparations has the ongoing effect of silencing and bending public discourse in ways that avoid dealing with the truth. (Waller and McCallum forthcoming, 1)

BOURDIEU AND HABITUS

It is also important to contextualize the Walkley Awards themselves within an overarching framework of race relations within Australia. Considered in Bourdieu's terms—that is, in the kind of cultural and social dispositions that define it—Australia's top journalism prize is, by definition, a highly subjective and elitist field (Wacquant 1992, 16). In my larger study of 23 long-form stories, six were written about Aboriginal issues. The judges of the feature writing category were, to my knowledge, all white and were in their turn selected by journalists who were also all white (Martin 2017).

Indigenous writer Melissa Lucashenko was one of the judges for the All Media: Coverage of Indigenous Affairs Walkley Award in 2014 (Blackman 2016, 2017).

In terms of Bourdieu's notion of habitus, which consists of 'a set of historical relations "deposited" within individual bodies' the judges have been moulded by the many factors a range of places, such as their upbringing, education and workplace' (Wacquant 1992, 16; Bourdieu 2005). Essentially the judges, who are part of the ruling settler culture, are acting from a position of privilege and power. They have the privileges of being white and of being professional journalists in the position of deciding what constitutes excellence in journalism. Just as they can be expected to hold the same ideals and aspirations as encapsulated in the Walkley Foundation's judging criteria, they must also be seen as part of a society that has a deeply troubled history and relationship with the Indigenous population. The feature writers are also part of the same society and are a salient example of white people writing about Indigenous people for an imagined virtuous community of predominately white readers. Five of the six feature articles about Indigenous people in my larger study of Walkley-winning long-form stories between 1988 and 2014 were authored by white journalists. The exception was Melissa Lucashenko, a writer of Aboriginal and European heritage. Her 2013 article tells the story of 3 women: one who came to Australia as a refugee at age 11 and had 4 children to an Aboriginal man, a second, who had Aboriginal ancestry on both sides of her family but identified as white, and a third, who was a white mother with four Aboriginal children. Lucashenko also positions herself and her teenage child firmly within her narrative, telling readers of her own struggles, which satisfies Habermas's validity criteria of being both truthful and sincere (Habermas 2001, Chap. 5). It is precisely because the question of Aboriginality is not an overt theme, rather an undeniable thread that connects the women in this feature, that Lucashenko's writing is a significant contribution to the ongoing narrative of Indigenous relations in Australia.

The Limits of the Imagined Virtuous Community

It is helpful at this juncture to examine the limits of my reworking of Anderson's concept of an imagined community, which is to consider how journalists such as Hooper are writing for their own imagined *virtuous* community of readers. Recent scholarship challenges the representations of the Indigenous public sphere as somehow existing separately from

8 DISADVANTAGED OR SOCIALLY MARGINALIZED: A CASE STUDY   189

other public spheres as highly problematic, because they do not include an understanding that Indigenous Australians are active consumers of and participants in the media (Latimore 2016). Nor is it helpful, as pointed out earlier, to view Aboriginal communities as a homogenous, unified group. Rather, extreme care must be taken when considering how Anderson's concept of an imagined virtuous community may apply to Indigenous Australians, or to the non-Indigenous audience of the articles. Just as there is no single, homogenous group of readers passively waiting to engage with the journalist's narrative (Anderson 1983, 48), the notion of the imagined community is particularly fraught when considered in relation to articles with an Indigenous theme. This is partly because European colonization cannot be considered as a rupture in an imagined Australian community because the nation did not exist prior to its being imagined. While there may certainly be, or may have been, an imagined Indigenous community, white citizens have no access to that community, and to assume they do so is to operate from a false premise that further denies Indigenous agency.

CASE STUDY

Chloe Hooper's 2006 article is about the death in custody of 36-year-old Cameron Doomadgee, an Indigenous man from Palm Island, a remote community about 65 kilometres northeast of Townsville in Far North Queensland. Beginning with Hooper's opening paragraph it is evident she has gone to the effort of presenting herself as a compassionate outsider on Palm Island:

> All I really knew about Palm Island were the headlines I'd been reading: 'Tropic of Despair', 'Island of Sorrow'. On 19 November 2004, a drunk Aboriginal man had been arrested for swearing at police. Less than an hour later he died with injuries like those of a road trauma victim. The Queensland State Coroner reported there was no sign of police brutality, backing up the police claim that the man had tripped on a step. The community did not agree, and a week later burnt down the police station. The state government immediately invoked emergency powers, flying in special police squads trained in counter-terrorist tactics who arrested countless locals, including teenagers and grandmothers. I went there two months later. (Hooper 2006a, 34)

190   J. MARTIN

Hooper's narrative voice performs two separate functions. First, it permits the many readers who may not be familiar with life on Palm Island, or who have had limited or no interaction with Indigenous people, to experience, through her personal observations about her own ignorance, a world very different from their own. Hooper's vivid scene-setting provides readers with the opportunity to be transported into her narrative. An example is the description of her arrival on Palm Island, which reads like the introduction to a literary novel rather than a news article, and recounts how 'the pale green sea seems so luminous and fecund' (4). Hooper informs readers that 'something is not quite right', using the literary device of foreshadowing to establish a sense of unease (34). By rendering herself highly visible as a narrator Hooper encourages her readers to position themselves alongside her in the article, identifying with her, viewing her scenic constructions through her eyes. This is further evident when Hooper writes that she notices the children's paintings on the wall with titles such as 'I feel safe when I'm not being hunted', consolidating a sense of foreboding for readers (34).

This particular combination of narrative devices establishes a strong connection with Hooper, for we as readers have been transported through her journalism to Palm Island and are relying on her for our narrative equilibrium in 'the most dangerous place on earth outside a combat zone' (34). Hooper's position as an outsider is emphasized further when she assumes that two brothers she sees 'stumbling around' are drunk, only to discover that they are blind (34). This reveals her as an observer who is very much a product of her own culture or habitus, susceptible to stereotypes about Indigenous people. Hooper demonstrates self-awareness and the virtue of *honesty* when she writes, 'my heart nearly stops. Not from fear but from shame' (34), providing a clear example of a journalist using narrative devices to express her own emotions for the purpose of establishing a bond with readers. That Hooper's choice of topic is expressed in such personal terms consolidates the importance of emotion as a means of creating a compelling narrative.

The second function of Hooper establishing herself as an empathetic eyewitness is that it positions her to write about Indigenous Australians in a manner sensitive to the cultural differences between the Palm Island community and her own experiences, or habitus, as a young, urban white woman. On the issue of white people writing on Indigenous Australians, Aboriginal researcher Jennifer Martiniello says:

8 DISADVANTAGED OR SOCIALLY MARGINALIZED: A CASE STUDY   191

> For many issues there is also a white story, not just a black story—after all, we didn't create the last 200 years of crap all by ourselves. So long as white writers are aware that there are boundaries they cannot cross when they are writing, and where or what the appropriate protocols are for dealing with Aboriginal people, their stories and their communities, then their work may be approved. (quoted by Heiss 2002, 200)

It is telling that the next moment in the narrative when Hooper expresses discomfort with her settler status is when another white woman smiles at her in the township and she is 'not sure' if she should smile back. She writes, 'I feel luminously white' (2006a, 36). Hooper's honest expression of her emotional state allows privileged white readers to imagine how they would feel if they were confronted with the reality of the disadvantage and social marginalization of Aboriginal people in remote communities like Palm Island. Hooper's use of the first-person voice, her willingness to take *responsibility* for the implications of her presence encourages readers to do the same.

Hooper then proceeds to outline Palm Island's brutal colonial history. Throughout the article, Hooper continually reinforces her viewpoint as an intruder into a community she admits she knew nothing about before her arrival. She educates and informs readers of the complex social and political context of her subject matter, as she learns about them herself, in line with the Australian journalists' code of ethics (MEAA 2020). She writes how, in 1916, the Chief Protector of Aborigines called Palm Island 'the ideal place for a delightful holiday' (Hooper 2006a, 36), which the Chief Protector qualified with the practical and disturbing statement that the shark-infested waters help to confine those 'we desire to punish' (36). Using the language of colonial discourse, Hooper delivers readers with a long list of what the 'blacks' were not allowed to do on Palm Island:

> Blacks were not allowed on Mango Avenue, where whites lived. Blacks were required to salute any white person they passed. White staff got choice cuts of meat; blacks got bones. Blacks had their milk watered down ... White day-trippers were carried to the shore on black backs ... Permits were needed to fish; permits were needed to swim. (36)

Hooper's reporting and mastery of narrative techniques provide readers with the context that life on Palm Island for an Indigenous person was one of servitude and poverty, where any protest or perceived act of

192   J. MARTIN

disobedience was met with swift, often violent, retribution. Historical facts, such as the existence of a leper colony and the 'lock hospital' for anyone with venereal disease on the island, further contribute to the readers' sense of a desolate place (36). Mention of the devastating effects of alcohol helps Hooper to consolidate the perception of Palm Island as having a traumatic history of colonial exploitation and misery. And that trauma continued, with Hooper explaining how,

> Even in the 1960s a man could be arrested for waving to his wife, or for laughing. A teenager whose cricket ball broke off a short length of branch would spend the night locked up. If anyone complained, they were sent to nearby Eclipse Island with only bread and water. On Eclipse prisoners tried to catch fish with their bare hands. (36)

After establishing her opening scene of arriving and then providing readers with a sense of the tyranny of colonial rule on Palm Island, Hooper shifts the focus to a description of the day that Doomadgee died. Hooper has positioned readers at the intersection of the historical truth of Australia's marginalization of its Indigenous people with the brutal reality of yet another black death in custody. Readers of Hooper's feature are left in no doubt that Australia's violent past reverberates in the present and into the future. She writes how Doomadgee was arrested, almost as an afterthought, for swearing at Senior Sergeant Chris Hurley and the Aboriginal Police Liaison Officer, Lloyd Bengaroo. Hooper describes Doomadgee as a 36-year-old 'happy-go-lucky character who loved to hunt and fish' and who had been drinking cask wine and '"goom"—methylated spirits mixed with water' (39). Hooper writes how witnesses outside of the police station said that: 'as Doomadgee was taken from the van, he was "going off, drunk, singing out and everything". Struggling, he hit the Senior Sergeant on the jaw. Two witnesses say they then saw Hurley punch Doomadgee back' (39). The men fell on the steps of the police station and Hurley then 'pulled his prisoner into the hallway'. Hooper writes that what Hurley did not know is that there was another Aboriginal man inside, waiting to be questioned. Roy Bramwell was at the police station about assaulting his de facto and her two sisters earlier in the day. His presence provided a glimpse into the prevalence of family violence among the Aboriginal community on Palm Island. Hooper quoted Roy Bramwell's description of Hurley beating Doomadgee:

8 DISADVANTAGED OR SOCIALLY MARGINALIZED: A CASE STUDY   193

Well, he tall, he tall, he tall, you know … just see the elbow going up and him down like that, you know, must have punched him pretty hard, didn't he? Well, he was a sober man, and he was a drunken man. (39)

When Hurley saw Bramwell, he asked him if he had seen anything. Hooper writes that Bramwell said he had not, and Hurley told him to leave. In this short exchange, Hooper presents readers with a revealing glimpse into the power structures of Palm Island and the complete lack of *responsibility* or *honesty* of Hurley. In Bramwell's case, although it can be said that he lacked the virtue of *courage* as well as *honesty* when he lied to Hurley that he hadn't seen anything, his behaviour can be understood as an act of self-preservation against getting beaten himself. Bramwell *does* tell his friends about Hurley beating Doomadgee and they *do* tell him to '"Go tell someone, tell the Justice Group". But none of them did anything. They went on drinking' (2006a, 39). While Bramwell and his friends clearly experienced an *emotional* empathy towards Doomadgee and expressed the need for someone to take *responsibility* to ensure his safety, they were unable to transform their emotions into virtue by taking action. Hooper then proceeds to describe Doomadgee's last conscious moments, calling 'help me!' (39). Hooper presents the shocking evidence of the security camera footage which shows: 'The officer kicks at Doomadgee a few times—later referred to (in the trial) as "an arousal technique"—then leans over him, realising he is dead' (40). Such a brutal end to the life of a defenceless man can be reasonably assumed to evoke the virtue of *empathy* from readers, and a desire for the virtues of *honesty* and *responsibility* to be fulfilled by the justice system. However, Hooper's detailed description of the long narrative of colonial brutality that has defined Palm Island does not instil faith that *honesty* will prevail and that justice will be served. As the Walkley judges noted, Hooper demonstrates a mastery of the narrative art of description, conveying a 'sense of threat' and providing readers with 'atmospheric details' that 'were exceptional' (Walkley Magazine 2006).

A further example of Hooper's use of atmospheric details and her ability to contrast mainstream white culture with Palm Island's Aboriginal community is how she uses the myth of the 'Tall Man' to frame her story. She recounts how, when asked about the 'Tall Man', a group of teenage boys:

194   J. MARTIN

In all sincerity, they point to a nearby light post to show the Tall Man's height. 'His feet as big as a giant's', one says. 'You can see his red eyes when the lights turned out on the football field.' Later I ask other children about the Tall Man and they report he's covered in hair, with shrivelled skin … (Hooper 2006a, 42)

Hooper describes how, in one witness statement, an old woman recalled, 'the tall man get out and arrest him. I saw the tall man grab him by the arm'. As discussed in Chap. 2, Hooper's use of a mythic element to frame her narrative strengthens the emotional connection to readers, as the imagery of this mythical discourse transports readers into her story (Green et al. 2004). Hooper employs this imagery again when she explains how Doomadgee's sister, Elizabeth Doomadgee, tells her that 'Aboriginal people have no choice but to be patient' and that it is her faith in a Christian God that helps her find the virtue of *resilience*. The island's Catholic priest, Father Tony, tells Hooper how Elizabeth demonstrated extraordinary *empathy* when she comforted a policeman who, after hearing her speak of her brother's death at a Townsville church meeting, got up to say how sorry he was and started to cry: 'Elizabeth went over and hugged him: "Brother I forgive you"' (Hooper 2006a, 46). But Elizabeth also had 'blackfella protocol', which means she could:

> put a curse on Lloyd Bengaroo [the Aboriginal Police Liaison Officer]. She could take an item of clothing off his washing line and send it to her relatives in the Northern Territory. They would make sure he'd grow sick and die. (41)

Elizabeth also tells Hooper of her community's need for the virtue of *honesty*: 'We want the truth. We want to hear the truth' (41). Later in the story Hooper recounted how the Doomadgees' paternal grandmother was Lizzy Daylight, whom the anthropologist David Trigger described as 'the grand old lady' of the Gangalidda people, a woman who 'was known to be in touch with the spiritual forces connected with Rainbow (Snake) Dreaming, and hence to such phenomena as storms, cyclones, lightning and so on' (49). Hooper's inclusion of such detail is evidence of her own sense of *responsibility* for representing the lives of the Indigenous members of the Palm Island community as more than a projection of 'settler common sense' which has traditionally categorized Aboriginal people as dependent upon alcohol and welfare. When Hooper has dinner at Elizabeth's home, she describes how she is served meat that was hunted

8 DISADVANTAGED OR SOCIALLY MARGINALIZED: A CASE STUDY   195

by Doomadgee, conveying his ability to provide for his family, to assume *responsibility*. Elizabeth ensures that Hooper and the lawyers eat first. Hooper writes, 'It is humbling to enjoy a dead man's bounty. Only after we refuse second helpings do the rest of the family also eat'. Hooper also describes Doomadgee's 15-year-old son, Eric Doomadgee, as 'a quiet, polite boy wearing an American basketball shirt'. Tragically, as Hooper wrote in an article on life on Palm Island after the death in custody inquest, Eric hanged himself on 31 July 2006, four days before what would be the final inquest into his father's death (Hooper 2006b). Sadly, on 14 January 2007, 24-year-old Patrick Bramwell, who was in the police lock-up with his uncle, Roy Bramwell (who was the man Hooper described as patting Doomadgee on the head as he died), also hanged himself (Brown 2007).

In Hooper's descriptions throughout her story of the daily lives of the Indigenous people on Palm Island, she conveys to readers their quiet *resilience*, expressing the 'immense empathy' that the Walkley judges commended her for. This *empathy* is communicated to readers who are given the opportunity to deepen their understanding of the hardships First Nation Australians face. When Hooper shifts the narrative into a description of a nightmare she would have as a child that one of her younger brothers was in danger, she allows readers to consider the shared human desire to protect those we love from harm:

> The terror came from believing I'd fail him. The fear swirled with an immediate desire for revenge. I suppose no one knows their own capacity for vengeance until the worst takes place. Elizabeth is both Christian and 'blackfella'; Old Testament and New. She can afford to love her enemy because she believes fiercely in divine retribution. ('I work for God, so he gotta work for me'). (Hooper 2006a, 41)

The intimate first-person narrative, in which the narrator explicitly shares her own experience with readers, has been referred to by researchers as adopting a 'romantic' or a 'cultural phenomenology' approach (Roberts and Giles 2014, 101–103). The effect of the device in this feature is to convey a range of complex emotions to readers through an exploration of the power relations that comprise the habitus of the lives of the Indigenous people on Palm Island. It also allows Hooper a means of introducing readers to different people on the island in a highly personal manner.

It is in Hooper's description of the coronial inquest that the gulf between the Indigenous and white communities are thrown into stark

196   J. MARTIN

relief. First of all, 'only local witnesses will give evidence on the island', with a makeshift court set up in the gymnasium, while the police, 'for security reasons, it is argued—will give theirs in Townsville' (2006a, 43). Hooper writes:

> It is distressing to watch the Aboriginal witnesses being examined and cross-examined. They are asked to read through and swear by their statements, which is impossible for the many who are illiterate. They are questioned in detail about the timing of events, but very few Palm Islanders wear watches. They are asked leading questions in complicated legalese and some of them, confused or intimidated, try to guess the correct answer. (2006a, 43)

And to ensure that the Aboriginal witnesses turned up to court sober, the lawyers, accompanied by Hooper, drove out to local homes. Hooper observes that 'What is happening here has nothing to do with justice. Most of the lawyers don't want to be on the island and some are even scared' (44). Further widening the cultural divide is the prevailing atmosphere of police protectionism. The court hears that Hurley has between 20 and 30 official complaints lodged against him, and the coroner has to stand aside 'when it is revealed he has presided over eight of these complaints, and each time adjudicated in Hurley's favour' (44). Hooper then recounts the stories mothers tell her about their sons being beaten by Hurley, including two young men who were mentally ill as well as a woman, Barbara Pilot, the deceased's cousin, who said Hurley had run over her foot with his car (44). Hooper later writes that 'Becoming a cop is a way for a man without a lot of education to gain a lot of power' and she includes the finding of the 1980s Royal Commission into police corruption in Queensland of the existence of a 'police code' which meant police did not enforce the law with each other (50). Hooper exposes this police culture by informing readers how Hurley contacted his 'good friend Detective Sergeant Darren Robinson' just 15 minutes after Doomadgee died. That officer in turn called another friend of Hurley's, Detective Senior Sergeant Kitching of the Townsville Crime and Investigation Bureau, and another policeman who also thought well of Hurley.

Hooper writes: 'It must have been reassuring for Hurley that he—the main suspect—would be investigated by old colleagues and friends' (50). Hurley even picked the men up from the airport and had dinner at his house with them. Even more damning, 'no part of the police station was made into a crime scene or sealed off. No areas were tested to see if there were matches with the blood from Doomadgee's eye. No photographs were taken of Hurley's hands or his boots and in the police transcript of Hurley's interview he is addressed as 'mate' or 'buddy' by the officer and he in turn calls the interviewer 'boss' (50). The cumulative impact on readers of Hooper's reporting and observations is to emphasize the lack of *honesty, responsibility* or any sense of *empathy* for the victim and his family or the community. By providing readers with insight into the poisonous police culture Hooper also allows readers to appreciate that within a dominant settler culture which so blatantly privileges white power, the simple fact that the Indigenous community has survived is, in and of itself, an act of *courage* and evidence of deep, ongoing *resilience* against formidable odds. With this deepened understanding comes the opportunity for readers, in turn, to experience full *empathy* for the Aboriginal community.

Hooper chooses to close her narrative with a description of the women in the courtroom who 'sit in the airless room emitting a low drumbeat of heartache', an echo of her opening reference when she thought her own heart would stop (53). This ending with such a descriptive scene communicates to readers the *resilience* and the *courage* of the Indigenous women of Palm Island to witness the process of justice. The 'airless room' can be read as indicative of the suffocating restrictions imposed upon the community by successive white authorities. Hooper writes that the women have an air of 'resigned grace' and that 'this grace is all that stands between them and chaos. It's too much: I want to leave' (53). The juxtaposition of the life of the people on Palm Island and her own is solidified in Hooper's final statement, of her relief at 'this not being my life' (53), showing how first-person narrative voice helps to convey a strong sense of place (Thomson et al. 2015) and at the same time the emotion of relief to readers (Aare 2016, 107). Hooper's description communicates her own privilege as well as the disadvantages faced by the Indigenous community she is leaving. Her narrative exemplifies the way in which journalists are able to 'seek and gain self-awareness through identifying where the self is located within a particular set of power relations and structures—in Bourdieu's terms, within a "field"' (Thomson et al. 2015, 153; Benson and Neveu 2005, 29–47). Hooper's combining of the narrative techniques of high visibility through the use of the first-person voice, along with her careful representation of her vulnerability, narrows the narratological gap between herself and the readers, providing a way for her to express emotion and notions of virtue like justice, *responsibility* and *honesty* (Aare 2016, 107).

EMOTIONAL LABOUR OF HOOPER

As we noted in Chap. 6, there is a growing appreciation within the wider study of journalism of the emotional labour invested by journalists in the creation of their stories (Pantti 2010a, b; Wahl-Jorgensen 2019). In Hooper's article, we have clear evidence of how integral the emotional investment of the writer can be, and the way in which the writer manages that investment to create a compelling narrative. It is timely to return to the judges' commendation of Hooper's respect for 'the world she visited' which is a tacit acknowledgement of the gap that exists between mainstream Australia and many of its First Nations people. As we have noted in our earlier discussions, it is action that distinguishes an emotion from a virtue. For Hooper, it is the act of writing, of creating long-form journalism that transforms her own emotional labour into the virtues of *courage, empathy, honesty, resilience, responsibility* and *phronesis* that are evident in her work. We have already discussed Hooper's use of the first-person voice to create a sense of immediacy and establish herself as a reliable narrator for readers. We will now deepen our understanding by noting how Hooper renders her own emotional labour to readers in order to communicate the challenges faced by an outsider—a white, female journalist—in writing about Indigenous Australians.

As noted earlier, Hooper establishes her outsider status from her opening paragraph, but it is when she describes her first encounter with Doomadgee's sister, Elizabeth Doomadgee, 'a handsome woman in her early forties', that we are given a sense of her crossing a threshold and accepting a sense of emotional *responsibility* for her role in covering the coronial inquest. She writes:

> Two naked toddlers are playing under a tap. Elizabeth stands at the door. She has an almost stately quality. But during this first meeting she seems fierce, as if controlling, just, a steady rage. Awkwardly, I tell her I am a writer hoping to follow the inquest into her brother's death. She is circumspect, but later in court I hear her complain to the island's chairwoman that people are taking notes. She asks for everyone other than me to be banned from writing: 'We got our writer here'. (Hooper 2006a, 40)

Hooper describes how she gets to know Elizabeth, sharing a meal with her, going out to collect taro roots, meeting other women in the community. She talks to teenagers and observes how an Aboriginal woman sitting

8 DISADVANTAGED OR SOCIALLY MARGINALIZED: A CASE STUDY   199

on the pier warns children that the man they are talking to is a policeman (40, 42, 44, 46). The cumulative effect of these scenes combined with Hooper's description of the violence that permeates Palm Island and her forensic reporting of Doomadgee's death is to leave readers in no doubt of the emotional intensity of covering such a story. But Hooper also makes this strikingly clear for the reader. We will recall how she wrote that it was 'distressing' to listen to the Aboriginal witnesses being cross-examined (43). When she writes about attending a church service, she conveys her incredulity at the words of a 'big, stern woman' who lists all the 'signs', such as murders, rapes, disease, pestilence, famine, floods and earthquakes, that show the end of the world was near (46). Hooper assumed the woman was talking about Palm Island, but when she hears her say 'We are fortunate in this community because nothing has happened to us yet', Hooper writes:

> 'Are you *serious*?' I thought. 'Are you *insane*?' ... I wanted to say, 'How much worse could things get?' In the previous month, a man had critically stabbed his brother over a beer. One woman had bitten another woman's lip off. A man had poured petrol on his partner and set her alight. There is 92% unemployment; 16 young people have killed themselves in eight months; half the men on the island will die before the age of 45. This place is like a black hole in the universe into which people have fallen. Rocks may as well have already rained down. There may as well have been an apocalypse ... We stood to sing: Yes, Jesus loves me | Yes, Jesus loves me Yes, Jesus love me | The Bible tells me so (46).

The overwhelming emotion expressed by Hooper in the above quote is frustration—frustration at the dire circumstances of the Palm Islanders and at how long they have been living with so much hardship and so little hope of improvement. Hooper's frustration conveys to readers the *resilience* of the Palm Islander community through surviving such hardship but also her outrage that they don't appear to realize the terrible extent of their own oppression. Key to the power of her emotional expression is the interweaving of hard facts to justify her outrage. Hooper then proceeds to ask if it is even possible to 'step into this dysfunction and desperation and not be corrupted in some way? Not made, in some way, mad', concluding with the searing observation that 'The church-going Palm Islanders pray to the Jesus who promised an afterlife, rather than the one who heals in the here and now, because *no one* could heal this place' (46). The extent

200   J. MARTIN

of Hooper's emotional investment, and the toll it took on her, is further evident when she tells readers: 'I thought I would be finished with this story within a few weeks. Instead, months of legal wrangling go by and part of me resents being dragged further into this grim parallel universe' (46). She further expresses her emotional fatigue when she recounts how the priest asks her if she has 'always been interested in the fate of the downtrodden' (49). She tells him no and then writes, 'I am becoming even less interested in those who are interested in the fate of the downtrodden' and recounts how 'One of them keeps talking of our spiritual journey. He thinks I'm in denial: "I can see it happening to you, even if you can't"' (49).

It is in the final section of her story that Hooper's emotional labour is palpable for readers. She describes the Palm Island women in the courtroom, how they look much older than their years and 'All of them are mothers with lost sons' and then explains how:

> I can feel their desperation for any tiny victory. 'You long for it. Long for it,' one woman tells me. She is another one who grew up in the Palm Island dormitory after she was taken from her parents. Like the others, she has a resigned grace about her. This grace is all that stands between them and chaos. It's too much: I want to leave. All I want to do is get on a plane and leave. And when I do, I feel myself shaking. I get home and I'm still shaking days later. It's overwhelming: the relief of being able to walk away from this, of this not being my life. (53)

But of course, we know that, despite wanting to 'get on a plane and leave', Hooper stayed and wrote her story, and, in the process, demonstrated her great capacity for emotional discipline. And although this was the end of her feature article, she did not walk away from the story of Palm Island and the death of Doomadgee and the wider issue of Aboriginal deaths in custody. Hooper went on to cover the second coronial inquest and the subsequent criminal trial of Hurley, who was eventually acquitted but left the police force years later following assault charges against him. Hooper published a book, *The Tall Man: Death and Life on Palm Island* (2008), and towards the end of 2019 she wrote about the death of Melbourne Indigenous woman Tanya Day in an article for the *Monthly* titled 'Remember Her Name' (2019a). Her article was a haunting echo of Bonita Mason's 1997 Walkley Award-winning feature article, 'The Girl in Cell 4' about the death in custody of 30-year-old Aboriginal woman Janet Beetson. Mason wrote her feature a decade after the 1987 Royal

Commission into Aboriginal Deaths in Custody, exposing how Beetson's death, just 72 hours after being imprisoned and caused by her not receiving her prescribed heart medication, could have been avoided if the recommendations of the Commission had been followed (Mason 1997). In her article, Mason quotes Beeston's mother-in-law, Dawn Delaney, who said, 'Through lack of care and consideration, that girl died. We can go to the moon but we can't be compassionate enough to take a girl who needs help to hospital' (61). Thirty-two years later Hooper wrote this description of Tanya Day:

> On December 5, 2017, Tanya Day, 55, boarded a Bendigo to Melbourne train. She was drunk and, as an Aboriginal woman, 10 times more likely to be arrested by Victoria Police for public drunkenness than a white woman. Half an hour later, as if in fulfilment of the statistic, four police officers were waiting for her on the Castlemaine platform. They took her from the train, put her in a divvy van and then a cell, where, barely monitored with a blood alcohol level of about 0.313, she fell, sustaining head injuries that killed her after 17 days in hospital. (Hooper 2019a).

In November of 2019 Hooper wrote an opinion piece for the *Sydney Morning Herald* titled 'Death in the Heart of the Desert Is Rewriting the Usual Script' about the death in custody of Aboriginal man Kumanjayi Walker in the remote Northern Territory community of Yuendumu. Hooper wrote how the Northern Territory Police Force's acting assistant commissioner, Travis Wurst, told a public meeting that '"Everything was recorded so what we need to do now is to find out what happened, for Kumanjayi, for your community, and for the police, so you know the truth"' (Hooper 2019b). Hooper compares Wurst's response to what happened on Palm Island 'almost exactly 15 years ago', when 'the then Queensland police commissioner, immediately pledged his support for senior sergeant Chris Hurley. He didn't send any emissary to the island, only the riot squad. There was no body camera on Hurley, there was only the seamless testimony of his colleagues'. She writes how Wurst 'sounded like a decent human being' and:

> At a moment when Australia seems ringed with fires, there's a public desire for politicians to deal with reality rather than entrenched ideology. There's also a sense that this death in the heart of the country can't just be treated like all the others. That whatever the truth—it will be brought to light. (Hooper 2019b)

202   J. MARTIN

On 27 September 2006, the Queensland Deputy State Coroner, Christine Clements, handed down her finding, which concluded that Doomadgee's death was caused by fatal injuries inflicted by Hurley. In a follow-up article, Hooper wrote:

> The courtroom took a deep collective breath. The Doomadgees all burst into tears. As one lawyer said, 'You got the sense it was the only time in a courtroom anything had ever gone their way'. (Hooper 2006b)

In her follow-up article, Hooper recounted the grim findings of a market research firm poll of more than 400 Townsville residents about their views of Aboriginal or Torres Strait Islanders in North Queensland. Just over 42 per cent of responses were 'negatively themed' and included comments such as:

> 'I don't have an opinion except to shoot them all'; 'Well something needs to be done—they have no respect, they want everything for nothing and most of them are better off than me'; 'They are mongrel dogs'. (Hooper 2006b)

Hurley was acquitted of manslaughter by a jury in June 2007. In 2016 Hurley was convicted and fined for assaulting a white man, Luke Cole, during a roadside arrest on the Gold Coast in 2013 (*SBS News* 2016). Hurley retired from the police on medical grounds in 2017 following a series of charges for assault and dangerous driving. District Court Judge Catherine Muir subsequently upheld Hurley's guilty verdict but ordered that no convictions be recorded because she accepted there was a 'direct link' between the offence and his post-traumatic stress disorder (Branco 2017). In yet another example of settler common sense, Hurley's career was reported as being in 'tatters' after assaulting a white man (*SBS News* 2016). In 2018, the Queensland government agreed to pay $30 million to settle a class action of 447 Palm Islanders over the 2004 riots following Doomadgee's death (Chen 2018). The mainstream commercial television station Channel 9 ran a story that claimed the Palm Island residents had wasted the money on 'luxury items including sports cars, luxury boats and dune buggies' (Heinke 2020). Founding managing editor of the *National Indigenous Times* and *Tracker* magazine, Chris Graham, condemned the reporting at the time as 'atrocious' and able to 'plumb new depths of gutter journalism' (Graham 2018).

The virtues of *honesty*, *empathy* and *responsibility* that we identified in Hooper's 2006 feature article are also evident in her subsequent writing. That she has continued to cover such an important and challenging issue as Aboriginal deaths in custody for years also demonstrates her *resilience*. Here, in Hooper's writing, is evidence of *phronetic* journalism, journalism that meets the four criteria discussed in Chap. 6. Her writing presents a narrative that 'is based on values, concerned with practical judgement and informed by reflection' (Kinsella and Pitman 2012, 2). Her article contributes to a debate that addresses the key question of how we live well together in a community and meets the Australian journalists' union standard of writing that seeks to 'search, disclose, record, question … suggest and remember' (MEAA 2020). And while there may not have been an immediate social justice outcome as a result of her 2006 article, what was clear, as shown in the judges' comments, was how Hooper's writing allowed her readers, through her creation of a 'sense of immense empathy' to 'immerse themselves in the lives and minds of Palm Island's people' (Walkley Magazine 2006). Finally, our discussion of Hooper's subsequent writing provides evidence for my opening argument that excellent long-form features can contribute to a body of journalism about an ongoing social justice issue—in this case Aboriginal deaths in custody—helping to raise community awareness of how the people whose livelihood and wealth we stole in order to ensure our own prosperity continue to suffer for our theft.

References

Aare, C. 2016. A Narratological Approach to Literary Journalism: How an Interplay between Voice and Point of View May Create Empathy with the Other. *Literary Journalism Studies* 8 (1): 106–139.

ABC News. 2020a. Australians Join Black Lives Matter Protests in Perth and Darwin as Refugee Rallies held in Sydney, Brisbane and Melbourne. *ABC News*, June 13. https://www.abc.net.au/news/2020-06-13/black-lives-matter-and-refugee-rights-protests-across-australia/12351952.

———. 2020b. George Floyd's Brother Says Donald Trump Barely Let Him Speak during Their Conversation. *ABC News*, May 31. https://www.abc.net.au/news/2020-05-31/george-floyd-brother-says-donald-trump-barely-let-him-speak/12305444.

[ACOSS] Australian Council of Social Services and the University of New South Wales. 2020. *Poverty in Australia 2020*. Sydney: ACOSS and UNSW. Accessed

204   J. MARTIN

May 21, 2020. http://povertyandinequality.acoss.org.au/wp-content/uploads/2020/02/Poverty-in-Australia-2020_Part-1_Overview.pdf.

Allam, L., C. Wahlquist, and N. Evershed. 2019. Indigenous Deaths in Custody Worsen in Year of Tracking by Deaths Inside Project. *Guardian*, August 23. https://www.theguardian.com/australia-news/2019/aug/23/indigenous-deaths-in-custody-worsen-over-year-of-tracking-by-deaths-inside-project.

Allam, L., C. Wahlquist, J. Bannister, and M. Herbert. 2020. Deaths Inside: Indigenous Australian Deaths in Custody 2020. *Guardian Australia*, June 5. https://www.theguardian.com/australia-news/ng-interactive/2018/aug/28/deaths-inside-indigenous-australian-deaths-in-custody.

Anderson, B. 1983. *Imagined Communities: Reflections on the Origin and Spread of Nationalism*. London: Verso.

Benson, R.D., and E. Neveu. 2005. *Bourdieu and the Journalistic Field*. Cambridge: Polity.

Black Lives Matter. n.d. About. Accessed July 29, 2020. https://blacklivesmatter.com/about/.

Blackman, B. 2016, 2017. Walkley Foundation Member's Emails to Author, April 6, 2016 and February 14, 2017.

Bourdieu, P. 2005. The Political Field, the Social Science Field, and the Journalistic Field. In *Bourdieu and the Journalistic Field*, ed. R. Benson and E. Neveu, 29–47. Cambridge: Polity Press.

Bourdieu, P., and L.J.D. Wacquant. 1992. *An Invitation to Reflexive Sociology*. Chicago: University of Chicago Press.

Branco, J. 2017. Former Cop Chris Hurley's Penalty for Assaulting a Motorist Reduced. *Brisbane Times*, December 11. https://www.brisbanetimes.com.au/national/queensland/former-cop-chris-hurley-s-penalty-for-assaulting-a-motorist-reduced-20171211-p4yxls.html.

Brown, M. 2007. Palm Island Mourns Third Death. *Sydney Morning Herald*, January 17. https://www.smh.com.au/national/palm-island-mourns-third-death-20070117-gdp9e9.html.

Chen, D. 2018. Palm Island Riots: Queensland Government to Pay $30m in Class Action Case. *ABC News*, May 1. https://www.abc.net.au/news/2018-05-01/palm-island-riots-qld-government-pay-$30m-class-action-decision/9714640.

Graham, C. 2018. A New Low: Channel 9 "Does a Sunrise" on $30m Palm Island Uprising Payout. *New Matilda*, May 8. https://newmatilda.com/2018/05/08/new-low-channel-9-sunrise-30m-palm-island-uprising-payout/.

Grant, S. 2015. Racism and the Australian Dream. *IQ2 Racism Debate*. Ethics Centre. https://ethics.org.au/stan-grants-speech/.

Green, M.C., T. Brock, and G. Kaufman. 2004. Understanding Media Enjoyment: The Role of Transportation into Narrative Worlds. *Communication Theory* 14 (4): 311–327.

Guardian. 2020. Black Lives Matter and Pro-refugee Events amid Covid-19 Warnings. *Guardian*, June 13. https://www.theguardian.com/world/2020/jun/13/australia-protests-thousands-take-part-in-black-lives-matter-and-pro-refugee-events-amid-health-warnings.

Guilliatt, R. 1999. The Lost Children v the Commonwealth. *Sydney Morning Herald, Good Weekend*, November 20, 18–23.

Habermas, J. 2001. Truth and Society: The Discursive Redemption of Factual Claims to Validity. In *On the Pragmatics of Social Interaction: Preliminary Studies in the Theory of Communicative Action*, trans. B. Fultner, ch. 5. Cambridge, MA: Polity Press.

Hage, G. 2003. *Against Paranoid Nationalism: Searching for Hope in a Shrinking Society*. Sydney: Pluto Press.

Hartsock, J.C. 2016. *Literary Journalism and the Aesthetics of Experience*. Amherst and Boston: University of Massachusetts Press.

Healing Foundation. 2020. Who are the Stolen Generations? https://healing-foundation.org.au/resources/who-are-the-stolen-generations/.

Heinke, A. 2020. Palm Island Riot Compensation Spent on Luxury Boats, Sports Cars and Motorbikes. Nine.com.au, May 18. https://www.9news.com.au/national/palm-island-riots-compensation-spent-on-luxury-boats-sports-cars-motorbikes-qld-news/2530e85e-8169-464f-a367-8810ec5ff0ff#:~:text=When%20Palm%20Island%20residents%20won,luxury%20boats%20and%20dune%20buggies.

Heiss, A. 2002. Writing about Indigenous Australia—Some Issues to Consider and Protocols to Follow! A Discussion Paper. *Southerly* 62 (2): 197–205.

Hooper, C. 2006a. The Tall Man. *Monthly*, no. 10 (Mar.): 34–53. https://www.themonthly.com.au/monthly-essays-chloe-hooper-tall-man-inside-palm-island039s-heart-darkness-185.

———. 2006b. Who Let the Dogs Out? Palm Island after the Inquest into a Death in Custody. *Monthly*, November 6. https://www.themonthly.com.au/issue/2006/november/1246441718/chloe-hooper/who-let-dogs-out.

———. 2008. *The Tall Man: Death and Life on Palm Island*. Melbourne: Penguin.

———. 2019a. Remember Her Name: Systemic Racism, Unconscious Bias, and the Death in Custody of Tanya Day. *Monthly*, December 2019–January 2020. https://www.themonthly.com.au/issue/2019/december/1575205200/chloe-hooper/remember-her-name.

———. 2019b. Death in the Heart of the Desert Is Rewriting the Usual Script. *Sydney Morning Herald*, November 16. https://www.smh.com.au/national/death-in-the-heart-of-the-desert-is-rewriting-the-usual-script-20191115-p53b26.html.

Jash, T. 2020. How to Learn from Indigenous People about the Black Lives Matter Movement in Australia. *ABC News*, June 22. https://www.abc.net.au/news/2020-06-22/how-to-engage-with-indigenous-content-black-lives-matter/12373408.

Johnson, D. 2020. The George Floyd Uprising Has Brought Us Hope. Now We Must Turn Protest to Policy. *Guardian*, June 30. https://www.theguardian.com/commentisfree/2020/jun/30/black-lives-matter-protests-voting-policy-change.

Kidd, J. 2020. NSW Police Investigate Officer Filmed Kicking, Pinning down Indigenous Teen during Arrest. *ABC News*, June 2. https://www.abc.net.au/news/2020-06-02/nsw-police-investigate-officer-over-arrest-of-indigenous-teen/12310758.

Kinsella, E.A., and A. Pitman, eds. 2012. *Phronesis as Professional Knowledge: Practical Wisdom in the Professions*. Rotterdam: Sense Publishers.

Latimore, J. 2016. Not an Event but a Structure. *Overland*, April 15. https://overland.org.au/2016/04/not-an-event-but-a-structure/.

Lucashenko, M. 2013. Sinking below Sight: Down and Out in Brisbane and Logan. *Griffith Review*, no. 41, 53–67.

Markham, F., and N. Biddle. 2018. *Income, Poverty and Inequality*. CAEPR 2016 Census Paper No. 2. Canberra: Centre for Aboriginal Economic Policy Research. Accessed June 23, 2020. https://caepr.cass.anu.edu.au/research/publications/income-poverty-and-inequality.

Martin, J. 2017. Inscribing Virtues in Australian Literary Journalism: An Investigation into How Journalists Communicate Emotions to Readers of the Magazine-style Walkley Award Winning Features, 1988–2014. PhD diss., University of Melbourne.

Martin, M. 2020. George Floyd's Death Brings Back Trauma for Family of Aboriginal Man Who Died in Custody. *ABC News*, June 1. https://www.abc.net.au/news/2020-06-01/david-dungays-family-traumatised-by-death-of-george-floyd/12307414.

Mason, B. 1997. The Girl in Cell 4. *HQ Magazine*, March/April, 56–61.

[MEAA] Media, Entertainment and Arts Alliance. 2020. *MEAA Journalist Code of Ethics*. Accessed May 20, 2020. https://www.meaa.org/meaa-media/code-of-ethics/.

Pantti, M. 2010a. Disaster News and Public Emotions. In *The Routledge Handbook of Emotions and Mass Media*, ed. K. Doveling, C. von Scheve, and E.A. Konjin, 221–236. London: Routledge.

———. 2010b. The Value of Emotion: An Examination of Television Journalists' Notions on Emotionality. *European Journal of Communication* 25 (2): 168–181.

Rifkin, M. 2014. *Settler Common Sense: Queerness and Everyday Colonialism in the American Renaissance*. Minneapolis: University of Minnesota Press.

Roberts, W., and F. Giles. 2014. Mapping Nonfiction Narrative: A New Theoretical Approach to Analyzing Literary Journalism. *Literary Journalism Studies* 6 (2): 101–117.

SBS News. 2016. Controversial Policeman Chris Hurley's Career in Tatters after Conviction. *SBS News*, December 2. https://www.sbs.com.au/news/controversial-policeman-chris-hurley-s-career-in-tatters-after-conviction.

Thomson, C., D. Bennett, M. Johnston, and B. Mason. 2015. Why the Where Matters: A Sense of Place Imperative for Teaching Better Indigenous Affairs Reporting. *Pacific Journalism Review* 21 (1): 141–161.

Tolj, B., and L. Huffadine. 2016. "It's at the Foundation of the Australian Dream": Indigenous TV Presenter Stan Grant Says RACISM Lies at the Heart of Society in Speech Taking the Internet by Storm … as Critics Slam Him for "hypocrisy". *Daily Mail*, January 24. https://www.dailymail.co.uk/news/article-3414024/Stan-Grant-s-passionate-speech-racism-goes-viral-hailed-Australia-s-Martin-Luther-King-moment.html.

Wacquant, L.J.D. 1992. Toward a Social Praxeology: The Structure and Logic of Bourdieu's Sociology. In *An Invitation to Reflexive Sociology*, by P. Bourdieu and L.J.D. Wacquant. Chicago: University of Chicago Press.

Wahl-Jorgensen, K. 2019. *Emotions, Media and Politics*. Cambridge, UK and Medford, MA: Polity.

Wahlquist, C., N. Evershed, and L. Allam. 2018. More than Half of 147 Indigenous People Who Died in Custody Had Not Been Found Guilty. *Guardian*, August 30. https://www.theguardian.com/australia-news/2018/aug/30/more-than-half-of-147-indigenous-people-who-died-in-custody-had-not-been-found-guilty.

Walkley Magazine. 2006. *The 2006 Walkley Awards*. Issue 42. December 2006/January 2007.

Waller, L., and K. McCallum. Forthcoming. 2021. Settler Colonial Representations of Indigenous Disadvantage. In *The Routledge Companion to Media and Poverty*, ed. S. Borden. London: Routledge.

Willing, J. 2020. 42 of the Most Powerful Photos from Black Lives Matter Protests around Australia. *Buzzfeed News*, June 10. https://www.buzzfeed.com/juliawilling/powerful-photos-from-blm-protests-in-australia.

CHAPTER 9

Citizen, Nation, World: A Case Study

INTRODUCTION

In this chapter I complete my analyses by demonstrating how the Virtue Paradigm and the Virtue Map can help illuminate the function of emotion in stories about what it means to belong to a local, national or even global community. Through a case study of the 2019 US Pulitzer Prize-winning feature article by Hannah Dreier, I will show the international relevance of the Virtue Map to interpreting how journalists construct compelling narratives. In Chap. 5 I discussed how, of the 23 feature articles included in my earlier Walkley study, I categorized 16 stories under the 'citizen' theme and 20 under the 'nation' theme. There were also at least 12 stories that contained elements of both themes, and in this chapter I will examine how these two themes entwine in Dreier's 2018 article about the plight of an immigrant teenage boy in the United States caught up in the notorious gang MS-13. Before beginning the analysis, I need to clarify that the definition I use of what it means to be a citizen includes an appreciation of the many ways a person can be considered part of a community. Inherent in the word 'community' is a strong emphasis on the reciprocal nature of everyday human relationships, whereas the word 'citizen' can be interpreted as being primarily focused on the public arena. I draw the

© The Author(s), under exclusive license to Springer Nature Switzerland AG 2021
J. Martin, *Emotions and Virtues in Feature Writing*,
https://doi.org/10.1007/978-3-030-62978-6_9

209

distinction between the terms 'citizen' and 'community' from my own foundational feminist belief that the 'personal is political' and that as much can be learned about those excluded from the privileges of citizenship as those who enjoy its entitlements (Hanisch 1970). The word 'community' also strongly resonates with my interest in how journalists construct stories that consider issues of identity, whether that is on a personal, national or global scale. This chapter begins with an examination of the challenges inherent in any attempt to map the genesis, existence and development of narrative journalism around the world—challenges that also offer the reader and researcher the rich reward of discovering beautifully written stories about people and situations far different from our own. The Virtue Map is offered as a compass to navigate these articles, and also as a means to challenge the way in which Anglo-centric assumptions have dominated the discourse within the discipline of literary journalism studies, and in that process, help to expand the canon of long-form stories.

Narrative Journalism Around the World

Narrative journalism is celebrated the world over, as evidenced by the plethora of awards for the form in countries such as Portugal, Greece, Italy, the Netherlands, Brazil and South Africa, and in Southeast Asia. The best-known award, often held up as a benchmark for other awards, is the US Pulitzer Prize. In the United Kingdom, the National Press Awards, formerly known as the British Press Awards and run by the Society of Editors, are considered among the top honours for journalists. France celebrates its reporters with the Albert-Londres Prize, Denmark has its coveted Cavling prize for journalism, there is the European Press Prize and Australia has the Walkley Awards. But while the existence of awards shows how honest stories that communicate the emotion of what it means to be human are acknowledged across borders as having great value, prizes should not be taken as proof that there is some internationally recognized 'gold standard' for what constitutes narrative journalism. Rather, as discussed in Chap. 2, prizes are an indication of what an organization considers laudable, and therefore careful scrutiny of the judging criteria is extremely valuable in discerning the journalistic values enshrined in a particular award.

9 CITIZEN, NATION, WORLD: A CASE STUDY   211

The diversity of long-form journalism around the globe, while too large a topic for a single chapter, is clearly evident in scholarship on the subject, such as Keeble and Tulloch's two-volume work of collected essays, *Global Literary Journalism: Exploring the Journalistic Imagination* (2012, 2014). As Richard Keeble wrote in the introduction to the second volume, while 'the early years of literary journalism scholarship was dominated by American and British academics: such as Thomas B. Connery (1992), John Hartsock (2000), Norman Sims and Mark Kramer (1984 and 1995) …, the focus has since broadened to include work from Australia, Brazil, France, India, Ireland and Portugal'. In 2011 John Bak and Bill Reynolds published *Literary Journalism across the Globe*, a collection of 16 essays from leading literary journalism scholars, which offered 'a look at how and where literary journalism varies (or does not), whether it is written in English, French, Portuguese, Spanish, Slovene, Finnish, Dutch, German, Polish, Russian or Mandarin' (Bak 2011, 2). And, in firm acknowledgement of the rich diversity of the form, Bak also pointed out in his introduction that when scholars of Anglo-American literary journalism have still not reached a consensus on what defines the form, 'we are logically a long way from determining what makes a literary journalism in the Netherlands negotiable to the form's Spanish or Portuguese heritage' (7).

From a historical perspective, two world wars resulted in European cultures developing under the influence of either American or Soviet superpowers, which in turn influenced how narrative journalism developed. The fundamental political divide between the US and the Soviet Union meant that 'western European presses leaned chauvinistically, if not propagandistically, toward the United States, while eastern European nations were forced to accept the state-controlled Pravda (truth) of the Soviet-influenced press' (Bak 2011, 9). And while the US was certainly a source of journalistic inspiration during the countercultural revolution of the 1960s and beyond, it is pertinent to remember that many European nations already had a literary journalistic tradition reaching back to the nineteenth century and sometimes earlier (Bak 2011, 16). Also, as discussed in Chap. 2, it is a mistake to conflate the existence of narrative journalism with primarily with the emergence or consolidation of democracy. Indeed, as international scholarship on literary journalism

212 J. MARTIN

has demonstrated, there is much evidence that the form found root in autocratic societies as a means of expression (Bak and Reynolds 2011). As John Bak notes:

> Just when it appears that the authorities have succeeded in trampling it out of existence in one culture, it goes underground, metamorphoses, and takes root in another. What grows in the different soil, and amid the new microclimatic changes, can never be exactly the same as it was prior to dislocation. But that it continues to reproduce elsewhere provides hope enough that international literary journalism, no matter how or where it blossoms, will ensure its longevity for the century to come. (Bak 2011, 17)

In 2012 Nancy Roberts, in her keynote address to the International Association of Literary Journalism Studies conference (IALJS) challenged the researchers and teachers present to look past the 'elite sources of literary journalism' such as Tom Wolfe, Truman Capote, Gay Talese and Joan Didion. In 2017, Gabrial and Amend published a survey of 33 teachers of narrative journalism from eight countries to find out whether a canon of writers existed and if so, which writers appeared most consistently. They discovered that 94 per cent of the books and 97 per cent of articles on class reading lists were written by writers from countries where English was the dominant spoken and written language. There was a strong preference for North American writers, who made up 81 per cent in combined categories of books and articles. Men wrote 74 per cent of the books and articles and 82 per cent of all writers were from the United States. While the authors acknowledged that their study was neither exhaustive nor definitive, they also highlighted the linguistic challenge of including narrative journalism in languages other than English in an expanded canon. They pointed out that, in terms of quality translations of narrative journalism, writers such as Gabriel García Márquez and Ryszard Kapuściński were 'the exception rather than the rule as they had close collaborative relationships with their translators' (95). Gabrial and Amend also noted that the IALJS was 'ideally equipped' for the task of recommending good translations (95). Indeed, the organization's recommended reading list includes works on narrative journalism from Bolivia, Brazil, China, Colombia, Cuba, the Czech Republic, Finland, France, Germany, Japan,

9 CITIZEN, NATION, WORLD: A CASE STUDY 213

the Netherlands, Poland, Portugal, Mexico, Russia, Spain and Slovenia, in addition to Australia, Canada, the United Kingdom and the United States (IALJS 2011).

While I look forward to the time when the Virtue Map can be applied more widely to narrative journalism written in languages other than English, for the practical purposes of my discussion I have chosen a Pulitzer Prize-winning feature article on the pragmatic grounds that the American awards are recognized internationally as a benchmark of excellence, and because the winning articles are freely available online. This is not to suggest that other award-winning features from elsewhere are any less worthy of analysis. Some recent examples of excellent long-form include Christina Lamb's series of articles for the UK's *Sunday Times Magazine* on children in poverty, which won the Society of Editors 2019 National Press Awards 'feature writer of the year—broadsheet'(Lamb 2019; National Press Awards 2019). The 2020 Pulitzer Prize in feature writing was won by Ben Taub for his 2019 feature, 'Guantánamo's Darkest Secret', which the judges described as a story that blended 'on-the-ground reporting and lyrical prose to offer a nuanced perspective on America's wider war on terror'; it provokes serious questions about issues of citizenship and nationhood. An extraordinary example of the power of the first-person voice is found in the writing of the 2018 Pulitzer winner, Rachel Kaadzi Ghansah, whose 2017 feature recounts her quest to discover why Dylann Roof walked into a Charleston church and started shooting, killing nine parishioners (Pulitzer Prizes n.d.). Then there is the 2019 European Press Prize for distinguished reporting, for a series on the experience of immigrants to the US, 'Fifty-Six Days of Separation', a poignant account of the trauma caused by government policy (Blasberg et al. 2018).

Significantly, in 2019 the first global prize for long-form non-fiction the 'True Story Award', one which claimed to have 'no editorial, economic or ideological agenda', but 'simply hopes to recognise first-class journalism' was held in Bern, Switzerland. The prize was created by independent Swiss journalists to 'broaden the predominately Western view of the world with other perspectives' (True Story Award 2019a). The Mission statement of the Award declared that:

214   J. MARTIN

Due to the nature of media coverage, readers in North America and Europe have a view of the world different to those in the Arab world, Africa and Asia. The prize encourages the broadening of our field of vision through the voices of reporters from different countries'. (True Story Award 2019a).

In its first year, the prize received more than 900 entries from stories from dozens of countries. Fifty jurors representing 29 countries selected 42 nominees which were sent to an 8-member panel of judges (Banaszynski 2019). The prize 'commends articles for excellence in research, reporting and relevance to society' and accepts entries in English, German, French, Italian, Spanish, Arabic, Hindi, Russian, Persian, Portuguese, Chinese and Japanese (True Story Award 2019a). The organizers said 'the prize should encourage and support the work of journalists the world over and that:

> In many places, the loss of pluralistic and independent reporting impairs freedom of speech. This is why courageous journalists and their investigative reporting combined with compelling storytelling is so important in all societies and countries. The True Story Award was created for them. (True Story Award 2019a)

The 2019 first prize of 30,000 Swiss francs was awarded to Russian reporter Shura Burtin. Second prize went to Mark Arax of the USA, and third prize to undercover Chinese journalist Du Qiang of China, with translated versions available on the True Story website (True Story Award 2019b; Burtin 2019; Arax 2018; Du 2018). Within the judging criteria of the prize is evidence of virtues common to the other journalism awards, such as US Pulitzers, the British Press Awards or Australia's Walkley Awards. The judges consider the research, quality and impact of the stories, taking into account the 'craft, truthfulness, narrative elegance' as well as the 'social, political and economic relevance'. In addition, the judges evaluate the country-specific circumstances (True Story Award 2019a). The establishment of a global prize for long-form is a welcome and overdue development and, just as I endeavour to do with my own discussion, I hope that the prize will encourage readers to seek out the many other examples of excellent feature writing from around the world, broadening the appreciation of long-form narrative journalism.

9 CITIZEN, NATION, WORLD: A CASE STUDY

CITIZEN, NATION, WORLD: A CASE STUDY

Hannah Dreier 'A Betrayal'
ProPublica, 2 April 2018 (co-published with *New York Magazine*)
Winner, 2019 Pulitzer Prize in Feature Writing.

The US$15,000 prize is awarded 'for distinguished writing giving prime consideration to quality of writing, originality and concision, using any available journalistic tool' (Pulitzer Prizes 2019).

Judges' comments: 'For a series of powerful, intimate narratives that followed Salvadoran immigrants on New York's Long Island whose lives were shattered by a botched federal crackdown on the international criminal gang MS-13.'

THE VIRTUE MAP

(Individual virtues are italicized for easy identification.)

- *Courage:* The courage of Henry Triste in handing his teacher his confession of his involvement in the MS-13 gang and his desire to escape their influence. His courage in agreeing to work with the FBI and to hand over the names of gang members. His courage in speaking to a journalist.
- *Empathy:* The empathy of Henry's teacher and the school principal in trying to assist by bringing the police in to help him, although it was a strategy that ultimately failed and led to Henry's arrest. The empathy of Dreier in covering Henry's story and exposing the many ways in which his case was mishandled. The empathy demonstrated by the public in response to Dreier's story.
- *Honesty:* Henry's honesty over his involvement in the gang. His honesty with Dreier and the free access he gave her to his text and Facebook messages. Dreier's own search for truth in seeking justice for Henry.
- *Responsibility:* Henry's ability to take responsibility for his actions. The responsibility demonstrated by Dreier and the *ProPublica* editorial team in how to report Henry's story without risking his life. The responsibility demonstrated by Henry's lawyer. The lack of responsi-

bility of US law enforcement and the government authorities, who used Henry to get information on MS-13 and then revealed his identity and used his admission of gang membership to seek his deportation. The lack of responsibility of the authorities in jailing Henry alongside those he had informed upon.

- *Resilience*: Henry's resilience in surviving the gangs in El Salvador and then in his new home in Long Island. His resilience in surviving in detention with the very gang members he had informed upon. His resilience in surviving the months in detention awaiting his court case.

- *Phronesis:* A deliberation that is 'based on values, concerned with practical judgement and informed by reflection' (Kinsella and Pitman 2012, 2); see also Chap. 6: Without the dedicated journalism of Dreier it is highly unlikely that Henry's case would have received the public attention and support that led to his eventually being able to begin a new life in Europe, free from the threats of MS-13. Dreier's reporting also led to a US government civil rights investigation and the Immigration and Customs Enforcement agency changing their policy. Henry was also able to find asylum in Europe instead of being returned to El Salvador where he faced being murdered by MS-13.

Table 9.1 Individual Virtue Map, Hannah Dreier 'A Betrayal'

Winning feature	Hannah Dreier 'A Betrayal'	
Publication	*ProPublica*	
Date	2 April 2018	
Categories	Children	•
	Marginalised and disadvantaged	•
	Citizens	•
	The nation	•
Virtues	Courage	•
	Empathy	•
	Honesty	•
	Resilience	•
	Responsibility	•
	Phronesis	•

9 CITIZEN, NATION, WORLD: A CASE STUDY   217

'A BETRAYAL'

The judges described Dreier's trilogy as 'powerful, intimate narratives that followed Salvadoran immigrants on New York's Long Island whose lives were shattered by a botched federal crackdown on the international criminal gang MS-13' (Pulitzer Prizes 2019). Dreier's three stories can be read in full online, and were jointly published with *New York Magazine*, *Newsday* and the *New York Times* (Dreier 2018a, b, c). The article chosen for my case study is the first in Dreier's three-part series and is entitled 'A Betrayal'. It is about 17-year-old immigrant, 'Henry Triste', who told police about his gang, MS-13, and in return was 'slated for deportation and marked by death' (2018a). Dreier's second article tells the story of 19-year-old Alex, an immigrant from Honduras, and 'How high schools have embraced the Trump administration's crackdown on MS-13 and destroyed immigrant students' American dreams' (2018b). The final story, 'The Disappeared', is a harrowing account of a mother's search to prove MS-13 gang members murdered her teenage son (2018c). Together, Dreier's body of work is a forensically researched, sensitively written and extraordinarily powerful account of the injustice suffered by immigrants coming to America for a better life.

In order to comprehensively demonstrate how the Virtue Map can be used to deepen our understanding of how journalists express emotion in their work, I have chosen for this case study to focus on the first article in Dreier's series, 'A Betrayal' (2018a). While I would certainly recommend reading Dreier's other two articles for a full appreciation of her exemplary reporting and writing skills, for my purposes of employing the Virtue Map in my analysis, it is more important to concentrate on a single story. By limiting my analysis to 'A Betrayal', I am able to explore in detail how Dreier's writing captures the Virtue Map themes of 'Citizen' and 'Nation' while appreciating how her work also concerns the topic of children and the socially marginalized and disadvantaged. What Dreier's feature article also shows is how award-winning narrative journalism transcends the daily news cycle to embrace globally shared virtues such as *courage, empathy, honesty, responsibility* and *resilience*. Dreier's writing is also an excellent example of *phronetic* journalism, as demonstrated by the testimony of *ProPublica*'s senior editor, Dan Golden in his nomination letter for Dreier's entry for the 2019 Anthony Shadid Award for Journalism Ethics':

218   J. MARTIN

The impact was extraordinary. Hundreds reached out, offering Henry jobs and a home, and donating to a fundraiser that raised $35,000 to help him find a safe place to live once he was released or deported. The Department of Homeland Security opened a civil rights investigation. ICE [Immigration and Customs Enforcement] said it would stop creating detailed gang memos, which jeopardize informants, and offered to move Henry into protective custody. Officials who had refused to testify on his behalf in immigration court suddenly were onboard. Amid intense public attention, the judge granted all parties an extension ... In the end, 'A Betrayal' didn't stop Henry's deportation to El Salvador, but, with the money that readers donated and the extra time allowed by delaying the hearing, he was able to set up a plan to go from there into hiding in a safe third country. (Golden 2019)

In regard to the theoretical frameworks that form the Virtue Paradigm for my analysis of Dreier's work, I can find, in Golden's praise of Dreier's writing, evidence of all seven of Schudson's criteria for news (Schudson 2008, 339). Dreier's *investigation* and *analysis* gave her audience new *information* which resulted in members of the public expressing *social empathy* through their engagement in *public forums* such as the comments section of the *ProPublica* website. Some members of the public then *mobilized* to help Henry, in the process *promoting a democracy* where people are treated fairly. And through her holding of authority to account and her intimate portrayal of Henry, Dreier also provided the conditions for readers to consider issues of identity in relation to how the United States treated some of its most vulnerable members, immigrant children. Dreier's article also meets Habermas's four validity claims of truth, appropriateness, sincerity and comprehension (Habermas 2001). Her forensic investigation of the facts about an issue that strikes at the heart of America's identity as a sanctuary for the persecuted—the unjust treatment of a child immigrant—satisfies Habermas's criteria of truth and appropriateness. Dreier's own expressions of her concerns for Henry's safety and the measures taken by *ProPublica* to protect his identity are evidence of sincerity. And finally, Dreier's success in winning the 2019 Pulitzer Prize for feature writing is strong testimony that her story meets Habermas's comprehension requirement.

Throughout the case study I will italicize the virtues as I identify them and, as further qualitative and contextual evidence of the phronetic strength of Dreier's 7000-word story, I include the paratextual information of the Pulitzer judges' comments, the editor's note that accompanied

9 CITIZEN, NATION, WORLD: A CASE STUDY   219

'A Betrayal', a brief selection of readers' comments, and Dreier's own follow-up article on her reporting (2018e). Paratext is material that is *about* a particular text but that exists *outside* the main body of the text. It provides insight into the way journalists communicate to readers how they would like their stories to be read (Ricketson 2014, 202–203; Genette 1997). In addition to co-publishing Dreier's article with *New York Magazine*, *ProPublica* also ran an eight-minute video in which Henry told his own story in Spanish, subtitled in English, while 'viewers watched it unfold in animation' and a series of arresting images (*ProPublica* 2018a). *ProPublica* also produced their first 'Twitter film' that told Henry's story though a series of animated slides that 'came alive with Henry's text messages', as well as releasing Henry's texts on Instagram (Beard 2018; *ProPublica* 2018b, c). In an interview with David Beard of *Poynter*, Dreier said she felt a *responsibility* to Henry to have his story reach as wide an audience as possible:

> I liked it because as a reporter you're always balancing brevity against rich storytelling. I felt like this helped me have it both ways—the story is sprawling and 7,000 words long, and the Tweetstorm hits the same story notes while being much quicker to take in. I feel like so often, these long reads circulate on Twitter but not everyone has time to actually get through them. Henry was really clear with us that he was taking the risks associated with doing this piece because he wanted people to understand how he came to be trapped between the gang and the law. (Beard 2018)

In an increasingly mediatized world, Dreier clearly embraced the opportunity to share Henry's story across a range of platforms to reach as wide an audience as possible to help the teenager get justice. Her enthusiasm shows that she had faith in her imagined community of readers and viewers and that they would bear witness to Henry's plight and be moved to act to help him. Dreier imagined her audience as a virtuous community who valued *honesty* and would respond to the *courage* and *resilience* shown by Henry with their own sense of *empathy* and *responsibility*. As the overwhelming response to Dreier's article demonstrated, her faith was not misplaced.

Dreier's article (2018a) includes all four of themes included in the Virtue Map. Her narrative concerns the plight of a child, she is writing about a marginalized and disadvantaged group of people (the Salvadoran immigrants), she raises questions about the requirements of citizenship and she prompts readers to consider the kind of nation they want the United States to be. For the purposes of my analysis, we will focus on how the Virtue Map themes of 'citizen' and 'nation' are at the heart of Dreier's article. Through telling Henry's story, Dreier is encouraging readers to face an uncomfortable truth—that the very authorities charged with protecting citizens and upholding the virtue of justice failed one of the most vulnerable members of society, a child immigrant. Dreier draws upon a discourse of civic responsibility and national identity throughout her article, providing readers with the opportunity to consider how the authorities failed to protect Henry, despite his having helped them in their fight against MS-13. Dreier's highly detailed account of Henry's life in El Salvador and the US town of Brentford in Suffolk County provides readers with the opportunity to empathize with Henry's individual plight but also to consider how his experience is not an isolated case but part of a wider immigrant story of displacement and injustice.

Thanks in large part to the huge public outpouring of support in response to Dreier's reporting, Henry is ultimately released from detention and sent to an undisclosed location in Europe for sanctuary. This is firm evidence of what Birgitta Höijer (2004) refers to as a 'discourse of global compassion'. According to Höijer, 'the media expose pictures of distant victims of civil wars, genocide, massacres and other violence against civil populations, and play a basic role in giving publicity to human suffering' and when they do so, 'the audience is expected to respond as good citizens with compassion and rational commitment' (513). By responding with a sense of civic responsibility, people become a part of 'global compassion', which Höijer rightly asserts is 'considered to be morally correct in the striving for cosmopolitan democracy', which is demonstrated in how the international community condemns 'crimes against humanity' (513). While Höijer defines compassion as 'reserved for the suffering of others in the public sphere' (514), for the purposes of my analysis I will adopt a more generous definition that encompasses the full sense of the meaning of the word 'community'. By considering what it means to belong to a community, we are better able to appreciate the power of the personal in Henry's life, as communicated to us by Dreier.

When readers learn about Henry's friends, his love for his grandfather, the kindness of his uncle and his classroom teacher, as well as his abandonment by his mother, they are invited to consider the teenager's full emotional life, which lays the foundation for engendering feelings of *empathy*. It is Dreier's ability to convey the personal that provides the opportunity for readers to consider the wider public, political consequences. Höijer's asserts that global compassion (or *empathy*) 'is a moral sensibility or concern for remote strangers from different contents, cultures and societies' (514) and I argue that it is this discourse that Dreier's story helps her audience consider. It is Dreier's ability to communicate emotion to readers that is key to their experience of global compassion.

Dreier tells Henry's story with a skilful combination of narrative authority, shifting scenes, evocative dialogue, forensic reporting and a keen eye for detail, or what Wolfe (1973, 31–32) refers to as recording the status details of a person's life. Her opening sentence is a shocking and dramatic statement: 'If Henry is killed, his death can be traced to a quiet moment in the fall of 2016, when he sat slouched in his usual seat by the door in 11th grade English class' (2018a). Dreier's description of a child facing death invites readers to consider the virtues of *responsibility* and *empathy*. Dreier then uses status markers to introduce readers to the subject of her story, Henry, a 'skinny kid with a shaggy haircut', who has, ominously, 'been thinking a lot about his life and about how it might end'. She follows with a line designed to shock readers even more with the realization that Henry is no ordinary schoolboy:

> It would have read like a journal entry by any 17-year-old, except this one detailed murder, committed with machetes, in the suburbs of Long Island. The gang Henry belonged to, MS-13, had already killed five students from Brentwood High School. The killers were his friends. And now they were demanding that he join in the rampage.

Dreier employs a discourse of universal justice when she guides readers to question how it is possible that a child in a classroom in the United States is a killer. Her opening sentences prompt readers to experience the emotions of shock, disbelief and outrage, which in turn allow readers to contemplate the virtues of *responsibility* and *empathy*. The fact that people felt sufficiently moved by Dreier's story to offer money, housing, free legal advice and employment, demonstrates how some readers were able to transform their emotions into virtuous action. The reader response to Dreier's telling of Henry's story is further evidence of how, as Höijer explains, 'The media may be seen as an intermediate link between the level of social situations, in which audiences' interpretations and responses develop, and humanitarian organizations and politics' (2004, 514).

222   J. MARTIN

Dreier then shifts between the detailed reconstructed scene of Henry in the classroom to providing forensic details about the background to his story. The context gives readers permission to *empathize* with the plight of a socially disadvantaged and marginalized child and also to grapple with the *responsibility* incumbent on being the citizen of a country where a teen is locked up for turning to the authorities for help. In the fourth paragraph, Dreier demonstrates the journalistic virtue of *honesty* with the information: 'For years, the gang had paid for Henry's school uniforms, protected him from rival gangs and given his grandmother meat for the family'. Dreier's account captures how the gang provided Henry with a sense of belonging and in return required absolute loyalty from him. This is evident in paragraph six, when Dreier shifts to dialogue in the voice of an MS-13 gang leader in El Salvador speaking to 12-year-old Henry:

> 'Your first killing will be hard,' El Destroyer told him. 'It will hurt. But I've killed 34 people. I'm too tired to do this one'. He said the devil was there in the grove and needed fresh blood. And if Henry didn't kill the man, the gang would kill them both.

Then Dreier shifts the scene again, using italics to bring readers back to Henry in the classroom, who explains: '*So to live a little longer, I had to do it.*' Dreier continues her narrative: 'But now, Henry wrote, he wanted to escape the life that had followed him from El Salvador. If he stayed in the gang, he knew he would die. He needed help.'

In these lines, Dreier communicates Henry's vulnerability and his *honesty* and his faith in entrusting her with his story and the subsequent *responsibility* she is charged with. Her writing encourages readers to *empathize* with the cruel injustice of Henry's plight.

Upon first reading Dreier's opening paragraphs, readers could rightly ask, '*How* does Dreier know what she knows? How *does* she know that 'classmates craned their necks to see what he was working on so furiously'? How does she know he 'pulled his hoodie over his earphones'? She could not possibly know these details because she was not there. Reconstructed scenes like these are not found in conventional news stories, but are found in literary journalism, and always demand a particular discipline from the writers (Ricketson 2014, 138–140). Ricketson argues journalists who create reconstructed scenes 'need to understand the misleading signals that an omniscient narrative voice sends in non-fiction and about when and in what ways such a narrative voice could be used' (151). Rather, the

9 CITIZEN, NATION, WORLD: A CASE STUDY 223

journalist must strike a balance between the facts of a story and the boundaries of a creative approach so that readers can reap one of the richest rewards of reading narrative journalism, which is to be drawn so deeply into the story that many are motivated to 'make sense of the chaos of life' (138–140). Dreier strikes her own balance in 'A Betrayal' by shifting readers' attention from the intimacy of the classroom scene with Henry to an authoritatively written paragraph that gives the history of the gang, and another that recounts details of Henry's childhood. Dreier constructs scenes for readers that communicate Henry's *resilience* in having survived his violent childhood, his *courage* in speaking out and the depths of Henry's fear and anguish—encouraging readers to feel *empathy*. She then uses her reporting skills to provide readers with a strong factual framework, evidence of the journalistic virtue of *honesty*, that conveys the danger facing the teenager, and establishes her authority as a reliable narrator.

Dreier's efforts in convincing readers of the veracity of her reporting are rewarded when, just over a third of the way into the article, she describes how Henry, after he hands his confession to his teacher and observes her from outside the classroom, he 'saw her cheeks flush and tears come to her eyes', a description that also conveys the woman's *empathy* for Henry. Dreier's description convincingly transports readers into her reconstructed scene and, in terms of narratorial presence (Lee 2011), readers are able to imagine themselves standing outside the classroom, observing the teacher as Henry does, or perhaps more intimately, positioned close to the teacher, reading Henry's confession. Dreier proceeds to provide readers with an account of Henry's dealings with MS-13, explaining how 'From the day he joined the gang, he was part of an operation that trafficked in a single product: violence'. Dreier explains to readers that MS-13 was originally established by Salvadoran refugees in Los Angeles 'who were seeking community after the civil war' and, crucially, that 'the gang offer[ed] a sense of security and belonging to its members, who kill[ed] to strengthen the group and move up the ranks' of the criminal organization. Dreier's explanation provides readers with the opportunity to consider the consequences to a community and a nation when the identity of being a good citizen is not as powerful as the lure of gang membership.

Dreier recounts the terrible reality that Henry had witnessed 'more than a dozen murders' in his first few years with the gang, how 'He learned how soft skin feels when you slice into it and how bodies, when they are sprayed with bullets, look like they are dancing'. Such vivid description creates an atmosphere of horror for readers, permitting them to experience *empathy* by imagining what it would be like to be a child, or perhaps be the parent of a child, in Henry's circumstances. Dreier then writes how Henry fled El Salvador after receiving a phone message telling him if he did not leave within 24 hours 'he would be disappeared—along with his grandparents'. Dreier contextualizes Henry's journey by informing readers that 'Some 200,000 unaccompanied children from Central America have shown up at the US border since 2013, and nearly 8,000 continued on to Long Island, most to join parents who had settled there years earlier'. Dreier establishes that Henry entered the US legally, which removes the opportunity for readers to engage in a discourse that he was an illegal immigrant and therefore less worthy of their sympathy. As Höijer's research into the reaction of viewers to television news found, people felt different levels of compassion for people depending on what kind of victim they were perceived to be. Children were considered the 'ideal' victim, and women also rated highly, but adult men begging for freedom from a detention camp were considered by respondents in Höijer's study as being 'selfish' as they were seen as capable of helping themselves and therefore less worthy recipients of compassion (2004, 516–517).

Dreier's bleak description of Henry's life after arriving in the US further encourages readers to empathize with the teen. His mother lives with an abusive partner; Henry works long hours and he is expected to hand over most of his money to her for rent and food. Dreier captures the hopelessness of Henry's situation and the lure of MS-13 with the words: 'At night, as he sat in the dark watching horror movies, he couldn't help but miss aspects of the gang—never being bored, always having backup'. Once again, Dreier emphasizes how a life belonging to a gang can become attractive to a teenager who is unable to find that sense of identity within his own family or community.

But school offers Henry salvation and a sense of belonging when he enrols at Brentwood High in 2014, where, 'At orientation, Henry learned that the school had a swimming pool and a music program. He had never touched an instrument before'. Dreier describes how Henry 'loved every minute of his freshman year: buying sandwiches at the deli with his friend, playing soccer in the park' but how, in his sophomore year, 'His new life began to fall apart' when a gang member from El Salvador that knew Henry enrolled at his school. Dreier recounts how Henry is pulled back into the gang and she writes how 'Henry felt guilty about breaking the promise he'd made his grandfather [not to rejoin the gang]' but also how it was 'a relief to fall back into his old ways' and 'Like any good franchise, MS-13 was comfortingly familiar'. Dreier then proceeds to describe the inner workings of MS-13 in El Salvador, where the gang 'was led by veterans hardened by decades of violence'. But in Suffolk County, the clique that was known as the 'Sailors' was 'led by a pair of teenage brothers who lived with their mom and kept the gang's cache of machetes, swords and hatchets buried in their backyard'.

As Henry became more entangled with the gang, his mother left him to live in a domestic violence shelter without saying goodbye. The gang told him 'We're your family' and 'we'll never abandon you'. But, Dreier writes, Henry 'knew that his relationship with his gang friends could crumble the moment he did anything to make them question his loyalty, no matter how simple the transgression—even being slow to answer a text message'. Dreier then illustrates the gang's dark discourse of family loyalty by describing how the Sailors became progressively more violent and were 'like any other bunch of bored and anxious and hormonal teenagers at school, only with machetes'. In these lines, Dreier captures the dangerous vacuum that a lack of any sense of being a part of community or a desire to contribute as citizens has created for the young people of Suffolk County. The identity of the Sailors lies far outside the bounds of the status of being US citizens. Dreier then goes on to describe how the gang brutally attacked and killed a girl that Henry had 'flagged' to the gang as being a potential threat. Dreier writes that the gang beat her so badly with baseball bats and machetes that 'police initially thought she had been hit by a car'. They also killed her friend to avoid leaving a witness.

Henry, becoming more and more frightened by the escalating violence, tried to join the army but was too young to enlist without parental permission. It was shortly after this moment that Henry wrote his confession to his teacher, staying away from school for the next week and then, upon his return, being relieved that his teacher wanted to help him. Henry's teacher demonstrates the virtues of *responsibility* and *empathy* in promising to help him. He is then called to the principal's office and introduced to a man he was told was from the FBI and that the FBI 'could give him a new identity and relocate him far from Long Island'. The man was Angel Rivera, a Suffolk County homicide detective with the FBI's Long Island Gang Task Force. He spoke Spanish and Henry trusted him and he became Rivera's informant, providing information that led to the arrest of MS-13 members and gave the names of '11 kids who had been marked for death by the Sailors'. Dreier provides readers with Trump's political discourse on gangs

226 J. MARTIN

and how, under his presidency, Immigration Customs Enforcement, or ICE, had, in 2017, arrested 'nearly four times more immigrants simply for being suspected of belonging to MS-13 than it did in 2016'. It was in this political climate that 'Suffolk County effectively began to serve as a local arm of ICE, rounding up immigrant kids for deportation'. Henry, who had now turned 18 and suffered the blow of his grandfather's death in El Salvador, thought his witness protection papers 'would be coming through any day'. But instead he was arrested by ICE and taken to a detention centre 'full of young men suspected of being MS-13 members—the very same ones he had snitched on'.

While confident at first that he would soon be released once the authorities realized he had been helping them, as the weeks passed Henry began to fear for his life, especially when MS-13 members demanded to see his 'memo', the document that detailed the reasons for his detainment. Dreier wrote that 'Henry's memo is so specific it amounts to a signed confession'. He asked his lawyer for help, who in turn contacted Rivera, who refused to testify on Henry's behalf. Dreier then explains to readers how turning an informant like Henry over to ICE sends a message to gang members that the police won't protect those who try to stand up against MS-13. The lack of *responsibility* towards Henry is voiced to Dreier by Robert Feliciano, the head of the Suffolk County school board, who tells her 'they certainly were taking advantage of what he had to offer … You can't just do that and then drop him'. Dreier then offers her own opinion on Henry's plight, writing:

> In fact, it appears that Henry's case was mishandled at almost every step along the way. Everyone involved places the blame on someone else. The school says it was required by law to tell the police that Henry was in danger. The police, who told ICE about Henry, blame the feds for trying to deport him. The FBI says that Rivera wasn't officially a member of the task force, even though he was working out of the bureau's office. And ICE says that it didn't know that Henry was an informant.

In a searing summary of Henry's circumstances, Dreier explains how a gang member, who, unlike Henry, had not admitted to being a member of MS-13, was released and that:

> a quarter of the 200 immigrants rounded up in ICE's anti-gang operation on Long Island last year [2016] have been released because of insufficient

9 CITIZEN, NATION, WORLD: A CASE STUDY   227

evidence. So Henry is marked for death and slated for deportation, while the gang members he helped his handler target go free.

Dreier shifts from her omnipotent narrative voice to the first-person in the final section of her article when she meets Henry in prison:

> Sitting across from me in ICE custody, Henry still looks like a boy. His orange jumpsuit pools at his feet, and he has stenciled 'Henry' on his shirt-sleeve in graffiti-style writing.

Dreier's use of the first-person encourages readers to deepen their *empathy* for Henry at his *courage* and *resilience* and to consolidate the reporter's position as an *honest* narrator who takes the *responsibility* of her reporting job seriously. This section also provides evidence of Dreier sharing some of the emotional load of the feature, while also doing what Wahl-Jorgensen described as 'outsourcing' the task to Henry and others in her story (Wahl-Jorgensen 2019, 39). Dreier's narrative choice allows readers to witness the considerable emotional labour she has invested in Henry and his story, and, through her empathic description of events, readers are guided to share her care and concern for his welfare. Dreier describes how Henry shares 'the most horrifying moments of his life in a flat, hyperdetailed way, as if he were watching a movie and narrating the plot'. She then contextualizes Henry's lack of emotion, which could otherwise risk being interpreted by readers as a lack of *responsibility* or *empathy*, by reporting that 'Like many children who have witnessed traumatic events, his mind has recorded the minutest details, but there are huge gaps in the emotional content'. As evidence, she writes how his answer to being asked how he feels about a killing is to calculate 'the number of bullets he thought had blasted apart the victim's body: 235'. She contrasts his detachment with the image of Henry's *courage* and *resilience* in daring to imagine 'a better future for himself', leaving readers with his dreams of 'graduating from high school and living by the ocean and fishing off a pier with children of his own' and doing 'Whatever gets him away from the gang, and the *federales* [*sic*], and allows him to live a little longer'. At the conclusion of Dreier's story, readers have been encouraged to empathize with Henry's plight and are left to consider the virtue of *responsibility* as the boy's fate rests upon the decision of the authorities who, until this point, have failed to protect him.

The editor's note at the end of the story, in conjunction with readers' comments and an article written by Dreier in the first person, published one week after 'A Betrayal', provides further evidence of the *phronetic* impact of the article as well as the emotional labour of the writer (Dreier 2018e). The *honesty* of the editor's explanation of how *ProPublica* 'wrestled with how to balance his [Henry's] desire to tell his story with the threat to his life', demonstrates a strong sense of institutional *responsibility* towards Henry (2018a). The editor informs readers how *ProPublica's* decision not to use the teenager's last name, but to include instead his real name, 'Henry' and his gang name, 'Triste', was made in consultation with his lawyers, as was the decision to photograph Henry in a way that hid his identity. The editor evokes a sense of Dreier's *honesty* by recounting how Dreier met twice with Henry in ICE custody and that he 'called her from his jail ward dozens of times in the weeks that followed', evidence of Henry's trust in Dreier but also proof of the emotional labour Dreier invested in writing Henry's story. The editor emphasizes Henry's *courage* and his *resilience* in telling his story despite the danger he faced by describing how he was 'whispering into the receiver as other MS-13 members tried to eavesdrop'. The editor's note provides evidence that the editorial team have displayed the Virtue Map virtues of *empathy, honesty, responsibility* as well as a sense of *phronesis* by providing a platform for Henry's story. But beyond this, the editor's note demonstrates *ProPublica's* acute awareness of Henry's *courage* in placing his trust in the publication, and emphasizes their awareness and appreciation of the emotional labour invested by Dreier.

Dreier's own follow-up article encapsulated the dilemma she faced as a journalist writing Henry's story: 'How do you write about a teenager who wants his story told, when there is no safe way to tell it?' (2018e). Her article also provides insight into the multidimensional context of the emotional work involved in constructing long-form journalism. Dreier writes that she first came across Henry's case while reporting on how the police on Long Island were working with immigration. She explains that when Henry's lawyer told her that it was not safe to write his story, she 'just kept tabs on the case' and that when Henry did agree to speak to her, he was 18 and 'eager to talk' (2018e). Dreier gives readers an *honest* insight into her research by explaining how, in addition to access to his phone and social media, Henry gave Dreier permission to contact his friends and family and those whose names recurred in the more than 2000 pages of his Facebook chat history. Dreier is demonstrating she has the determination to thoroughly and *responsibly* investigate the facts of the case as well as the *honesty* to verify information before publishing. Dreier stresses how

9 CITIZEN, NATION, WORLD: A CASE STUDY   **229**

seriously she takes her sense of professional *responsibility* towards Henry through her observation that: 'It was more access than any source has ever allowed me. And given Henry's youth and vulnerable position, I often wondered if it was too much.' Implicit in Dreier's article, as well as in 'A Betrayal', is her own emotional labour involved in pursuing Henry's story, a process that required *courage, empathy, honesty, resilience, responsibility* and *phronesis*. The writer's accounting of her process allows readers to 'dovetail' or overlay Dreier's expressed virtues with those who are the subjects of her story. When Dreier ends her article by explaining how adamant Henry was that he wanted his story told, she is providing readers once more with insight into her emotional labour and the virtue of *responsibility* that she felt towards her subject:

> I consulted with gang and law enforcement experts and with Henry's lawyer to ensure we were doing the right thing. I became convinced that what Henry said was true: He was a dead man walking. A story promised a sliver of hope that someone might intervene. (2018e)

The function of emotion in connecting readers with Henry's story was demonstrated by the massive outpouring of public support—*empathy*—that followed the article's publication. Around **300,000** readers spent an average of **27** minutes on the article, four times the site's average. In the Comments section, one reader wrote 'For the first time, I feel *compassion* [my emphasis] for an illegal alien'. Another reader demonstrated *empathy* by writing: 'What a horrific story. So many people failed this child, and no one is willing to take *responsibility* [my emphasis] for the failure' and another confirmed Henry's *honesty*: 'Yep, that's exactly what happens with gangs. You don't kill, they will kill you or a family member'. When unsympathetic comments were posted, one reader evoked the virtues of empathy and responsibility: 'A child is coerced into committing a crime by hardened criminals under the threat of death, and you blame the child? That's pretty cold and unempathetic'.

Just three days after 'A Betrayal' went to press, Dreier wrote a followup article detailing how strongly the community responded to Henry's *honesty* and *courage* at telling his story (2018d). The immigration officials at the jail showed a sense of *responsibility* for Henry by contacting *ProPublica* and asking for his surname so that they could offer to move him into protective custody. Henry's former FBI handler demonstrated the virtues of *empathy, honesty* and *responsibility* when he agreed to testify

230   J. MARTIN

at this hearing, as did Henry's former school principal after having spoken to the teen in jail. An expert witness on gang culture also embodied the virtues of *empathy* and *responsibility* when he agreed to work on Henry's case for free. Hundreds of people showed their *empathy* by writing to *ProPublica* asking how they could help Henry, and in response, his lawyer (who also worked pro bono) set up a campaign which eventually raised tens of thousands of dollars:

> Families in Connecticut, Illinois, Wisconsin, Washington and California have offered to take him in if he wins asylum. One reader offered to set him up with a job in the Midwest. Another said she is working on getting him a visa to move to Canada (Dreier 2018d).

Dreier reinforces the sense of community *responsibility* expressed towards Henry in her reporting of how the story 'galvanized' activists and advocacy groups, how local politicians also came to his defence, how the story was translated into Spanish. Dreier wrote that Henry would like to join the US Army and 'was especially heartened' to hear from a first-generation Mexican-American infantryman who said 'Henry is the kind of kid I want to lead in my platoon. An underdog who is trying to survive and do the right thing' (2018d). The infantryman's words recognize Henry's *honesty* and *courage* and his *resilience* in 'trying to survive'. In the first few days after Henry's story was published there is evidence that the public and those in authority were moved by the teenager's *courage*, *honesty*, *resilience* and the sense of *responsibility* Henry showed in owning up to his actions. In a follow-up article published on 22 January 2019, Dreier's reporting of the decision of the Department of Homeland Security to open a civil rights investigation into Henry's case is yet more evidence of *phronesis*.

In the same 22 January article Dreier writes that despite the rejection, the judge showed *empathy* for Henry when he delivered an 'unusually emotional decision' in which he was 'very sympathetic' to Henry's case; but the court, because of a government crackdown, did 'not have the discretionary authority to take such humanitarian factors into consideration'. In a final demonstration of the virtue of *responsibility*, Dreier reports how Henry's lawyer arranged for a team to meet the teenager at the airport in El Salvador to safely deport him to Europe. Dreier also establishes that *ProPublica* displayed a sense of *responsibility* when, 'Out of concern for Henry's safety, *ProPublica* held this story until he left El Salvador'. The

9 CITIZEN, NATION, WORLD: A CASE STUDY   231

money raised for Henry was used to help him set up life in a European city where he was seeking asylum, evidence of the *empathy* aroused in people who felt driven to help Henry when the US judicial process failed him. Finally, Dreier ends the story with an emotional quote from Henry that summarizes the *courage, honesty, responsibility* and *resilience* of the young man: 'I have broken with the gang forever now, that's one good thing to have come of all this,' he said.

My examination of Dreier's article 'A Betrayal' through the lens of the Virtue Map has illuminated how emotions and virtues are inscribed in a story that exposes the gross injustice suffered by a teenage immigrant at the hands of the US authorities he had taken considerable personal risk to help. I have shown how Dreier's feature is anchored in questions of identity and how she created, through her ability to convey emotion, the opportunity for readers to consider the injustice of Henry's treatment by the authorities he had helped with his information. I have demonstrated how the Virtue Map is a tool for analysing how journalists communicate emotions, including their own, in order to ignite emotion and evoke virtuous responses in readers. The model helps us recognize the universal nature of the virtues of *courage, empathy, honesty, resilience, responsibility* and *phronesis*, providing insight into how the journalist uses them to guide our understanding and responses as readers of themes that are otherwise often difficult to grasp in their complexity and abstraction. The Virtue Map also provides a means by which to appreciate the emotional labour of the journalist and provides a more multifaceted perspective of emotional work within contemporary journalism. My analysis of Dreier's long-form narrative, 'A Betrayal', as well as the editor's comments, Dreier's own follow-up story and the multimedia elements *ProPublica* included in the online version, has demonstrated how the Virtue Map can illuminate social justice themes about what it means to be a citizen as part of a local, national and global community. On one level, Henry's story is about the plight of one teenage immigrant in Long Island. But 'A Betrayal' also raises important questions about how violence and crime cross borders and impact communities. And ultimately, it was the international community that provided a safe haven for Henry after he was marked for deportation from the US. In conclusion, my analysis of Dreier's 'A Betrayal' has demonstrated how the Virtue Map can provide insight into the synergy that is created when forensic reporting skills are fused with well-written prose on subjects of critical significance about humankind, forcing us to focus on who we think we are and what type of people we want to be.

REFERENCES

Arax, M. 2018. A Kingdom from Dust. *California Sunday Magazine*, January 31. https://story.californiasunday.com/resnick-a-kingdom-from-dust.

Bak, J.S. 2011. Introduction. In *Literary Journalism across the Globe: Journalistic Traditions and Transnational Influences*, ed. J.S. Bak and B. Reynolds. Amherst, MA: University of Massachusetts Press.

Bak, J.S., and B. Reynolds, eds. 2011. *Literary Journalism across the Globe: Journalistic Traditions and Transnational Influences*. Amherst, MA: University of Massachusetts Press.

Banaszynski, J. 2019. A New "true story" Award Honors Longform Nonfiction from Around the World. *NiemanStoryboard: Narrative News*, September 6. https://niemanstoryboard.org/stories/a-new-true-story-award-honors-longform-nonfiction-from-around-the-world/

Beard, D. 2018. A Devastating Story, the Hope of New Readers: Why ProPublica Did 2 Versions of "A Betrayal". *Poynter*, April 5. https://www.poynter.org/reporting-editing/2018/a-devastating-story-the-hope-of-new-readers-why-propublica-did-2-versions-of-%C2%91a-betrayal%C2%92/.

Blasberg, M., K. Kuntz, and C. Scheuermann. 2018. Fifty-Six Days of Separation. *Spiegel International*, September 11. https://www.spiegel.de/international/world/u-s-family-separation-policy-leaves-deep-scars-a-1226050.html.

Burtin, S. 2019. Monitor 1. Translated by A.O. Fisher. *True Story Award Winners 2019*. Originally Published Meduza, Russia, September 26, 2018. https://truestoryaward.org/story/63.

Connery, T.B., ed. 1992. *A Sourcebook of American Literary Journalism: Representative Writers in an Emerging Genre*. New York: Greenwood Press.

Dreier, H. 2018a. A Betrayal. *ProPublica*, April 2. Accessed February 6, 2020. https://features.propublica.org/ms-13/a-betrayal-ms13-gang-police-fbi-ice-deportation/.

———. 2018b. He Drew His School Mascot—and ICE Labelled Him a Gang Member. *ProPublica*, December 27. https://features.propublica.org/ms-13-immigrant-students/huntington-school-deportations-ice-honduras/.

———. 2018c. The Disappeared. *ProPublica*, September 20. https://features.propublica.org/ms13-miguel/the-disappeared/.

———. 2018d. Teenage MS-13 Gang Informant Heads into Final Asylum Hearing. *ProPublica*, April 5. Accessed February 6, 2020. https://www.propublica.org/article/triste-henry-teenage-ms-13-gang-informant-heads-into-final-asylum-hearing/.

———. 2018e. What It Was Like Reporting on a Teenager Marked for Death by Gang MS-13. *ProPublica*, April 10. Accessed February 6, 2020. https://www.propublica.org/article/what-it-was-like-reporting-on-a-teenager-marked-for-death-by-the-gang-ms-13/.

9 CITIZEN, NATION, WORLD: A CASE STUDY   233

———. 2019. Former MS-13 Member Who Secretly Helped Police Is Deported. *ProPublica*, January 22. Accessed February 6, 2020. https://www.propublica.org/article/ms-13-member-who-secretly-helped-police-is-deported/.

Du, Q. 2018. The Vagabond Club. Translated by D. Li. *True Story Award Winners 2019.* https://truestoryaward.org/story/57. (Awarded third prize)

Gabrial, B., and E. Amend. 2017. The Ammo for the Canon: What Literary Journalism Educators Teach'. *Literary Journalism Studies* 9 (1): 83–99.

Genette, G. 1997. *Paratexts: Thresholds of Interpretation.* Translated by J. Lewin. Cambridge: Cambridge University Press.

Ghansah Kaadzi, R. 2017. A Most American Terrorist: The Making of Dylann Roof. *GQ Magazine*, August 21. Accessed June 19, 2020. https://www.gq.com/story/dylann-roof-making-of-an-american-terrorist.

Golden, D. 2019. Letter to the Judges of the Andrew Shadid Award 2019. https://ethics.journalism.wisc.edu/files/2019/02/HannahDrier_ProPublica.pdf

Habermas, J. 2001. Truth and Society: The Discursive Redemption of Factual Claims to Validity. In *On the Pragmatics of Social Interaction: Preliminary Studies in the Theory of Communicative Action*, ed. B. Fultner, 85–103. Cambridge, MA: MIT Press.

Hanisch, C. 1970. The Personal is Political. In *Notes from the Second Year: Women's Liberation*, ed. S. Firestone and A. Koedt. New York: Radical Feminism. http://carolhanisch.org/CHwritings/PIP.html.

Hartsock, J.C. 2000. *A History of American Literary Journalism.* Amherst: University of Massachusetts Press.

Höijer, B. 2004. The Discourse of Global Compassion: The Audience and Media Reporting of Human Suffering. *Media, Culture & Society* 26 (4): 513–531.

International Association of Literary Journalism Studies (IALJS). 2011. Selected Bibliography of Literary Journalism Scholarship. Accessed July 18, 2020. https://ialjs.org/wp-content/uploads/2011/06/123-141_Bibliography.pdf.

Keeble, R., and J. Tulloch, eds. 2012. *Global Literary Journalism: Exploring the Journalistic Imagination.* Vol. 1. New York: Peter Lang Publishers.

———, eds. 2014. *Global Literary Journalism: Exploring the Journalistic Imagination.* Vol. 2. New York: Peter Lang Publishers.

Kinsella, E.A., and A. Pitman. 2012. Engaging Phronesis in Professional Practice and Education. In *Phronesis as Professional Knowledge. Professional Practice and Education: A Diversity of Voices*, ed. E.A. Kinsella and A. Pitman, vol. 1, 1–11. Rotterdam: Sense Publishers.

Lamb, C. 2019. Doctor Miracle: Meet the Man Who Has Saved Thousands of Rape Victims—Many of Them Children and Babies. *Sunday Times*, November 17. https://www.thetimes.co.uk/article/doctor-miracle-meet-the-man-who-

234   J. MARTIN

has-saved-thousands-of-rape-victims-many-of-them-children-and-babies-kxs8q2scq.

Lee, C. 2011. *Our Very Own Adventure: Towards a Poetics of the Short Story.* Melbourne: Melbourne University Press.

National Press Awards. 2019. Gallery of Winners for 2019: Feature Writer of the Year—Broadsheet. Winner: Christina Lamb, The Sunday Times Magazine. https://www.societyofeditors.org/events/national-press-awards-2019/winners-gallery/.

ProPublica. 2018a. The Teenager Told Police All About His Gang, MS-13. In Return, He Was Slated for Deportation and Marked For Death. *YouTube,* April 2. https://www.youtube.com/watch?v=Yi2lfa3L1MA.

——— (@propublica). 2018b. If Henry Is Killed, His Death Can be Traced to a Quiet Moment in the Fall of 2016 When He Decided to Spill What He Knew About MS-13. *Twitter,* April 4. https://twitter.com/ProPublica/status/981178287367049216.

———. 2018c. Henry, a High School Student on Long Island, Wanted Out of MS-13. But Without Protection, the Only Way Out is Death. *Instagram,* April 4. https://www.instagram.com/p/BhHklNNB0-H/.

Pulitzer Prizes. 2019. The 2019 Pulitzer Prize Winner in Feature Writing: Hannah Dreier of ProPublica. Accessed February 25, 2020. https://www.pulitzer.org/winners/hannah-dreier-propublica/.

———. 2020. The 2020 Pulitzer Prize Winner in Feature Writing: Ben Taub of the New Yorker. https://www.pulitzer.org/winners/ben-taub-new-yorker/.

———. n.d. The 2018 Pulitzer Prize Winner in Feature Writing: Rachel Kaadzi Ghansah, Freelance Reporter, GQ. Accessed August 4, 2020. https://www.pulitzer.org/winners/rachel-kaadzi-ghansah-freelance-reporter-gq.

Ricketson, M. 2014. *Telling True Stories: Navigating the Challenges of Writing Narrative Non-Fiction.* Sydney: Allen & Unwin.

Roberts, N. 2012. Firing the Canon: The Historical Search for Journalism's Missing Links. Keynote address, International Association for Literary Journalism Studies, Toronto, Canada, May 2012. *Literary Journalism Studies* 4 (2, Fall): 82, 90.

Schudson, M. 2008. *Why Democracies Need an Unlovable Press.* Malden, MA: Polity Press.

Sims, N., ed. 1984. *The Literary Journalists.* New York: Ballantine Books.

Sims, N., and M. Kramer, eds. 1995. *Literary Journalism.* New York: Ballantine Books.

Taub, B. 2019. Guantánamo's Darkest Secret. *New Yorker,* April 15. https://www.newyorker.com/magazine/2019/04/22/guantanamos-darkest-secret/.

True Story Award. 2019a. True Story Award, About: Mission. Accessed August 30, 2020. https://truestoryaward.org/about#mission
———. 2019b. True Story Award: Winners 2019. Accessed August 30, 2020. https://truestoryaward.org/winners
Wahl-Jorgensen, K. 2019. *Emotions, Media and Politics*. Cambridge, UK, and Medford, MA: Polity.
Wolfe, T. 1973. The New Journalism. In *The New Journalism*, ed. T. Wolfe and E.W. Johnson, 3–36. New York: Harper and Row.

CHAPTER 10

Conclusion

Just prior to writing this conclusion, I listened to an episode of *The Sunday Read*, a weekly event on the *New York Times*'s podcast *The Daily*, in which a journalist introduces their long-form article to be read aloud by a professional voice actor. *The Sunday Read* is an excellent example of how the long-form narrative lends itself to formats other than text, such as the podcast. In the episode I listened to, 'The Accusation', I found not only evocative prose but also keen insight into why virtues, both in journalism and in society, matter (Viren 2020a). The podcast was an audio version of an article (2020b) published in March 2020 by the *New York Times Magazine*, 'The Accusations were Lies. But Could We Prove It?'; it was written by Sarah Viren, a journalist and assistant professor of creative non-fiction writing at Arizona State University. Viren told the story of how her wife, Marta, also a scholar who worked at the same university, was falsely accused of sexual harassment and the ordeal they both went through to try and clear her name. They eventually did discover who had spread the lies, which grew to also accusing Viren of sexual harassment. But although both Marta and Viren were cleared of any wrongdoing, it was not before they had undergone a gruelling internal investigation by the university. The couple ultimately decided not to 'pay for more truth' by pursuing a court case against the person responsible, and under the terms of the out-of-court settlement they were free to tell their story but not name their harasser. Viren explained at the start of the podcast episode how, as a writer of creative non-fiction, she was 'obsessed' with one of the central

© The Author(s), under exclusive license to Springer Nature Switzerland AG 2021
J. Martin, *Emotions and Virtues in Feature Writing*,
https://doi.org/10.1007/978-3-030-62978-6_10

237

questions in the field: 'How do we tell true stories and what is the relationship between truth telling and story-telling?' She said, 'That experience and everything that followed afterwards changed my understanding, not only of storytelling and of truth but also lies'. Viren also recounted how she was asked before her ordeal, in a job interview for a university position, what she thought her responsibility was as a creative non-fiction writer in a post-truth world. At the time, she said she had given a broad-sweeping answer that she knew had failed to impress her potential employers. But she said that after what she and Marta had endured, she now knew exactly what her answer would be:

> Our allegiance as nonfiction writers is not so much to truth as it is to honesty. Because truth can be spoken into a void, while honesty implies an audience, a reader, real people to whom you commit to tell your story as accurately and truthfully as you can so that they can then differentiate for themselves the facts from the lies, the truth from the fiction.
>
> I've done that here. Now the story belongs to you. (Viren 2020b)

Viren's words capture beautifully the integral role virtues play in helping us live well and flourish together in a community. She also illuminates how important it is that the journalist be dedicated to communicating stories to readers that are not just *true*, a simple recounting of the facts, but are as *honest* an account of what happened as it is possible to give. That is, the facts are presented as part of a complex and nuanced whole, so that readers can decide for themselves where the 'truth' lies. Viren's last two sentences of the above quote, which close her article, capture one of my central arguments in this book, that the journalist has in mind an 'imagined virtuous community' when they construct their narrative. When Viren declares she has told her story as 'accurately and truthfully' as she can, in the line 'I've done that here', she immediately follows her statement by saying: 'Now the story belongs to you'. Viren, after giving her audience the gift of the virtue of her honesty, charges those who have borne witness to her story with the virtue of social responsibility. In her own words, Viren makes it clear that she hopes that, through the telling of her story, others may be protected from going through the same ordeal that she and her wife endured. Viren's hope that her story will make a difference also provided me with a powerful example of the relevance of the virtue of phronesis, or practical wisdom, to journalism. As the master virtue of the Virtue Map, phronesis encapsulates one of journalism's highest

10 CONCLUSION 239

aims, to effect positive change in society. It is significant that in my study of 23 Walkley award-winning magazine-style features, I found that more than half contained elements of phronetic journalism.

My book began with a simple aim, to investigate how journalists of award-winning long-form narratives use their reporting and narrative skills to make us feel something when we read their work. My interest lies in exploring the ways in which celebrated narratives are constructed so that they transcend the news cycle and become important cultural markers of our collective history. Drawing upon the work of neo-Aristotelian theorists such as MacIntyre and Couldry, I asked to what extent prize-winning features contribute towards the nourishing of community by performing the important cultural work of helping people live well together, to flourish, both with and through the media (Couldry 2012; Couldry et al. 2013, 1). I agree wholeheartedly with Couldry's argument that 'We cannot live so intensively with media without generating questions about the ethical dimensions of that life, questions that, as with other aspects of our lives, hold no promise of consensual answers' (Couldry et al. 2013, 3). Like Couldry, I do not lay claim to any definitive answers on how we can live well, with and through the media, but I do, like him, believe that this is a profoundly important and compelling question to be asking in our increasingly mediatized world. I propose the Virtue Map as one means of examining how journalists use emotion to achieve their goal of connecting with readers and also motivating them to consider change.

As I explained in Chap. 1, this book has its genesis in my earlier research project into the role of emotion in a selection of 23 Walkley-Award winning magazine-style long-form feature articles published between 1988 and 2014. It was through my close textual analysis of these stories that I began to appreciate the role emotion plays in the construction of these compelling narratives on topics that are part of the warp and weft of the social fabric that forms my own country, Australia. From my reading, I discerned the journalists were communicating particular virtues to readers in their stories, virtues such as courage, empathy, honesty, responsibility, resilience and the aforementioned master virtue of phronesis, which I then transformed into the basis of my Virtue Map model. From my own experience as a journalist I was acutely aware of the relationship between the writer and the reader and of how each story was always crafted with a particular audience in mind. Put simply, writers write to be read. I argue that in the kind of stories that are given prizes (which are often judged by fellow journalists), those that are written on themes that matter to society, the writer is writing for a reader who they imagine will care about the topic, or who might be encouraged to care. The journalist is writing, to draw upon Benedict Anderson's notion of an imagined community, for an imagined *virtuous* community of readers (Anderson 1983).

This first half of my book is devoted to providing my rationale for developing my theoretical framework, the Virtue Paradigm and my new analytical tool, the Virtue Map. My model is a fresh lens which researchers and readers of narrative journalism can use to identify how journalists communicate emotion in their stories. Beyond this, I advocate that my model is effective in identifying how journalists, in the process of communicating emotions, may also be framing a particular set of values for their imagined readership. While I acknowledge the need for further research into the way in which journalists around the globe use narrative and reporting devices to help readers feel emotion—and, importantly, how it is in the experiencing of that emotion that readers are given the opportunity to change their world view—my model provides a sound base camp for that journey. This is not to suggest that the Virtue Paradigm or Virtue Map can or should be used in the same configuration for each and every example of long-form narrative journalism, regardless of topic or origin. As I have demonstrated throughout the book in my discussion of the Virtue Paradigm, every feature article must be considered on its own terms, taking into account the contents of the story as constructed by the writer, but also paying attention to the wider political, social and cultural context in which the text is produced and consumed. While I have been clear throughout this research that the Virtue Paradigm is a means of considering a number of theoretical approaches that may be helpful in analysing how journalists construct narratives, it is never going to be able to encapsulate every relevant theory for each and every story. Rather, it is a helpful guide for researchers and a demonstration of how different theories across different disciplines, such as virtue ethics, sociology and the study of emotion, as well as media theory, can be brought together to provide insight into how journalists construct their narratives. The choice of a theoretical lens can and should vary depending upon the article chosen. While Bourdieu's notion of habitus may provide insight into one story's cultural underpinnings, critical discourse analysis or Habermas's theory of validity may give greater insight into another (Bourdieu and Wacquant 1992; Habermas 1984). Or, as I have shown in the analysis chapters of the second half of this book, a combination of theoretical approaches may be used to explore a single story.

The Virtue Map is also a powerful vehicle to provide insight into the significant emotional labour invested in the story by the journalist. Its application will lead to a greater appreciation of the journalist's sense of responsibility to write as honest a story for the reader as possible. The Virtue Map helps us address questions about the journalists' own relationships with their subject matter. Do the writers insert themselves into the narrative? If so, when and how do they do this and what is the overall effect? Or do the journalists keep a distance from the people they are writing about and if they do, to what end? The Virtue Map can help us track whether the perspective of the writer changes throughout the article. By focusing on what virtues are being communicated in the story, we can consider what values are considered important by both the journalist and the readers that the journalist is addressing, what I have referred to as an 'imagined virtuous community of readers'. A thoughtful application of the Virtue Map allows a critical consideration of what virtues are embodied in a particular text. For example, a narrative that communicates the virtue of resilience could prompt questions on who is being resilient and why. In Chloe Hooper's article about an Aboriginal death in custody, the resilience shown by the Palm Island community by the sheer act of their survival, let alone the maintenance of parts of their culture, must be viewed as evidence of the trauma caused by colonization.

The particular virtues included in my iteration of the Virtue Map should not be considered as a formal template to be applied to every long-form narrative regardless of where it is written, who it is written about and who it is written for. The Virtue Map is a preliminary analytical tool whose purpose is to provide a more nuanced understanding of how journalists achieve the effects they do in their stories. The list of virtues is neither definitive nor exhaustive and, for the sake of clarity, I limited my list by encapsulating the virtues of compassion, kindness and sympathy into the overall virtue of 'full empathy'. This is a potential limitation and I would encourage any future study to consider expanding or recasting this list of virtues. It is my sincere hope that the Virtue Map will encourage readers and researchers to think critically about the six virtues I have selected and assess whether they do indeed apply to the long-form narratives they are reading—or whether they consider that other virtues are being communicated by the story, perhaps virtues such as leadership, loyalty or patriotism. Whatever the narrative scenario, the central value of the Virtue Map to the study of journalism is a deeper appreciation of the integral role that emotion plays in constructing a compelling story.

Just as I suggested a study of the presence of virtues across all Walkley Awards categories would be a valuable avenue of future research, a focus on the presence of the virtue of phronesis may be helpful in identifying examples of stories using different media such as radio or television, or internet and social media platforms that endeavour to connect citizens with important social issues. The Virtue Map provides an analytical tool that can be applied to media outside the selective realm of award-winning long-form journalism, a focus deliberately chosen for this book in order to best demonstrate the model. Both the Virtue Paradigm and the Virtue Map are, moreover, effective teaching tools which can help journalism students better understand how and why journalists strive to engage with our emotions.

In writing this book, I set out to investigate the under-researched and under-theorized question of how journalists communicate emotions to readers—in particular, journalists who produce what have been judged as well-written, compelling magazine-style features. My research then went one step further to map how the journalist, through the use of reporting and narrative devices, created a compelling story that transported readers into the particular context of the article. I argued that, in the category of exemplary, award-winning features included in this book, the writer's goal has been to encourage readers to connect with issues significant to a modern democratic society. My discussion has established that throughout the history of the long-form narrative, emotion has never been absent and was always a means of writers connecting with readers; the question was to what degree this was done and what narrative tools that were used to do it. As my discussion of the case studies in Part II of this book has shown, a key narrative device was the way in which journalists positioned themselves in the stories in order to communicate emotion. Equally significant was the combined effect of narrative devices such as scene setting, dialogue and the use of status markers upon influencing the imagined position of the reader within the story, a position that was shown to shift, often many times, to give readers a range of perspectives. What this book has shown is that within award-winning narratives, journalists can be seen to use their professional writing skills to strive towards encouraging their imagined community of virtuous readers to engage with the subjects of the articles, an act that constitutes a small contribution towards nourishing Australian society.

There is also much scope for the Virtue Map to be used in investigating how emotion is used in long-form narrative journalism across a range of digital platforms. In Chap. 5 I discussed the emergence of online aggregation sites such as *Longreads* in 2009 and *Longform* in 2010 as providing expanded opportunities for the publication of long-form narrative journalism. As David Dowling states in his 2019 book *Immersive Longform Storytelling*, narrative journalism has entered something of a golden age in the digital era. Dowling argues that, just as the so-called New Journalists of the 1960s (writers such as Tom Wolfe, Joan Didion and Hunter S. Thompson) employed fictional techniques in their writing to create compelling stories:

> Journalism now borrows from the grammar of cinema and photography in hybridized online forms such as the multimedia feature, a rapidly evolving genre that began with the *New York Times'* 2012 'Snow Fall: Avalanche at Tunnel Creek'. (Dowling 2019, 2)

The impact of 'Snow Fall' should not be underestimated, and the term 'snow fall' became journalistic shorthand for creating a multi-media experience for readers online (Dowling and Vogan 2015, 209–224).

Narrative journalism in the digital age represents a new frontier of storytelling, one in which podcasts such as This American Life's *Serial* or *S-Town* place the subjectivity of the reporting and the journalistic process at the centre. A number of long-form articles have inspired movies, such as Jessica Pressler's 2015 article 'The Hustlers at Scores', which was made into the 2019 film *Hustlers* (Cusick 2020). Other examples of long-form narratives being made into Hollywood moves include Tom Junod's 1998 article on the children's television entertainer, Fred Rogers, which became the 2019 film *A Beautiful Day in the Neighborhood* and the 2015 movie *Spotlight*, which was inspired by and based upon the 2002 *Boston Globe* Spotlight Team that investigated child sexual abuse in the Catholic Church (Cusick 2020). Again, the Virtue Map provides a powerful model to explore how the emotional labour of the reporter is used as a narrative device in long-form narratives online.

Of course, just as Jonathan Mahler lamented in an opinion piece for the *New York Times* in 2014 titled 'When "Long-Form" is Bad Form', the length of an article online or the extent to which it embeds multimedia elements does not guarantee that it will qualify as quality narrative journalism (Mahler 2014). But, as Giles and Hitch (2017, 87) argue,

> Where a narrative attends to the techniques of affective writing, fosters readers' engagement, maintains continuity to preserve this connection, and respects readers' autonomy in navigating the story, its qualification as literary journalism remains uncompromised.

In conclusion, the model's contribution to the field of journalism studies is as a tool that helps us better understand the synergy that is created when forensic reporting skills are fused with well-written prose that has the potential, through the communication of emotion, to spark the imaginations of readers and encourage them to consider what it means to be a citizen in this globalized, mediatized society. It is my hope that the Virtue Map will provide a compass with which scholars, students and readers of long-form features can better map how journalists write award-winning stories and perhaps, through that process, more deeply understand why some stories resonate with readers, challenging their own personal, political and community landscape. The Virtue Map and the Virtue Paradigm can help guide readers towards those examples of multimedia long-form journalism stories where the writers use the alchemy of their words to move us to joy, to tears, to anger and even, most miraculously, to action, contributing to society's ongoing conversation it has with itself over how we can live a virtuous, or 'good' life.

REFERENCES

Anderson, B. 1983. *Imagined Communities: Reflections on the Origin and Spread of Nationalism.* London: Verso.

Aristotle. 2019. *Nicomachean Ethics*, 3rd ed. Translated by T. Irwin. Indianapolis: Hackett.

Bourdieu, P., and L.J.D. Wacquant. 1992. *An Invitation to Reflexive Sociology.* Chicago: University of Chicago Press.

Couldry, N. 2012. *Media, Society, World: Social Theory and Digital Media Practice.* Cambridge, UK and Malden, MA: Polity.

Couldry, N., M. Madianou, and A. Pinchevski. 2013. *Ethics of Media.* New York: Palgrave Macmillan.

Cusick C. 2020. 25 Movies and the Magazine Stories That Inspired Them. Longreads.com, February 28. https://longreads.com/2020/02/28/movies-based-on-articles/.

Dowling, D. 2019. *Immersive Longform Storytelling: Media, Technology, Audience.* New York: Routledge.

Dowling, D., and T. Vogan. 2015. Can We 'Snowfall' This?: Digital Longform and the Race for the Tablet Market. *Digital Journalism* 3 (2): 209–224.

Giles, F., and G. Hitch. 2017. Multimedia Features as 'Narra-descriptive' Texts: Exploring the Relationship between Literary Journalism and Multimedia. *Literary. Journalism Studies* 9 (2): 74–91.

Habermas, J. 1984. *The Theory of Communicative Action. Vol. 1, Reason and the Rationalization of Society.* Boston: Beacon Press.

Mahler, J. 2014. When 'Long-Form' is Bad Form. *New York Times*, January 24. https://www.nytimes.com/2014/01/25/opinion/when-long-form-is-bad-form.html?_r=0.

Viren, S. 2020a. The Sunday Read: 'The Accusation'. *The Daily* podcast, *New York Times*, July 26, 2020. Produced by Kelly Prime; edited by Dave Shaw; written by Sarah Viren; narrated by Gabra Zackman. https://www.nytimes.com/2020/07/26/podcasts/the-daily/the-accusation-the-sunday-read.html.

———. 2020b. The Accusations Were Lies. But Could We Prove It? *New York Times Magazine*, March 18. https://www.nytimes.com/2020/03/18/magazine/title-ix-sexual-harassment-accusations.html?searchResultPosition=6.

Appendix: List of Recommended Reading by Chapter

Chapter 7: Children

Elliott, A. 2013. Invisible Child. *New York Times*, December 9. http://www.nytimes.com/projects/2013/invisible-child/index.html#/?chapt=1.

Garner, H. 2017. Why She Broke: The Woman, Her Children and the Lake: Akon Guode's Tragic Story. *Monthly*, June. https://www.the-monthly.com.au/issue/2017/june/1496239200/helen-garner/why-she-broke. (Winner of 2017 Walkley Award for Feature Writing Long, Over 4000 Words).

Legge, K. 2002. Patrick: A Case in the Life of a Family Court Judge. *Weekend Australian Magazine*, December 7, 34–37. (Winner of 2003 Walkley Award for Magazine Feature Writing).

Linnell, G. 1997. Hope Lives Here. *Sunday Age, Sunday Life Supplement*, October 5, 8–16. (Winner of 1998 Walkley Award for Best Feature Writing).

Rule, B. 2008. Crusade for Kaitlin. *Sunday Times, STM Supplement*, March 2, 14–18. (Winner of 2008 Walkley Award for Magazine Feature Writing).

Simons, M. 2019. Do You Ever Think about Me? The Children Sex Tourists Leave Behind. *Guardian*, March 20. Accessed May 21, 2020. https://www.theguardian.com/society/2019/mar/02/children-sex-tourists-leave-behind-fathers-visited-philippines.

© The Author(s), under exclusive license to Springer Nature Switzerland AG 2021
J. Martin, *Emotions and Virtues in Feature Writing*, https://doi.org/10.1007/978-3-030-62978-6

248 APPENDIX: LIST OF RECOMMENDED READING BY CHAPTER

Whittaker, M. 2005. Ordinary Heroes. *Weekend Australian Magazine*, June 18, 26–31. (Winner of 2005 Walkley Award for Magazine Feature Writing).

CHAPTER 8: DISADVANTAGED OR SOCIALLY MARGINALIZED

Davey, M. 2018. "I Still Feel Mutilated": Victims of Disgraced Gynaecologist Emil Gayed Speak Out. *Guardian Australia*, June 25. https://www.theguardian.com/australia-news/2018/jun/25/i-still-feel-mutilated-victims-of-disgraced-gynaecologist-emil-gayed-speak-out. (Winner of 2019 Walkley Award for Women's Leadership in Media).

Guilliatt, R. 1999. The Lost Children v the Commonwealth. *Sydney Morning Herald, Good Weekend*, November 20, 18–23. (Winner of 2000 Walkley Award for Magazine Feature Writing).

Lucashenko, M. 2013. Sinking below Sight: Down and Out in Brisbane and Logan. *Griffith Review*, no. 41, 53–67. (Winner of 2013 Walkley Award for Feature Writing Long, Over 4000 Words).

Mason, B. 1997. The Girl in Cell 4. *HQ Magazine*, March/April, 56–61. (Winner of 1997 Walkley Award for Magazine Feature Writing).

Tippet, G. 1997. Slaying the Monster. *Sunday Age: Agenda*, June 22, 1–2. (Winner, 1997 Walkley Award for Best Feature Writing).

Toohey, P. 2001. Highly Inflammable. *Weekend Australian Magazine*, November 24, 24–28. (Winner of 2002 Walkley Award for Magazine Feature Writing).

CHAPTER 9: CITIZEN. NATION. WORLD

Arax, M. 2018. A Kingdom from Dust. *California Sunday Magazine*, January 31. https://story.californiasunday.com/resnick-a-kingdom-from-dust. (Second Place in 2019 True Story Award).

Bearup, G. 2001. Death Surrounds Her. *Sydney Morning Herald, Good Weekend Magazine*, May 19, 26–31. (Winner of 2001 Walkley Award for Magazine Feature Writing).

Blackwood, S. 2015. Here We Are. *Chicago Magazine*, October 26. https://www.chicagomag.com/Chicago-Magazine/November-2015/Pembroke/.

Blasberg, M., K. Kuntz, and C. Scheuermann. 2018. Fifty-Six Days of Separation. *Spiegel International*, September 11. https://www.spiegel.

APPENDIX: LIST OF RECOMMENDED READING BY CHAPTER   **249**

de/international/world/u-s-family-separation-policy-leaves-deep-scars-a-1226050.html.

Burtin, S. 2019. Monitor 1. Translated by A.O. Fisher. *True Story Award Winners 2019*. Originally published Meduza, Russia, September 26, 2018. https://truestoryaward.org/story/63.

Button, J. 2018. Angels or Arrogant Gods: Dutton, Immigration and the Triumph of Border Protection. *Monthly*, February. https://www.the-monthly.com.au/issue/2018/february/1517403600/james-button/dutton-s-dark-victory. (Winner of 2018 Walkley Award for Feature Writing Long).

Cadzow, J. 2004. The Right Thing. *Age, Good Weekend*, August 14, 32–36. (Winner of 2004 Walkley Award for Magazine Feature Writing).

Cadzow, J. 2012. The World According to Bryce. *Sydney Morning Herald*, March 17. https://www.smh.com.au/entertainment/books/the-world-according-to-bryce-20120312-1utb7.html. (Winner of 2012 Walkley Award for Best Magazine Feature).

Carlyon, P. 2009. Where the Hell is Everyone?. *Herald Sun*, February 14. http://www.news.com.au/news/where-the-hell-is-everyone/story-fna7dq6e-1111118849619. (Winner of 2012 Walkley Award for Newspaper Feature Writing).

Castillo, M., N. Roldan, and M. Ureste. 2018. The Master Scam. *Animal Politico*. https://www.animalpolitico.com/estafa-maestra/.

Colman, M. 2011. Tree of Life. *Courier Mail, QWeekend Magazine*, April 23, 10–14. (Winner of 2011 Walkley Award for Magazine Feature Writing).

Crabb, A. 2009. Stop at Nothing: The Life and Adventures of Malcolm Turnbull. *Quarterly Essay*, no. 34 (June): 1–100. (Winner of 2009 Walkley Award for Magazine Feature Writing).

Doolittle, R. 2017. Unfounded: Why Police Dismiss 1 in 5 Sexual Assault Claims as Baseless. *Global Mail*, February 3. https://www.theglo-beandmail.com/news/investigations/unfounded-sexual-assault-canada-main/article33891309/.

Du, Q. 2018. The Vagabond Club. Translated by D. Li. *True Story Award Winners 2019*. https://truestoryaward.org/story/57. (Awarded third prize).

Gawenda, M. 1988. Echoes of a Darker Age: Australia's Nazi War Crime Trials. *Time Australia Magazine*, May 23, 12–19.

250 APPENDIX: LIST OF RECOMMENDED READING BY CHAPTER

Ghansah Kaadzi, R. 2017. A Most American Terrorist: The Making of Dylann Roof. *GQ Magazine*, August 21. https://www.gq.com/story/dylann-roof-making-of-an-american-terrorist.

Hartcher, P. 1996. How the Enemy Became an Ally. *Australian Financial Review*, July 4, 18–19. (Winner of 1996 Walkley Award for Best Feature Writing).

Harvey, A. 2000. Heartbreak Hotel: Eight Days in Childers. *Daily Telegraph, Weekend Extra*, July 1, 42–43. (Winner of 2000 Walkley Award for Newspaper Feature Writing).

Hawley, J. 1988. Lloyd Rees: The Final Interview. *Sydney Morning Herald, Good Weekend Magazine*, October 15, 39–48. http://www.smh.com.au/good-weekend/gw-classics/lloyd-rees-the-final-interview-20140917-10bd9n.html. (Winner of 1989 Walkley Award for Best Feature Writing).

Hawley, J. 1990. A Portrait in Pain. *Sydney Morning Herald, Good Weekend Magazine*, August 18, 18–29. http://www.smh.com.au/good-weekend/gw-classics/a-portrait-in-pain-20140903-10c76n.html. (Winner of 1990 Walkley Award for Best Feature Writing and the Gold Walkley Award).

Hill, J. 2015. Suffer the Children: Trouble in the Family Court. *Monthly*, November. https://www.themonthly.com.au/issue/2015/november/1446296400/jess-hill/suffer-children. (Winner of 2016 Walkley Award for Feature Writing Long, Over 4000 Words).

Hooper, C. 2013. On the Road with Julia Gillard. *Monthly*, August. https://www.themonthly.com.au/issue/2013/august/1375315200/chloe-hooper/road-julia-gillard#mtr.

Kilcullen, D. 2015. Blood Year: Terror and the Islamic State. *Quarterly Essay*, no. 58, May. https://www.quarterlyessay.com.au/essay/2015/05/blood-year. (Winner of 2015 Walkley Award for Feature Writing Long, Over 4000 Words).

Knox, M. 2006. Cruising. *Monthly*, September, 26–36. https://www.themonthly.com.au/issue/2006/september/1166764350/malcolm-knox/cruising. (Winner of 2007 Walkley Award for Magazine Feature Writing).

Leser, D. 1998. Who's Afraid of Alan Jones? *Age, Good Weekend Magazine*, November 14, 26–37. (Winner of 1999 Walkley Award for Magazine Feature Writing).

APPENDIX: LIST OF RECOMMENDED READING BY CHAPTER   251

Marr, D. 2010. Power Trip: The Political Journey of Kevin Rudd. *Quarterly Essay* 38 (June): 1–91. (Winner of 2010 Walkley Award for Magazine Feature Writing).

Marx, J. 2006. I Was Russell Crowe's Stooge. *Sydney Morning Herald*, June 7. http://www.smh.com.au/news/national/when-i-was-russell-crowes-stooge/2006/06/06/1149359738242.html. (Winner of 2006 Walkley for Best Newspaper Feature Writing).

Robson, F. 1995. Standing Accused. *Sydney Morning Herald*, March 15, 13. (Winner of 1995 Walkley Award for Best Feature Writing).

Simons, M. 2020. Cry Me a River: The Tragedy of the Murray–Darling Basin. *Quarterly Essay*, no. 77 (March): 1–114. https://www.quarterlyessay.com.au/essay/2020/03/cry-me-a-river.

Taub, B. 2019. Guantánamo's Darkest Secret. *New Yorker*, April 15. https://www.newyorker.com/magazine/2019/04/22/guantanamos-darkest-secret/.

This American Life. 2020. Our Pulitzer Winning Episode. https://www.thisamericanlife.org/704/our-pulitzer-winning-episode.

Toohey, P. 2014. That Sinking Feeling. *Quarterly Essay*, no. 53, 1–94. (Winner of 2014 Walkley Award for Feature Writing Long, Over 4000 Words).

Vincent, S. 2018. "A Nagging Doubt": The Retrial of David Eastman. *Monthly*, December 2018–January 2019. https://www.themonthly.com.au/issue/2018/december/1543582800/sam-vincent/retrial-david-eastman. (Winner of 2019 Walkley Award for Feature Writing Long).

Viren, S. 2020a. The Sunday Read: "The Accusation". *The Daily* podcast, *New York Times*, July 26. Produced by Kelly Prime; edited by Dave Shaw; written by Sarah Viren; narrated by Gabra Zackman. https://www.nytimes.com/2020/07/26/podcasts/the-daily/the-accusation-the-sunday-read.html.

Viren, S. 2020b. The Accusations Were Lies. But Could We Prove It? *New York Times Magazine*, March 18. https://www.nytimes.com/2020/03/18/magazine/title-ix-sexual-harassment-accusations.html?searchResultPosition=6.

Younge, G. 2017. My Travels in White America—A Land of Anxiety, Division and Pockets of Pain. *Guardian*, November 7. https://www.theguardian.com/us-news/2017/nov/06/my-travels-in-white-america-a-land-of-anxiety-division-and-pockets-of-pain.

INDEX

A

Aare, C., 173

Abelson, R.P., 69

Aboriginal population
deaths in custody, 184–186
imagined virtuous community
and, 188–189
long-form writing about, 187–188
poverty rate, 186
Stolen Generation, 183
views on, 202
white nationalism and outsider
status of, 58–59
white people writing
about, 190–191
writing concerning injustice against,
183–184 (*see also* 'Tall Man,
The' (Hooper))

Abuse, child, *see* Child abuse

Accountable Journalism website, 131

'Accusations were Lies, The. But
Could We Prove It?'
(Viren), 237–239

After Virtue (MacIntyre), 3

Age, 91, 161–163

Ahmed, Sara, 110, 175

Aiton, Paul Leslie, 148, 149,
154, 158–159, 163–167,
173, 175

Albert Londres Prize, 124

Al Jazeera, 128

Amazon, 93

Amend, E., 212

American Society of Editors, 30

Amiel, Barbara, 91

Analysis (Schudson's function of
news), 171, 218

Anderson, Benedict, 7, 57, 172, 174,
188–189, 240

Anderson, C.W., 4, 133

Animal Politico, 135

Appropriateness (validity claim), 55,
169, 218

Arax, Mark, 214

Aretaic ethics, *see* Virtue ethics

Argus, 83

© The Author(s), under exclusive license to Springer Nature
Switzerland AG 2021
J. Martin, *Emotions and Virtues in Feature Writing*,
https://doi.org/10.1007/978-3-030-62978-6

254 INDEX

Aristotle
'cognitive core' of
emotions, 112–113
on emotions and virtues, 47
eudaimonia, 5, 28
intellectual virtues, 46, 133
moral virtues, 46, 128, 132, 133
Nicomachean Ethics, 46
on *phronesis*, 6–7, 74–75, 126
'stable and eternal' world of, 74
on theoretical reason, 75
on virtue education, 117–118
virtue ethics (*see* Virtue ethics)
world of, 126
See also Phronesis (practical wisdom)
(virtue)
Australia
Convergence Review into media
ownership, 52
magazine culture in, 88–94
narrative journalism's development
in, 82–83
Royal Commissions (*see* Royal
Commissions)
Australian Colonial Narrative
Journalism (ACNJ), 82–83
Australian Journalists Association
(AJA), 84, 85, 89
Avieson, Bunty, 82, 83, 150
Awards, journalism
'background consensus' and, 55, 56
criteria, 29, 30, 36, 55, 76
culture surrounding, 34–38
examples, 4, 30–31, 210
feature writing category in, 87,
89–91, 96–97
global, 213–214
See also specific awards
Award-winning journalism
case studies, 147–176
civic morals in, 50
communicative action facilitated
by, 53–54

imagined virtuous community
and, 57–59
judging criteria, analysing, 30–33
methods for analysing, 66–68
as phronetic journalism, 7,
71–72, 239
societal role and impact of, 5–6, 28,
45, 46, 54–55, 117 (*see also
Eudaimonia*)
themes, 97, 99
validity claims applied to, 57
virtues, 47–49, 98–99
See also specific titles

B
'Background consensus,' 54–56
Bak, John, 24, 211, 212
Baker, Jill, 96
Barber, Lynn, 91
Batson, C.D., 129
Batty, Luke, 151
Beard, David, 219
Bearup, Greg, 101
Beautiful Day in the Neighborhood, A
(film), 243
Beetson, Janet, 183, 200
'*Behind the Text, Candid Conversations
with Australian Creative
Nonfiction Writers*' (Joseph), 23
Bell, E., 4, 133
Bengaroo, Lloyd, 192, 194
'Betrayal, A' (Dreier)
case study, 215–231
comments on, 215
description in, 222–224
editor's note to, 227–228
follow-up articles, 228–231
narrative voice in, 222, 227
paratextual information, 218–219
as phronetic journalism,
217, 228–231
reconstructed scenes in, 222–223

INDEX 255

theoretical frameworks
applied to, 218
'transportation' affected in, 68
virtues in, 215–216
'Birth of the New Journalism, The:
eyewitness report by Tom Wolfe'
(Wolfe), 18
Black Inc. Books, 91–92
Black Lives Matter movement, 184
Blackwood, Scott, 134
Blair, Jayson, 19, 132
Bly, Nellie, 25–26, 83, 119
Bogart, L., 33
Book-length journalism, 18–22, 93
Book publishing (Australia), 93
Borden, S.L., 58
Boston Globe, 243
Bourdieu, Pierre
field theory, 34–38, 187, 197
habitus (*see Habitus*)
symbolic capital, 34–38
Bramwell, Patrick, 195
Bramwell, Roy, 192–193, 195
'Brand New Day' (Button), 95
Broadcasting, awards for, 31
Brock, 69
Bulletin, 92
Burtin, Shura, 214
Butcher, Cheryl, 148, 149, 155–156,
163–167, 173
Button, J., 95

C
Cadzow, Jane, 91, 101, 102
Calvi, P., 17
Canberra Times, 158
Capote, Truman, 18–20, 25
Carey, James, 45
Carlton, Mike, 183
Carlyon, Patrick, 96
Carrington, Thomas, 83
Carson, Andrea, 32

Case studies
'Betrayal, A' (Dreier), 215–231
'Did Daniel Have to Die?'
(Garner), 147–176
'Tall Man, The' (Hooper),
181–182, 189–203
Cavling Prize (Denmark), 34, 35, 85
Cawthon, D., 28, 29
Character education (virtue
education), 117–118
Character (in a story), use of term, 24
Character (quality), 115
Chicago Magazine, 134
Child abuse
discourses around, challenges
to, 164–165
features covering, 7, 128–129
growing awareness of, 151
media representation of, 157–163
reforms around, 157–158, 162
writing about (*see* 'Did Daniel Have
to Die?' (Garner))
'Children' theme, 99, 147–176,
217, 219
Citizen, defining, 209
Citizenship, ideal practices of, 58
See also Imagined virtuous
community
'Citizen' theme, 99, 209, 217, 219–220
Civic responsibility, discourse
of, 219–221
Civic values/morals, 48, 50
Clark, Roy Peter, 67
Clements, Christine, 202
Cleo, 90
Cochran, Elizabeth, *see* Bly, Nellie
Codes of ethics, for journalists
award criteria and, 88
courage in, 128
examples, 49
neo-Aristotelian approach
to, 118–119
phronetic journalism and, 127

256 INDEX

Collective guilt, 174–176
Colman, Mike, 102
Colonialism/colonial
  discourse, 186–187
  See also 'Settler common sense'/
    settler discourse
Common sense, *phronesis*
  and, 115–116
Communicative action, theory of
  (Habermas), 52–57
Communicative power, 52
Communicative reason, 53
Community/-ies
  collective guilt in, 176
  defining a, 58, 209–210, 220
  emotion's fostering of, 125
  imagined virtuous (*see* Imagined
    virtuous community)
  responsibility of,
    162–165, 228–230
Compassion, 220–221, 223–224
  See also Empathy (virtue)
Comprehension (validity claim), 55,
  169, 218
Confessional journalism, 121
Consensus of truth, 56–57
Context-setting, 191–193
Context studies, 67–68
Convergence Review into media
  ownership (Australia), 52
Coplan, A., 173
Copyright Agency Cultural Fund, 87
Coronial inquest, writing
  about, 195–197
  See also 'Tall Man, The' (Hooper)
Coté, W., 131
Couldry, N., 25, 28, 36, 46–52,
  118–119, 128, 239
Courage (virtue), 128–129
  in 'Betrayal, A' (Dreier), 215,
    223, 226–227
  in 'Did Daniel Have to Die?'
    (Garner), 148

in 'Tall Man, The' (Hooper),
  181, 197
Coward, Rosalind, 121
Crabb, Annabel, 92, 102
Creative non-fiction, 22–23
  See also Narrative journalism
Creech, B., 133
Critical discourse analysis, 66–67,
  160–161, 187–188
'Cruising' (Knox), 101
'Crusade for Kaitlin' (Rule), 102
Cry Me a River (Simons), 94
Csikszentmihalyi, M., 69
Cultural capital (Bourdieu),
  34, 37–38
Cultural differences, writing
  about, 190–197
Cultural phenomenology approach
  (narrative tool), 195
Culture, award-giving, 34–38

D
Dart Center for Journalism and
  Trauma, 167
Davies, Kerrie, 82, 150
Day, Tanya, 200–201
Daylight, Lizzy, 194
De Vries, Rink Jacob, 158–159
'Death in the Heart of the Desert Is
  Rewriting the Usual Script'
  (Hooper), 201
'Death Surrounds Her' (Bearup), 101
Deconstructionist approach (media
  studies), 68
Delaney, Dawn, 201
Democracy
  journalism and, 45, 50–51, 211
  promoting (Schudson's function of
    news), 218
Department of Homeland Security
  (US), 230
Der Spiegel, 132

INDEX 257

'Did Daniel Have to Die?'
(Garner), 95, 98
case study, 147–176
comments on, 147–148
community responsibility evoked
by, 162–165
cover, 160
description in, 175
discourse analysis related to, 153–184
framing of, 152
imagined virtuous community
and, 172–176
layout, 152–153
mainstream media coverage
and, 158–160
narrative structure, 158–160
scenes, 153
Schudson's functions of news
applied to, 170–172
validity claims and, 169–170
virtues in, 98, 148
Digital news, 52
See also Online content
Dillard, J.P., 110–111
'Disadvantaged or socially
marginalized people' theme
in 'Betrayal, A' (Dreier), 217, 219
case study, 181–182, 189–203
journalism's commitment
to, 183–184
wider application of, 99, 186
'Disappeared, The' (Dreier), 217
Disaster reporting, 122
Discourse analysis (DA), 66–68,
160–167, 186–187
Discourse(s)
around Daniel Valerio's
death, 161–163
civic responsibility, 219–221
family loyalty, 225
Garner's writing as challenge to
dominant, 164–165
global compassion, 220–221

the term, defined, 65
universal justice, 221
Dispatches (Herr), 18–20
Dobell, William, 98
Domestic violence, 151
See also Child abuse
Doolittle, Robyn, 135
Doomadgee, Cameron
death of, details surrounding,
192–193, 202
writing about (*see* 'Tall Man, The'
(Hooper))
Doomadgee, Elizabeth, 181,
193–195, 198–199
Doomadgee, Eric, 195
Dowling, David, 243
Dreier, Hannah
'Betrayal, A' (*see* 'Betrayal, A'
(Dreier))
case study, 215–231
'Disappeared, The,' 217
emotional labour of, 226–229
Du Qiang, 214
Dungay, David, 184
Durkheim, Emile, 48, 50, 110

E

Echoes of a Darker Age: Australia's
Nazi War Crime Trials'
(Gawenda), 97–98
Edgar, A., 53
Ellett, F.S., 74–75
Ellie Awards, 30–31
Ellingsen, P., 95
Elliott, Andrea, 134
Emotional discipline, 122–125, 129,
160, 200
Emotional labour
of journalists, 113, 120–121, 129,
167–169, 198–203, 226–229
Virtue Map's insight into, 6, 241
Emotional legitimacy, 174

258 INDEX

Emotions
  cognitive core of, 112–113
  collective guilt, 174–176
  defining, 110–112, 175
  facts balanced with, 122–125
  in long-form narrative journalism,
    37–38, 110–111, 113,
    119–125, 242
  mythic themes informed by, 28
  narrative's role in
    understanding, 109–111
  'outsourcing' of (narrative tool),
    120–121, 227
  political or moral action
    founded on, 122
  social cohesion and, 125
  states of, 115
  transportation theory and, 68–70
  virtues and, 6, 47, 110–112,
    153–156, 198
Empathy (virtue), 129–131
  in 'Betrayal, A' (Dreier),
    215, 220–227
  defined, 129–131
  in 'Did Daniel Have to Die?'
    (Garner), 148
  'full empathy,' 118–119, 173
  long-form's alchemy and,
    38, 130–131
  social empathy, 171, 218
  sympathy contrasted with, 130
  in 'Tall Man, The' (Hooper), 181,
    185, 193–195, 197
  transportation theory and, 70
Episteme, 70–71, 74, 77
Ethical Journalism Network, 135
Ethics, 47–48
  Aristotle's (see Virtue ethics)
  codes of (see Codes of ethics, for
    journalists)
  media (see under Media)
Eudaimonia, 5, 28

European Press Prize, 125, 213
Excellence in writing
  defining, 31–33
  quality of, in journalism, 45–46
  See also Virtue ethics

F
Facts, 18–22, 122–125, 191–193
Fake news, 52
Family loyalty, discourse of, 225
Family violence, 151
  See also Child abuse
Farquharson, Robert, 152
Feature writing
  awards recognizing, 82–83, 87,
    89, 96–97
  award-winning (see Award-winning
    journalism)
  constructing, 6, 73
  disturbance in, 55–56
  elements, 24
  emotions' role in, 119–125 (see also
    Emotions)
  history, in Australia, 82–83
  as 'ideal speech situations,' 56–57
  magazine-style (see Magazine-style
    features)
  news stories and magazine,
    compared, 89–91,
    95–97, 158–160
  as phronetic journalism (see
    Phronetic journalism)
  the term, discussed, 22
  'transportation' in, 68–70
  validity claims for analysing, 54–55
  Walkley entries of, 96–97
  See also Long-form narrative
    journalism
Feelings, see Emotions
Feliciano, Robert, 226
Feminist social studies, 73

Fico, F., 33
Fictionalization, in long-form journalism, 18–22
Fictional techniques, *see* Narrative tools
Field theory (Bourdieu), 34–38, 187, 197
'Fifty-Six Days of Separation' (Balsberg et al.), 213
'Finkelstein Report' (Australia), 52
First Nations people (Australia), *see* Aboriginal population
First-person narrative voice
  in 'Betrayal, A' (Dreier), 226–227
  in 'Did Daniel Have to Die?' (Garner), 173, 174
  emotional authority of, 121
  example, 213
  in 'Tall Man, The' (Hooper), 189–197
  third-person voice and, 120
First Stone, The (Garner), 18, 20–22, 152
Fitterer, R.J., 111–116
Floyd, George, 184
Flyvbjerg, Bent, 71–73
Folk-devil framework, 162, 163
Forde, K.R., 35–36
Foreign Press Media Association Award, 93
Foreshadowing, 190
'Free Press Unlimited' foundation, 133
'Full empathy,' 118–119
  See also Empathy (virtue)
Fursich, E., 67, 68

G
Gabrial, B., 212
Garner, Helen
  awards for, 98
  career of, 151–152
  case study, 147–176
  creative non-fiction label, views on, 22–23
  'Did Daniel Have to Die?' (*see* 'Did Daniel Have to Die?' (Garner))
  emotional labour of, 167–169
  First Stone, The, 18, 20–22, 152
  Monkey Grip, 152
  This House of Grief, 152, 172
  True Stories, 21
  Walkley judges on, 123
Gawenda, Michael, 97–98, 147, 172
George Polk Award, 134
Ghansah, Rachel Kaadzi, 121–122
Giles, Fiona, 93, 244
'Girl in Cell 4, The' (Mason), 200–201
Global compassion, discourse of, 220–221
  See also Empathy (virtue)
Globe and Mail, 135
Gluck, A., 130
Go, Marina, 86
Goddard, C., 157, 161
Golden, Dan, 217
Golden Pear Award (Poland), 76
Gold Walkley Award, 7, 31, 87, 89, 98, 152
Good Weekend (*Age*), 91
Good Weekend (*Sydney Morning Herald*), 98
Goodyer, Paula, 90
Graham, Chris, 202
Graham, Louisa, 86
Grant, Stan, 183–184
Greek dramatic tradition, 25
Green, M.C., 69
Griffith Review, 92
'Guantánamo's Darkest Secret' (Taub), 213
Guardian Australia, 93, 185

260 INDEX

Guardian Weekend magazine, 93
Guilliatt, Richard, 183
Guilt, 174–176
Guode, Akon, 152

H
Habermas, J.
  'background consensus,' 54–56
  communicative action theory, 52–57
  public spheres theory,
    53–55, 67, 188
  validity claims (*see* Validity claims
    (Habermas))
Habitus
  award judging and, 188
  emotional life and, 114
  individual as collective and, 50
  in 'Tall Man, The' (Hooper),
    190, 195
Hage, Ghassan, 58–59, 125, 184
Harris, Ted, 85
Hartcher, P., 95
Hartsock, John, 17, 24, 25
Hawley, Janet, 98
Hay Thomson, Catherine, 83
Helleman, John, 25
Herald-Sun, 157, 161–163, 167, 172
'Here We Are' (Blackwood), 134
Herr, Michael, 18–20
'Highly Inflammable' (Toohey),
  59, 92, 101
Hill, Jes, 151
Historical facts, 191–193
Hitch, G., 244
Höijer, Birgitta, 220, 221, 223–224
Honesty (virtue), 131–132
  in 'Betrayal, A' (Dreier), 215, 222,
    223, 226–231
  in 'Did Daniel Have to Die?'
    (Garner), 148
  Garner's demonstration of, 153

in long-form narrative
  journalism, 48
narrative construction and,
  132, 238–239
in 'Tall Man, The' (Hooper), 181,
  185, 190, 193, 194, 197
See also Truth
Hooper, Chloe
  awards for, 92
  case study, 181–182, 189–190
  creative non-fiction label, views
    on, 22–23
  emotional labour of, 198–203
  other writings of, 200–201
  'Remember Her Name,' 200
  'Tall Man, The' (Hooper) (*see* 'Tall
    Man, The' (Hooper))
  work of, as phronetic
    journalism, 203
'Hope Lives Here' (Linnell), 100
'Horizon of concern,' 117
Howard, John, 186
Howe, George, 82
'How the Enemy Became an Ally'
  (Hartcher), 95
Hughes, George, 82
Hurley, Chris, 192–193,
  195–197, 200–202
Hurst, John, 84–85, 89, 90, 94, 95
'Hustlers at Scores, The'
  (Pressler), 243
Hustlers (film), 243

I
'Ideal speech situation' (Habermas),
  54–57, 75
Identity
  emotion and collective, 122
  national, 220
  as news function, 75, 170,
    172, 218

story construction and issues of, 210
virtues' informing of, 115
Imagined virtuous community, 57–58
Aboriginal population
and, 188–189
in 'Betrayal, A' (Dreier) and, 219
defined, 7
in 'Did Daniel Have to Die?'
(Garner), 150, 172–176
narrative construction and, 7,
238, 240
Immigrants, writing on, *see* 'Betrayal,
A' (Dreier)
Immigration Customs Enforcement
(ICE), 226
Impact, defining, 29–30
In Cold Blood (Capote), 18–20, 25
Independent Media Inquiry
(Australia), 52
Indigenous population (Australia), *see*
Aboriginal population
Information
as Schudson's function of news,
170–171, 218
as 'social good,' 135
Injustice
protests against, 184
racial, 183–186
writing addressing, 183–185 (*see
also* 'Betrayal, A' (Dreier); 'Tall
Man, The' (Hooper))
Instagram, 219
Intellectual virtues, 46, 133
International Association of Literary
Journalism Studies (IALJS), 212
International Principles of Professional
Ethics in Journalism
(UNESCO), 134
Interviewee, use of term, 24
Investigation (Schudson's function of
news), 171, 218
Investigative journalism, 32, 48

'Invisible Child' (Elliott), 134
'I Was Russell Crowe's Stooge'
(Marx), 96

J
James, John Stanley, 83
Janda, Michael, 86
Joseph, Sue, 18, 22, 23, 25, 37–38, 131
Journalism
aretaic (excellence) quality in, 45–46
award culture's impact on field
of, 34–38
awards (*see* Awards, journalism)
award-winning (*see* Award-winning
journalism)
codes of ethics (*see* Codes of ethics,
for journalists)
democracy and, 45, 50–51, 211
feature (*see* Feature writing)
injustice challenged by, 183–185
investigative journalism, 32, 48
long-form (*see* Long-form narrative
journalism)
methodology, understandings
about, 122–124
narrative (*see* Narrative journalism)
phronesis and (*see* Phronetic journalism)
as a practice, 50
principles guiding, 48–49, 75–76, 126
purpose and role of, 4
'quality writing' defined in, 30–33
resilience required of, 133–134
resistance to labels in, 22–23
social advocacy role of, 73, 76–77
subjective or confessional, 121
techne of, 73
truth as central to, 21–22
virtues' role in, 45–52 (*see also
specific virtues*)
*Journalism: Theory, Practice and
Criticism*, 133

262 INDEX

Journalists
  as agents of change, 135
  courage of, 128
  emotional labour of, 113, 120–121,
    129, 167–169,
    198–203, 226–229
  key tasks of, in feature writing, 109
  principle duties of, 58, 115
  traumatic issues toll on, 167
  'yellow journalists,' 119
Junod, Tom, 243
Justice, discourse of universal, 221

K
Kafka, Franz, 117
*Kandy-Kolored Tangerine-Flake
  Streamline Baby* (Wolfe), 25
Keeble, Richard, 211
Kelly, Ned, 83
Kindle Singles (Amazon), 93
Kinsella, Elizabeth, 71–74, 77
Kissane, Karen, 159–160, 170–171
Knowledge, virtues and, 116–117
Knox, Malcolm, 101
Koenig, Sarah, 94
Kotisova, J., 129
Kovach, B., 4, 48, 75, 115, 126
Kristjánsson, Kristján, 112–115, 117

L
Lacy, S., 33
Lamb, Christina, 213
Language, authority of, 56–57
Legge, Kate, 54, 101
Le Monde, 124
Leser, David, 101
Liddell, M., 157, 161
'Life on the Pension'
  (Whitton), 89–90
Linnell, Garry, 100
Literary devices, 190

Literary journalism, 22
  See also Narrative journalism
Literary Journalism across the Globe
  (Bak and Reynolds), 211
'Lloyd Rees: the final interview, the
  final works' (Hawley), 100
Lock, Tony, 27, 98, 124
Lonergan, Bernard, 116, 117
Longform, 93
Long-form narrative journalism
  awards recognizing (*see* Awards,
    journalism)
  award-winning (*see* Award-winning
    journalism)
  diversity of, 211–214
  emotions' role in (*see* Emotions)
  examples, 18, 213 (*see also* Case
    studies)
  fictionalization in, 18–22
  knowing facilitated by, 117
  multimedia formats, 237, 243–244
  narrative tools used in (*see*
    Narrative tools)
  in newspaper features, 96
  news stories compared
    to, 158–160
  phronesis usefulness in
    analysing, 74–77
  publishing landscape for, in
    Australia, 91–94
  rising popularity of, 119
  understanding emotional
    construction in (*see* Virtue Map)
  unique properties of, 24–25
  as a 'virtue compass,' 114
  virtues and (*see* Virtue(s))
  Walkley judging criteria, 36
Longform National Magazine
  Awards, 134
Longform, 243
Longreads, 93, 243
Los Angeles Times, 56
Losowsky, Andrew, 133–134

INDEX   263

Lucashenko, Melissa, 54, 92, 102, 183, 188
Lule, J., 28–29

M
MacIntyre, Alasdair, 3, 46–48, 50, 51, 75, 109, 128–129, 132
Magazine-style features
  awards recognizing, 89–91, 96–97
  case studies (*see* Case studies)
  increased recognition of, in Australia, 88–94
  news stories compared to, 89–91, 95–97, 158–160
  selection criteria for, 32
  themes, 97, 99
  virtues, 47–49, 98–99
  Walkley entries of, 97
  Walkley Project and, 94–99
  See also Feature writing
Mahler, Jonathan, 243
Making Social Science Matter (Flyvbjerg), 71
Maras, S., 33
'Marginalized or disadvantaged people' theme
  in 'Betrayal, A' (Dreier), 217, 219
  case study, 181–182, 189–203
  journalism's commitment to, 183–184
  wider application of, 99, 186
Marr, David, 92, 102
Marsh, Charles, 26, 29
Martiniello, Jennifer, 190
Marx, Jack, 96
Mason, Bonita, 183, 200–201
'Master Scam, The' (*Animal Politico*), 135
McCallum, Kerry, 99, 186, 187
McCarthy, Joanne, 7
McChesney, R.W., 37, 51
McDonald, Willa, 82, 83, 150

McGeough, Paul, 22
Mead, Jenna, 20–21
Media
  civic role of, 50
  communicative power of, 53
  ethics for, global, 51–52, 118–119, 127, 128, 135 (*see also* Codes of ethics, for journalists)
  guidelines, 166
Media, Entertainment and Arts Alliance (MEAA), 84, 86, 88
Media studies, 67–68
Mendes, Philip, 161–162, 167
Michener Awards (Canada), 76, 135
Mobilization (Schudson's function of news), 172, 218
Molina, P., 66
Monkey Grip (Garner), 152
Monthly, 92, 181–182, 189–201
Morality/moral philosophy, 117
Moral panic framework, 161–162
Moral virtues, 46, 128, 132, 133
Movies, long-form inspired, 243
Muir, Catherine, 202
Mythic themes
  defining, 29
  effect and impact of, 27–29
  examples, 27–29, 193–194
  Greek dramatic tradition, 25
  virtue ethics and, 28

N
Nadler, A.M., 133
Narrative
  devices (*see* Narrative tools)
  distance in, 120, 172, 174, 241
  emotions understood through, 110–111
  perspective in, 120
  structure in, 158–160
  transformational quality of, 69–70
  voice in (*see* Narrative voice)

264 INDEX

Narrative journalism
  awards recognizing (*see* Awards, journalism)
  canon associated with, 212–213
  communicative action theory and, 52–57
  defined, 23–24
  democracy and, 211
  diverse lineage of, 17
  emotions' role in, 119–125 (*see also* Emotions)
  empathy in, 130–131 (*see also* Empathy (virtue))
  ethnocentric attitudes towards, 29
  fictionalization in, 18–22
  global perspective on, 210–214
  historical perspective, 211–212
  history, in Australia, 82–83
  internal logic of, 55
  long-form (*see* Long-form narrative journalism)
  methods for analysing, 66–68
  multimedia formats, 237, 243–244
  mythic themes in, 27, 29
  narrative tools used in (*see* Narrative tools)
  New Journalism and, 17
  origins, 25–29
  phronesis in, 46
  rising popularity of, 119
  theoretical approaches to, 5, 240 (*see also* Virtue Paradigm)
  'transportation' in, 68–70, 117
  truth as central to, 21–22
  validity claims (Habermas) applied to, 54–57
Narrative tools, 119–121
  in 'Betrayal, A' (Dreier), 221
  in 'Did Daniel Have to Die' (Garner), 172–176
  honest story crafted using, 132
  'outsourcing' of emotion, 120–121, 227
  as preferred term, 24

  purpose, 24, 242
  scene-setting (*see* Scene-setting)
  status markers, 166, 221
  in 'Tall Man, The' (Hooper), 189–197
Narrative voice
  in 'Betrayal, A' (Dreier), 222, 227
  in 'Did Daniel Have to Die?' (Garner), 172–174
  omniscient, 120, 222
  in 'Tall Man, The' (Hooper), 189–197
  third-person, 120, 173
Narratorial presence, 120, 152
  in 'Betrayal, A' (Dreier), 223
  in 'Did Daniel Have to Die?' (Garner), 173
  narrative tools' relationship with, 242
  in 'Tall Man, The' (Hooper), 185, 189–190
Narrator, reliable, 153, 167–168, 173, 223
National Association of Broadcasters, 31
National identity discourse, 220
National Indigenous Times, 202
Nationalism, 57, 58
National Magazine Awards (Canada), 31
National Magazine Awards (US), 30
National Newspaper Awards (Canada), 31
National Press Awards (Britain), 48, 56, 213
National Public Radio (NPR), 31, 93
'Nation' theme, 99, 209, 217, 219–220
National Union of French Journalists, 131
Neill, R., 95
Nell, Victor, 69
Neveu, E., 51
Newcastle Herald, 7

INDEX 265

New Journalism, 17, 18, 25, 90, 119
New Matilda, 92
News functions, in a democratic society, 75, 126, 170–172, 218
New South Wales Advertiser, 82
Newspapers, history of (Australia), 82
News stories
  long-form examples, 96
  magazine features and, 89–91, 95–97, 158–160
  Walkley entries of, 97
  See also Feature writing
New Yorker, 88, 128
New York Magazine, 219
New York Times, 20, 56, 76, 128, 132, 134, 243
New York Times Magazine, 237
Nicomachean Ethics (Aristotle), 46
'No Place Like Home' (Kissane), 170–171
Northern Protector of Aboriginals, 186
Northern Territory Emergency Response (2007), 186
Nussbaum, Martha, 110–112, 130

O
Oakes, Laurie, 96–97
Oatley, K., 115
Obert, Michael, 125
Objectivity
  narrative voice and, 120
  rejection of pure, 123
O'Donnell, Penny, 31, 32, 34
Omniscient narrative voice, 120, 223
Online content, 31, 52, 93, 243–244
'Ordinary Heroes' (Whittaker), 101
Ortega y Gasset Awards (Spain), 76, 135
Our Watch (organization), 166
'Outsourcing' of emotion (narrative tool), 120–121, 227

P
Palm Island, 202
  See also 'Tall Man, The' (Hooper)
Pantti, M., 76, 122
Papacharissi, Z., 129–130
Paratext, 218–219
Paterson, A.B. (Banjo), 83
'Patrick: A case in the life of a family court judge' (Legge), 54, 101
Peabody Awards, 31
Percy, Karen, 86
Peters, Chris, 119
Phone-hacking scandal (UK), 51–52
Phronesis (practical wisdom) (virtue)
  across academic disciplines and professions, 71–77
  in 'Betrayal, A' (Dreier), 216, 228–231
  common sense contrasted with, 115–116
  definitions, 6–7, 71, 74–75, 126
  in 'Did Daniel Have to Die?' (Garner), 148
  as human action, 116
  journalism application of, 73, 238
  (*see also* Phronetic journalism)
  as a master virtue, 46, 99
  in a modern context, 74–75
  in 'Tall Man, The'(Hooper), 182
Phronetic journalism, 6–7, 53, 72–77
  aretaic quality in, 46
  attributes, 7, 46
  award-winning features as, 7, 239
  'Betrayal, A' (Dreier) as, 217, 228–231
  criteria, 127
  'Did Daniel Have to Die?' (Garner) as, 170–172
  Hooper's writing as, 203
  value of, 126
Phronetic questions, 71–72
Phronetic social science, 71–73
Phronesis (practical wisdom) (virtue)
Pilot, Barbara, 196

266 INDEX

Pitman, Alan, 71–74, 77
Podcasts, 93–94
Police culture, 195–197
'Portrait in pain, A' (Hawley), 100
Post-structuralism, 68
Poupeau, Franck, 57
Power
  communicative power, 52
  phronetic approach to, 71–72
  relations of, 195–197
  social and cultural
    construction of, 50
  symbolic, of journalists,
    34, 37–38
'Power Trip: The political journey of
  Kevin Rudd' (Marr), 92, 102
  See also Phronesis (practical wisdom)
    (virtue)
Poynter, 219
Practical wisdom (phronesis), see
  Phronesis (practical wisdom)
    (virtue)
Pressler, Jessica, 243
Preston, N., 46, 47, 50
Prizes, journalism, see Awards,
  journalism
Promoting a democracy (Schudson's
  function of news), 172
ProPublica, 215–231
Public forum (Schudson's function of
  news), 172, 218
Public spheres (Habermas),
  53–55, 67, 188
Publishing industry (Australia), 93
Pulitzer Prize (US)
  exclusivity of, historically, 30–31
  feature writing category,
    87, 89, 213
  journalism influenced by, 35–36
  for Public Service journalism, 128
  winning articles, analysis of, 56,
    120–121, 213

Q
Quality writing, 30–33, 69
Quarterly Essay, 91–92, 94

R
Race
  injustice related to, 183–186
  settler cultural discourse and,
    186–187, 190–197, 202
  Walkley Awards and, 187–188
Raney, A.A., 69, 70
Readers
  imagined virtuous community of (see
    Imagined virtuous community)
  meaning created by, 164–165
  narratorial presence and (see
    Narratorial presence)
Real Social Science (Flyvbjerg), 73
Reconstructed scenes, 222–223
Rees, Lloyd, 98
Relevance (validity claim), 55
Reliable narrator, 153, 167–168,
  173, 223
Relotius, Claas, 19, 132
'Remember Her Name'
  (Hooper), 200
Reporting devices, see Narrative tools
Research methods, 65–68
Resilience (virtue), 133–134
  in 'Betrayal, A' (Dreier), 216,
    223, 226–231
  defined, 133
  in 'Did Daniel Have to Die?'
    (Garner), 148
  Garner's demonstration of,
    152, 153
  in long-form narrative
    journalism, 134
  in 'Tall Man, The' (Hooper), 182,
    194, 195, 197, 199, 241
Responsibility (virtue), 134–136

in 'Betrayal, A' (Dreier), 215, 219, 221–222, 225–231
in 'Did Daniel Have to Die?' (Garner), 148, 154, 162–165
Garner's demonstration of, 153–156
in long-form narrative journalism, 48, 135–136
in 'Tall Man, The' (Hooper), 182, 185, 191, 193, 194, 197
Reynolds, Bill, 211
Ricketson, Matthew, 18, 21, 25, 91, 93, 120, 222
Rifkin, Mark, 186
'Right Thing, The' (Cadzow), 91, 101, 102
Rivera, Angel, 225, 226
Roberts, Nancy, 212
Robson, F., 95
Romantic approach (narrative tool), 195
Roof, Dylann, 121–122, 213
Roseneil, Sasha, 73
Rosenstiel, T., 4, 48, 75, 115, 126
Royal Commissions
into Aboriginal Deaths in Custody (1991), 185
into Institutional Responses to Child Sexual Abuse (2017), 7, 151
into Police Corruption, 196
Rule, Billy, 102

S
Salon, 93
Sarbin, Ted, 49, 109, 164
'Save Our Children' campaign *(Herald-Sun)*, 157, 161–163, 172
Scene-setting
in 'Betrayal, A' (Dreier), 222–223

in 'Did Daniel Have to Die?' (Garner), 153, 173
in 'Tall Man, The' (Hooper), 190
Schank, R.C., 69
Schudson, M., 75, 126, 170–172, 218
Schwartz, Morry, 92
Seaman, Elizabeth Cochrane, *see* Bly, Nellie
See What You Made Me Do: Power, Control and Domestic Abuse (Hill), 151
Semiotics, 68
Serial (NPR), 94
'Settler common sense'/settler discourse, 186–187, 190–197, 202
Shapiro, S., 25
Shepard, A., 35
Shirky, C., 4, 133
Simmons, A., 130, 173
Simons, Margaret, 91–94
Simpson, R., 131
Sims, Norman, 17–19, 21
Sincerity (validity claim), 55, 169, 188, 218
'Sinking below sight: Down and out in Brisbane and Logan' (Lucashenko), 54, 92, 102, 183, 188
Slate, 93
'Slaying the Monster' (Tippet), 98, 124
Smith, Joshua, 98
Snow Fall: Avalanche at Tunnel Creek' (Branch), 243
Snowden, Edward, 52
Snyder, Julie, 94
Social context, in media analysis, 68
Social discourses, *see* Discourse(s)
Social empathy (Schudson's function of news), 171, 218, 227
See also Empathy (virtue)

268 INDEX

Social justice narrative, 99, 186
'Social justice' theme, 99, 197
Sommer, Eva, 84
Southwell-Keely, Terry, 84
Spooner, John, 152–153
Spotlight (film), 243
Status markers, 166, 221
Steensen, S., 24
Stoicism, 112
Stolen Generation, 183
'Stop at Nothing: The Life and
  Adventures of Malcolm Turnbull'
  (Crabb), 92, 102
Storytelling
  human connections forged
    through, 4
  in journalism (*see* Narrative
    journalism)
  truth's relationship with, 237–239
Strom, Marcus, 86
Subjective journalism, 121
Subjectivity, in media analysis, 68
Subject, use of term, 24
Sunday Read, The, 237
Sunday Times Magazine (UK), 213
Sydney Gazette, 82
Sydney Morning Herald, 84,
  91, 98, 201
Symbolic capital (Bourdieu), 34–38
Symbolic power (Bourdieu),
  34, 37–38
Sympathy, 130

T
Tabloid newspapers, 161
'Tall Man, The' (Hooper), 27
  case study, 181–182, 189–201
  comments on, 181
  emotional investment in, 198–201
  narrative tools in, 189–197
  virtues in, 181–182, 241

Taub, Ben, 213
Taylor, J., 24
Taylor, Lenore, 86
Techne, 7, 70–71, 73–74, 77
'Ten Days in a Madhouse' (Bly), 83
Textual analysis, 67–68
Themes, of Walkley articles,
  97, 99, 119
  See also specific themes
Theoretical approaches to
  narrative, 5, 240
  See also Virtue Paradigm
Third-person narrative voice, 120, 173
This American Life (podcast), 31
This House of Grief (Garner), 152, 172
Time Australia, 97, 147–176
Tippet, Gary, 27, 98, 124
Titchener, Edward Bradford, 130
'To Anyone Who Thinks Journalism
  Can't Change the World' (*New
  York Times*), 76
Tofel, R.J., 29
Toohey, Paul, 59, 92, 101
Torres Strait Islander population, 202
Tracker, 202
Transportation (term), 69
Transportation theory, 68–70, 117,
  127, 190
Trauma subjects, 130–131, 167
'Tree of life' (Colman), 102
Trigger, David, 194
Triste, Henry, *see* 'Betrayal, A' (Dreier)
True Stories (Garner), 21
'True Story Award,' 213–214
Trump, Donald (President), 52
Truth
  consensus of, 56–57
  implicit in journalistic
    expectations, 20, 123
  media charters' use of the word, 131
  storytelling's relationship
    with, 237–239

as validity claim, 55, 169, 188, 218
See also Honesty (virtue)
Tulloch, J., 211
Twitter, 219

U
Universal justice discourse, 221

V
Valerio, Daniel
feature writing about, 98, 103 (*see also* 'Did Daniel Have to Die?' (Garner))
media coverage of death, 157–163, 167, 172
Validity claims (Habermas)
in 'Betrayal, A' (Dreier), 218
in 'Did Daniel Have to Die?' (Garner), 169–170
feature writing analysis using, 54–55
in Lucashenko's writing, 188
phronesis and, 75
truth as, 132
Values
in phronetic journalism, 127
virtues related to, 114–115, 241
van Dijk, Teun A., 66–67, 161
Vincent, Elise, 124
Violence, family, 151
See also Child abuse
Viren, Sarah, 237–239
Virtue education (character education), 117–118
Virtue ethics, 28, 45–47, 50, 112–119
See also Eudaimonia; Phronesis (practical wisdom) (virtue)
Virtue Map
about, 240–241
advantages, 121, 122

applications of, 5–7, 66, 115, 117–119, 244
contribution of, 125
diverse use of, 136, 242–244
origin of, 239
phronesis and, 76–77, 99
virtues comprising, 99, 125–136, 241 (*see also* Virtue(s))
Walkley winners analysed using, 5, 148, 181–182, 215–231
Virtue Paradigm
applications of, 66, 240–241, 244
basis, 117
central aspects of, 58
diverse use of, 242–244
Schudson's functions of news and, 170
transportation theory and, 69
Walkley winners analysed using, 160–176, 218
Virtue(s)
action and, 153–156
in award-winning articles, 47–49, 98–99
communicative action theory and, 52–57
as culturally specific, 47
deliberate choosing of, 115
emotions and, 6, 47, 110–112, 153–156, 198
intellectual, 46, 133
in journalism, 45–52
knowledge and, 116–117
moral, 46, 128, 132, 133
non-exhaustive nature of, in Virtue Map, 241
transportation theory and, 68–70
values related to, 114–115, 241
See also Virtue Map; Virtue Paradigm; *specific virtues*
Virtuous Emotions (Kristjánsson), 112

270 INDEX

W

Wahl-Jorgensen, K., 120–121, 129, 227
Walker, Kumanjayi, 201
Walkley, William Gaston (Bill), 84–85, 89
Walkley Awards
award culture and, 35–37
as basis for Walkley Project (*see* Magazine-style features)
Book Award, 93
changes to, 85–89, 95, 96
courage recognized by, 128
criticism related to, 35–36
entry fees, 86
entry numbers, 96–97
feature writing category, 89–91, 96
format of articles winning, 33
Gold Walkley Award (*see* Gold Walkley Award)
history, 84–85
investigative journalism category in, 32
judging criteria, 30, 36, 88, 117
judging system, 86–88
perceptions of, 31
race relations context framing, 187–188
virtues identified in recipients, 48, 98–99
Walkley Foundation, 86, 96
Walkley Project, 94–95

Waller, Lisa, 99, 186, 187
Wasserman, H., 133
West, Iain, 163, 166
'When "Long-Form" is Bad Form' (Mahler), 243
'Where the Hell is Everyone?' (Carlyon), 96
White nationalism, 58
Whittaker, Mark, 101
Whitton, Evan, 89–90
'Who's Afraid of Alan Jones' (Leser), 101
WikiLeaks, 52
Williams, Sylvia, 155–156
Williams, Wayne, 154–155
Willig, Ida, 34–36, 85
Wolfe, Tom, 18, 25, 26, 120, 160, 221
Words, authority of, 56–57
'World according to Bryce, The' (Cadzow), 91, 101, 102
Wright, Kate, 118–119
Wurst, Travis, 201

X

X-ray technique, 67

Y

'Yellow journalists,' 119

Printed in the United States
by Baker & Taylor Publisher Services